PHILOSOPHICALLY
SPEAKING

PHILOSOPHICALLY SPEAKING

SPEAKING

RICHARD L. PURTILL

Western Washington State College

PRENTICE-HALL, INC.   *Englewood Cliffs, New Jersey*

Library of Congress Cataloging in Publication Data

Purtill, Richard L, 1931-
  Philosophically speaking.

  Includes bibliographies and index.
  1. Philosophy—Introductions. I. Title.
BD21.P87   190   74-20565
ISBN 0-13-662551-7

10 9 8 7 6 5 4 3 2 1

Prentice-Hall International, Inc., London
Prentice-Hall of Australia, Pty. Ltd., Sydney
Prentice-Hall of Canada, Ltd., Toronto
Prentice-Hall of India Private Limited, New Delhi
Prentice-Hall of Japan, Inc., Tokyo

To my wife
Elizabeth Banks Purtill

For in her is a spirit intelligent, holy, unique, manifold, subtle, agile, clear, unstained, certain, invulnerable, loving the good, keen, unhampered, beneficent, kindly, firm, secure, tranquil.

Wisdom 7:22–23

Contents

Preface

Most of us who teach philosophy think of our subject as exciting and absorbing. If we did not we would probably be doing something other than teaching philosophy. But we often have trouble getting this excitement across to our students. This is partly because the problems that interest us now are often no longer the problems that interest beginners in philosophy. We have seen that to answer the big, important questions a good many small, technical questions must first be answered. And since these technical questions have their own fascination sometimes the big questions can be forgotten or indefinitely postponed.

Yet it is useless to expect that the beginner will find the technical questions as fascinating as the teacher may find them. This is not just because these questions are difficult, although they are. It is not just because they require rigorous thinking, although they do. It is mainly because the students do not see the *point* of these questions, cannot relate them to anything they are interested in or feel that they could be interested in. The teacher must start from where the student is, not from where the teacher is. (Socrates was very good at this, as Plato and especially Xenophon show.)

Does this mean that the teacher of introductory classes in philosophy must deal only with the big subjects and avoid rigorous treatment? No, for once the relevance of the technical questions has been established most students are willing to work on them, and once the advantages of rigor have been shown, they will be willing to attempt it. Of course some students expect only to be entertained, some students are unwilling to work hard; and some students do not have the abilities needed to do philosophy. But the average student is quite capable of working at philosophy and profiting from the experience. However the student must first be convinced that philosophy is worth working at.

The way of attacking problems which the teachers have learned in graduate school and which they may employ in their own writing may need modification in order not to "turn off" students at the beginning. We all know the sort of paper which consists of giving six possible interpretations of a philosophical claim and showing that each of them is open to serious objections. Some papers like that are extremely important, and many of them are at least useful. But if you go to work in that way in an introductory class, at least at the beginning, you run the risk of losing your class. On the other hand almost everyone is interested in a good sharp debate, and if different interpretations of a position can be developed in the course of a reasonably lifelike discussion, then the relevance of the points becomes clearer to the beginner.

For this reason dialogues are a natural introduction to philosophy, and many teachers find the dialogues of Plato, Berkeley, or Hume good starting points for an introductory class. But students, for a variety of reasons, find many barriers to understanding in such dialogues, and philosophy can be lost sight of while the mores of Greece in the fifth century B.C., or the theological controversies of the eighteenth century are explained. Because of this, I have written my own dialogues and have tried to keep them contemporary and lively. "Snoopy is a beagle" will do as well for illustration as "Socrates is mortal," and it has a more familiar ring to the student, if not to the teacher.

I have also tried to choose subjects, such as the existence of God or the nature of man, which are perennially interesting, or subjects such as crime and punishment or the justice of war, which are closely tied to contemporary problems. Also, by showing the relevance of more specialized problems to those of wider interest, I hope to show that a philosophy which tries to deal *only* with "burning issues" is seriously incomplete.

The drawback of the dialogue method is that it is time-consuming— more material can be covered by straight exposition than by dialogue. Thus, a dialogue treatment of a topic is often incomplete. But this need not be a defect in an introductory book. An incomplete discussion invites readers to fill in the missing parts for themselves. I have not deliberately used bad arguments nor have I tried to be provocative, but you or your students may find some of the arguments in these dialogues to be bad ones or find the state in which I leave certain questions quite provocative. So much the better—correct my mistakes and carry on the discussion from where I leave it. And you of course have the advantage over me, for while you can reply to *my* arguments, I cannot reply to yours!

My first aim, then, is to interest students; my second aim is to get them involved in doing philosophy on their own. To help them do this I have tried to give exercises which are clear-cut and, especially near the beginning of the book, fairly limited in scope. Once students have had the experience of doing philosophy they may love it or hate it, but at least they will have some idea of what it is.

This book can be used in several ways for an introductory philosophy course:

a. As the sole text.

b. Together with a paperback book of readings. The best now available is John Hosper's *Readings in Introductory Philosophical Analysis* (Prentice-Hall, 1964). The combined cost will be less than many hardback books of readings.

c. Together with a hardcover book of readings. The best book now available is *Philosophy, An Introduction,* edited by Margaret Wilson, Dan Brock, and Richard Kuhns (Appleton-Century-Crofts, 1972). If cost to the students is an important factor, multiple copies of this book or a similar one can be ordered for the library, and put on reserve for student use. (Some copies should be ordered for the Bookstore for those students who wish to buy the book of readings.)

d. Together with one or more good single-author books on specific areas of philosophy. All of those in the Prentice-Hall "Foundations of Philosophy" series are excellent. Thus a teacher who wished to cover Philosophy of Religion and Metaphysics in depth could use my chapters 1, 2, 3, 7 and 10 in this book with John Hicks' *Philosophy of Religion,* 2nd ed. (Prentice-Hall, 1973), and Richard Taylor's *Metaphysics,* 2nd ed. (Prentice-Hall, 1973). A teacher interested in covering ethical problems in more depth could use chapters 2, 4, 5, 6 and 10 in this book with William Frankena's *Ethics,* 2nd ed. (Prentice-Hall, 1973) and Joel Feinberg's *Social Philosophy* (Prentice-Hall, 1973). A variety of other combinations are possible.

For those who wish to use this book in the last three ways, I have given a Further Readings list at the end of each chapter, keyed to the books I have mentioned. For those who wish to use other books I have given a select bibliography in Appendix B. Finally, I have given in Appendix A brief biographical notes on philosophers mentioned throughout the book. I hope that these features will make the book more usable. Students should, at the very least, carry away from their philosophy class an increased awareness of good and bad arguments, and a clearer notion of their own position on a number of important issues. Despite initial puzzlement, and even in the face of their own resistance to philosophy, a large number of students find at least something of value in their experience of philosophy. Only a small number, of course, will go on to become professional philosophers, but if the class is a good one many will also carry away at least a respect for rigorous, critical thinking. If they also carry away a love of wisdom, that will be as much as we can expect and more, perhaps, than we deserve.

My thanks to the Bureau for Faculty Research at Western Washington State College for assistance in the preparation of this book and to Mrs. Ann Drake and Mrs. Mary Sutterman who did the typing. Thanks also to Norwell F. Therien, Jr. and Teru Uyeyama of Prentice-Hall and to all the students who used preliminary versions of the book in classes and who made helpful comments.

Richard L. Purtill

Prologue

STUDENT: Professor Home, this may sound silly but I feel very interested in philosophy and at the same time I'm not really sure that I know what philosophy is.

HOME: Perhaps you're interested in philosophy just because you don't know much about it. Things which are mysterious or unknown often fascinate people.

STUDENT: Well, I really feel I should know more about philosophy than I do.

HOME: It's not surprising that you don't know more. After all, almost every other course you have in college has at least some resemblance to courses you had in high school or even in grade school. History, English, mathematics, even most science courses, are somewhat like courses you have had before. But philosophy is something entirely new to most college students. So an introductory course, or an introductory book, in philosophy has the job of giving you your first idea of what philosophy is all about, as well as the job of starting you on doing philosophy.

STUDENT: I'm a little puzzled when you speak about *doing* philosophy instead of *learning* philosophy.

HOME: Well, that's not a bad place to start. Think of some subject you're familiar with—history, for example. Now in grade school history is often largely a matter of learning dates, names, and places. Later on you may learn something about the explanation of historical events.

STUDENT: Yes, in high school we had a history textbook that explained the American Revolution as the result of economic factors.

HOME: But you realize, of course, that someone has to work out these explanations and discover these dates, select some events as worth writing about and reject others. That's the job of a historian, who studies what happened in the past, and why. They're "doing history," doing the job of a historian, while you were merely "learning history," learning the *results* of their discoveries.

STUDENT: Yes, I can see that.

HOME: Now take a class in mathematics. You can't merely learn the things that mathematicians have come up with in the sense of just learning the results of mathematical computations; you have to do a certain amount of mathematics yourself.

STUDENT: Of course you couldn't learn the answers to all the problems. There are too many different ones.

HOME: Not only that, but you wouldn't really understand how the results were arrived at. You'd be inclined to regard the mathematician's work as a sort of magic. That's just what happened in the early days of mathematics when only expert mathematicians with years of study behind them could do things like long division. Those who wanted the results of the calculations had to simply take it on faith that the mathematician was doing the calculation correctly.

STUDENT: Lots of people still think of scientists in just that way.

HOME: True, and that's why most good courses in science try to give you some laboratory experience, so that besides learning what scientists have discovered you can get some idea of how these results were arrived at. But now let's get back to philosophy. Do you think it would be enough just to learn the results that philosophers have arrived at?

STUDENT: Do philosophers agree on any results?

HOME: Quite often they do, after they've argued out the pros and cons of a question. But suppose you were an atheist and I simply told you that philosophers agreed that God existed, or suppose you were a pacifist and I simply told you that philosophers agreed that war is sometimes justified. What would be your reaction?

STUDENT: Well—I'd want to hear your reasons.

HOME: Precisely. That's the whole point. Philosophers don't claim to have a message from God as some religious teachers do, or some mystical experience of enlightenment as others do. Whatever conclusions philosophers have arrived at were reached on the basis of reason. Now here's the thing about rational arguments. If you see that an argument is a good one, it doesn't really matter who you hear it from—me, another student, a bus driver, or an old man in the park. Once you understand the argument, the argument itself is your basis for accepting the conclusion, not the authority of the person who gave it to you.

STUDENT: Then do philosophers spend most of their time arguing?

HOME: Yes, I think it's fair to say they do, so long as we make it clear that what we mean by "arguing" is not just quarreling or disagreeing, but looking at reasons pro and con and trying to reach a decision on the basis of those reasons. Philosophers do other things also. They spend quite a lot of time clarifying questions and statements, so that they'll know what they're arguing about, and some time looking for assumptions and preconceptions that can lead us astray in argument. But most of their other activities help or lead up to argument in one way or another.

STUDENT: But how do you know that arguing will get you the conclusions you want?

HOME: Let's do a little clarifying on that question. You might mean "How do you know in advance that you'll get conclusions you'll like?" The answer to that is that you don't. Philosophers have to follow the argument where it leads them. If they don't they stop being philosophers and start being special pleaders for some point of view, looking only at evidence that supports their view. On the other hand, you might mean "How do you know that argument will give me answers to questions I'm interested in?" Again the answer is that you don't. Some questions can only be settled by experience, for example, "Would I really enjoy living in Hawaii?" Others can be settled by experiment or calculation, or in other ways. But there are many important questions that can be settled by argument, if they can be settled at all. And the only way of seeing whether they can be is to seriously try.

STUDENT: But aren't there arguments on both sides of every question in philosophy?

HOME: Yes, and there are arguments on both sides of every case in the law courts too. I'm not speaking about the legal issues—just about the facts of the case, who did what, where, when, how, and so on. In some cases we have a hard time making up our minds which side is right. But in the majority of cases we can reach a decision and be reasonably sure of being right.

STUDENT: Is philosophy like law, then?

HOME: In some important ways it is. At any rate it's less misleading to think of philosophical arguments as like legal arguments than to think of philosophy as being like science or mathematics.

STUDENT: But if philosophers are like the lawyers in a case . . .

HOME: You might say that the teacher in a class has to play the part of lawyer for both sides of the case as well as being the judge who sees that justice is done to both sides. But each student is a jury of one, who has to think through the case for himself or herself. Here's what one very good contemporary philosopher, J. R. Lucas,[1] says at the beginning of his book called *The Freedom of the Will:*

> Philosophy has to be self-thought if it is to be thought at all. It is an activity, rather than a set of propositions. Each man needs to think out the problems and their solutions for himself, and although another man's philosophizing may help him in his own, he cannot accept their conclusions, or even understand their arguments, until he has already argued a lot with himself.

Of course, outside of a class the jury in a particular instance might be the reader of a book or article, or a professional philosopher listening to another professional philosopher.

STUDENT: Then it's all up to the individual?

HOME: Not in the way I think you may mean that. Facts are facts, whatever the jury says. Juries sometimes give verdicts that are silly or unreasonable. In one sense it is "all up to the jury," but the jury can be right or wrong, reasonable or unreasonable. In the same way, no one can force you to come to a particular conclusion by arguing with you. You have the choice of being unreasonable. Some things in philosophy are sufficiently well established so that only a very unreasonable person would reject them. Other things are still a matter of debate and reasonable people can disagree about them. What is and isn't settled beyond reasonable doubt is itself sometimes a matter of debate, though.

STUDENT: But how can you come to any conclusion with all these arguments?

[1] Brief biographical notes on philosophers mentioned in this book appear in Appendix A.

HOME: Don't give up too easily. In fact that's a good slogan for the beginner in philosophy to keep in mind. Many people start off being dogmatic in philosophy and as soon as they find out that there are arguments on the other side they rush to the other extreme of complete skepticism. Don't be satisfied with easy answers, but don't give up hope of an answer just because getting it involves a little work. As Spinoza [2] said, "All things which are worthwhile are both difficult and rare."

STUDENT: I've read a little about Spinoza and some of the other great philosophers in the past, and I'm finding what I read a little hard to fit in with what you've said. Do philosophers nowadays still read Spinoza?

HOME: All of them have read him as students. Whether they still read him depends a great deal on whether they're interested in the sort of problems he was interested in. Philosophy is like a great public debate, going on all through the ages. Lots of people have contributed to the debate and some, the great philosophers, have contributed more than others. It's no use trying to get in on a debate unless you know at least the more important points that have been made. This is why a knowledge of the history of philosophy is one of the two essential tools for a philosopher. The other is logic, which is the study of argument.

STUDENT: But are there philosophers today who agree with Spinoza?

HOME: By "agree with" do you mean "agree with in every detail?" Any philosopher who did that wouldn't be a very good philosopher, since objections were made to some of Spinoza's positions, and they showed that those positions were wrong and needed to be changed. Anyone who held all of Spinoza's views today would need to have answered all those objections and come up with new arguments. So it would no longer be Spinoza's position. If you just mean, do some philosophers accept *some* of Spinoza's positions, of course some philosophers do. In fact, some great philosophers, like Aristotle [3] or Kant,[4] made such a contribution to philosophy that there are philosophers today who would feel that they are continuing their work and therefore call themselves Aristotelians or Kantians. But most philosophers today don't feel that they belong to a school or a party within philosophy.

STUDENT: But couldn't somebody still come up with new arguments for a position held in the past?

HOME: Yes, that's in the nature of philosophy. Philosophy is *dialecti-*

---

[2] Baruch Spinoza: see Biography (Appendix A).
[3] Aristotle: see Biography (Appendix A).
[4] Immanuel Kant: see Biography (Appendix A) and Further Readings at the end of Chapter 4.

cal: it arrives at conclusions by considering pros and cons, and if there is a new pro or con to be considered this may alter a previous conclusion.

STUDENT: How does all this apply to a philosopher's thinking about things outside of philosophy, politics for example?

HOME: Philosophers differ among themselves about politics, like any group. Any political decision involves a great many matters of fact and views about what will be successful in practice, as well as matters of principle. And political principles themselves are one of the things that philosophers disagree about.

STUDENT: Well, it's clear enough that philosophers argue; but what sorts of things do they argue about?

HOME: All the traditional things are still debated: God, Freedom and Immortality, Right and Wrong, Knowledge, Truth, and Beauty. Then there are problems raised by our modern world, for example whether computers could be said to think, or what art should aim at now that we can "imitate nature" mechanically with cameras and other devices.

STUDENT: And do they find answers to those questions?

HOME: In many cases, yes. I've found answers to many problems that satisfy me completely, answers to others that seem reasonably satisfactory. Other questions I'm still working on. If my answers don't satisfy another philosopher, he can argue with me. If I'm wrong, I'll be glad to be convinced of it. Argument is the philosopher's laboratory. An argument that can stand up to the criticism of the philosophical community has a pretty good chance of being close to the truth, if not the whole truth.

STUDENT: Where does this kind of argument go on?

HOME: In all kinds of settings of course— dorm rooms, faculty offices, the Student Union, at people's homes. But especially in philosophy classrooms, even in introductory classes, because arguing something with beginners is often a better test of your real understanding of it than arguing with other professionals. It also takes place in philosophical books and journals. The debate is slow motion, of course, but each side can present its own view at length. And at philosophical meetings of all kinds, either meetings of philosophical societies or special meetings of different kinds.

STUDENT: We're having such a meeting here soon, aren't we?

HOME: Yes, and you have an unusual opportunity of seeing a real philosophical debate. Three very distinguished philosophers are here for our annual colloquium. This year, after consulting with the students, we decided to have a series of debates on general topics instead of having each philosopher present a paper on a specialized topic. So you'll have an opportunity of getting an introduction to philosophical thinking from a number of different points of view on some very important topics.

STUDENT: Could you tell me a little about what kind of philosophers they are? I mean are any of them existentialists, for example?

HOME: No, none of them are existentialists. One of them, Professor Kirk, is a philosopher of a fairly traditional kind. He's interested in philosophy of religion and you'll find him discussing great philosophers of the past like Aristotle, Plato,[5] and Aquinas.[6] He's somewhat interested in existentialist writers, but he couldn't call himself an existentialist. The other two are analytic philosophers, although of rather different kinds.

STUDENT: I've heard that term—"analytic" philosopher or "analytic" philosophy used before but I've never been quite sure what it meant. Could you explain a bit?

HOME: Well, I'll try, but I'll have to go back a bit into history. Around the turn of the century philosophy in most parts of the world was rather like religions in some ways. Philosophers belonged to schools of philosophy associated with the names of great philosophers of the past, just as people belonged to various religious sects. There wasn't much debate or discussion between different schools of philosophy and not even much debate within schools. Many philosophy teachers felt that their job was to expound the ideas of the founder of their school, not to argue with or about them. Professor Venner was one of a group of young students and teachers in Vienna after World War I who began to challenge this view of philosophy. The group became known as the "Vienna Circle." Many of them had started out in science or mathematics and their chief point of agreement was the principle that all meaningful statements were either true or false by definition—which was supposed to cover the statements of mathematics—or provable as true or false by sense experience, by observation and experiment; more or less, you can say, by the methods of science. This was called the verification principle—that's a very rough statement of it, of course.

STUDENT: But isn't that a scientific principle—I know I've heard my science teachers talk in just that way.

---

[5] Plato: see Biography (Appendix A) and Further Readings at the end of Chapter 10.
[6] Aquinas: see Biography (Appendix A) and Further Readings at the end of Chapter 1.

HOME: No, it's a philosophical principle, put forward by the Vienna Circle and their supporters—the whole group is often called the logical positivists, by the way. A good many scientists have seized on it, but most philosophers since the time of the Vienna Circle have rejected it, for a number of reasons.

STUDENT: Is the other philosopher a logical positivist too?

HOME: No, Professor Oxmore—who, by the way, is a woman—is what's called an ordinary language philosopher. After the verification principle was argued about and largely rejected, philosophers in England began to look more closely at the way we use and misuse words, and many of them came to the conclusion that a lot of philosophical problems arise because we misuse ordinary language in various ways. Ordinary language philosophy was the next stage after logical positivism and learned from its successes and failures. They form two stages in a new approach to philosophy, concerned with language, suspicious of grand generalizations and systems, trying to solve problems bit by bit instead of all at once. Those are some of the characteristics of analytic philosophy. But analytic philosophers disagree on all sorts of things.

STUDENT: And do our three visitors disagree?

HOME: Yes, I can hardly think of any subject they don't hold different views on. The discussion among them—which I'll be involved in too—ought to be pretty lively.

STUDENT: It sounds fascinating—I'll be looking forward to it.

HOME: We'll be glad to have you attend the sessions. But remember that there's no substitute for doing your own philosophizing in a regular philosophy class or outside of one. The advantage of a class is that you'll get help and criticism. By all means come and talk to me again about philosophy any time you like, but you may want to take some regular philosophy courses too. Perhaps I'll see you in one of my classes next session.

STUDENT: Perhaps you will.

Note: The colloquium, described in this book, and the four philosophers, who are members of the panel, are all fictional. No resemblance is implied or intended to any actual philosophers or any actual philosophical meeting. Personal details about the fictional philosophers are intended purely for dramatic purposes.

PHILOSOPHICALLY SPEAKING

1

Is God a "Great Pumpkin"?

HOME: Perhaps I should open this colloquium by making clear just what we hope to do. For some years our annual colloquium has followed the usual pattern for affairs of this sort. We've invited several distinguished philosophers from other universities to present specialized papers, followed by discussion of points raised by the papers. Our colloquium has put a special emphasis on giving plenty of time for discussion, and on involving all of our guests in the discussion of all of the papers, not just their own. But the papers have taken up a good deal of the time, and some of them have been on highly specialized or highly technical topics. This year, on the urging of an advisory committee composed of philosophy students, we've decided to do things somewhat differently. We've invited three distinguished guests, with myself to make up a fourth member of the panel. This group will simply discuss a number of separate topics, with no one reading papers or giving formal presentations. For each session, one of us four will act as chairman, to keep the discussion on the rails and call time at the end, but the chairman isn't expected to stay out of the discussion if he has anything to contribute. The first part of the discussion will take place only between the members of the panel; after that we'll throw the discussion open for questions or comments from the floor. You'll find details about the arrangements in the printed program.

Because our audience is a varied one, and not all of you are well-versed in philosophy, even when I'm not the chairman I'll try to interrupt if I think that we're getting too technical or talking over the heads of the audience. This may slow up the discussion a little at times, but I think that it's an excellent idea—it's very easy for us to get interested in technical problems and forget that the discussion is for the benefit of the audience and not just for our own benefit. I'll also go over the transcript of our discussion which will be typed up from the tapes which are being made, and insert some additional information about things like dates of philosophers we mention or publication dates of books we refer to. This ought to be useful to those who use the transcript for various purposes— I know I'll plan to use it for some of my classes.

The first of our three guests is Professor Karl Venner, who was one of the original members of the Vienna Circle group of philosophers and has had a long and distinguished career at many European and American universities. He specializes in logic and philosophy of science and is the author of many books and articles. The second guest is Professor Elizabeth Oxmore, who has taught at the University of Oxford for many years, with occasional visits to American universities. Her papers have appeared in many journals and in the Proceedings of the Aristotelian Society. Her specialties are philosophy of language and philosophy of mind. Our third guest is Professor Timothy Kirk, who has taught both in Great Britain and in the United States. He specializes in philosophy of religion and is the author of several books. He has also published in both philosophical and theological journals. I am Mark Home of the philosophy department here; I take it that most of you are aware of my qualifications and disqualifications. I don't want to be mock-modest about the distinguished company I'm in, but perhaps I ought to tell you that both Professor Venner and Professor Oxmore have been my teachers and that I have learned a great deal from Professor Kirk on several topics. I'm heartily in awe of all three of them, but I hope that this won't have too repressive an effect on me. You'll find more details about our guests in the program.

Our first topic is philosophy of religion; the title of the session is "Is God a 'Great Pumpkin'?"

For the sake of those unfamiliar with the allusion in our title for today's discussion, let me set the scene briefly. Linus, a small boy in the *Peanuts* comic strip, believes in a Great Pumpkin who brings toys and gifts to children on Hallowe'en. The other children laugh at him, but Linus stays in a pumpkin patch all night on Hallowe'en, missing out on trick-or-treating and a party with his friends. When the Great Pumpkin fails to appear, Linus still believes in him, saying that the pumpkin patch he chose was not "sincere" enough, and that next year the Great Pumpkin will surely come. The view of the other children, and presumably the view of most grownups, is that Linus is foolish to continue to believe in the Great Pumpkin. I suppose that another way of posing our question for debate would be, "Are theists as foolish in their belief in God as Linus seems to be in his belief in the Great Pumpkin?" Professor Venner, perhaps you might begin.

VENNER: Yes. As Professor Home knows, my view is that God is like the Great Pumpkin and those who believe in God are foolish to do so. It seems to me that all of the arguments for the existence of God are bad ones, and that there are good arguments against the existence of God. I have great affection and respect for many people, like Professor Home and Professor Kirk, who are believers in God. But I think that they are like the stubborn small boy, Linus. They are standing in the pumpkin patch waiting for good things that will never come, instead of being with their friends seeking for good things within their reach. I invite them to come out of the pumpkin patch and come to the party with the rest of us.

KIRK: For my own part, I want to decline the invitation; I'll let Home speak for himself. I won't try to compete with Professor Venner in making use of the Great Pumpkin analogy, although I will note that Linus' interest in the Great Pumpkin seems pretty much confined to the toys and gifts, and that I don't want to align myself with those who are interested in God merely for what they can get out of Him. More to the point, Charles Schultz, the creator of Peanuts, has never really told us *why* Linus believes in the Great Pumpkin. Whether his reasons are good ones I don't know, but I want to challenge Professor Venner's claim that all of the arguments for God's existence are bad ones. I am myself quite satisfied with some of the traditional arguments.

VENNER: You would defend, for example, Anselm's ontological argument [1] or Aquinas' Five Ways? [2]

KIRK: No, not the ontological argument, but . . .

HOME: Excuse me for interrupting, Professor Kirk, but perhaps you could help some of the audience follow the discussion if you briefly described the main arguments for the existence of God, and said why you reject the ontological argument.

KIRK: Alright, if you like. The clearest and shortest way I know of stating the ontological argument is this. Plainly there are things that exist and are thought about, like the building we're in. There are also

---

[1] St. Anselm, see Biography (Appendix A) and Further Readings at the end of this chapter.
[2] St. Thomas Aquinas, see Biography (Appendix A) and Further Readings at the end of this chapter.

presumably things that exist but which nobody thinks about. Again there are things, like Tolkien's imaginary hobbits, in his book *Lord of the Rings,* for instance, which people think about but which don't exist, and there are things which neither exist nor are thought about. That gives us four classes: which one is God in? Since lots of people think about God, presumably God is not in either of the classes of not thought about things, existent or nonexistent. So presumably God is either in the class "existing and thought about" or in the class "not existing but thought about." So far this is all very simple. But now comes the tricky part. The ontological argument asks us to examine our idea or concept of God. Isn't our idea of God the idea of the greatest possible being—a being than whom there *could be* no greater? It would seem that this is just what we *mean* by God. Well then, the argument goes, it must be the case that God both exists and is thought of. For if God were fictional—not existing but thought of, like the hobbits—then God wouldn't be the greatest being possible, because a real, existing God would be greater than a fictional God. But we've agreed that by definition God is the greatest possible being. So we've eliminated all of the possibilities but one—God must both exist and be thought of!

OXMORE: That's a very ingenious statement of the argument. You rather slipped in the premise that a real God would be in some sense greater than a fictional God, though. Is that where your objections to the argument come in?

KIRK: No, actually I think that bit can be argued for with at least some degree of convincingness. My objection is that the whole argument is a bit of verbal sleight of hand, an attempt to get from the realm of definitions to the realm of existence. What the argument *does* show, I think, is that if we use the term "God" to refer to something fictional or to something or someone in some way imperfect, then we're misusing the term. It's quite all right to say that the term "God" with a capital "G" can only refer to something existent. But the whole question is whether the term does refer to anything. And you can't tell whether a word refers to something merely by looking at the word. I think that's the basic fallacy behind all versions of the ontological argument.

HOME: Of course people have attacked it from all sorts of angles.

KIRK: Yes, the curious thing about the ontological argument is that while it's provoked all sorts of interesting arguments, it's probably never convinced anyone. But there are arguments for the existence of God which have convinced people who previously disbelieved in the existence of God that God really does exist. I'd classify these in three main groups. First, variations on what is usually called the cosmological argument—

attempts to start with very general features of the universe like change or causality and argue from them to the existence of God. Second, attempts to argue from the apparent order and understandability of the universe to a designer or lawgiver—what's often called the teleological argument or argument from design.

VENNER: This argument has some appeal even for scientifically minded philosophers like myself, since it has some resemblance to scientific arguments. But as Hume [3] pointed out, the hypothesis of a designer is quite consistent with many possibilities that would be quite unwelcome to a theist like yourself. For example, that the universe was designed by many gods or that it was designed by a being who then grew old and died.

KIRK: I think there are some replies to Hume's arguments on that point, but I wouldn't rely on this argument by itself. Similarly the third class of arguments for the existence of God—those that try to argue from moral experience to the existence of a moral lawgiver—seems to me not to be convincing independent of other arguments. But a combination of arguments, beginning with an argument along the lines of the cosmological argument and bringing in elements of the design argument and moral argument, can be shown to be very strong indeed. You mentioned Aquinas' Five Ways, Venner. It seems to me that although they're presented as independent arguments, Aquinas is actually presenting a sort of cumulative argument.

HOME: Perhaps you could briefly indicate what the Five Ways are, for those who haven't heard of them.

KIRK: Aquinas' Five Ways are five arguments for the existence of God, proposed by Saint Thomas Aquinas in the thirteenth century. The first three are arguments from very general features of the universe, like causality or change, to the existence of a First Cause, an unchanged source of change, and so on. The fourth one is an argument from the existence of various degrees of goodness to a Supreme Good, and the last one is an argument from the apparent order and regularity of the universe to the existence of a designer of the universe. I wouldn't always defend Aquinas' own version of these arguments, although I'd defend expanded and up-to-date versions of all five. By the way, it seems to me that critics of theism, especially in introductory books and classes, often play a rather shabby trick here. They take a "question" from Aquinas' *Summa Theologica*, something which covers at most two pages taken out of something about on the scale of an encyclopedia. They take something written in Aristotelian terminology for sound Aristotelians—people

---

[3] David Hume, see Biography (Appendix A) and Further Readings at the end of Chapter 2.

who agreed on Aristotle's philosophy even though they disagreed on much else. Then they couple this with long and elaborate analyses written much later, which criticize Aquinas' argument, and conclude without giving any contemporary theist a chance for a reply. No wonder the impression is given that the theistic arguments are refuted.

VENNER: I agree that this is unfair, but it is no longer so much done, I think.

KIRK: Perhaps not, but no widely used introductory book in philosophy gives the theist what I would call a fair shake.

VENNER: Well, you are here in person to repair the deficiency, Professor Kirk. Perhaps you will state your version of the traditional proofs that you do find satisfactory.

KIRK: I'd be happy to. The sort of thing I want to try to do is argue from various things we know about the universe around us to the existence of a being with at least some of the characteristics of the Christian God. This kind of argument from the world to God has certain severe limitations at best, and it's rather in disfavor in some circles nowadays, but philosophers have given such arguments ever since Socrates. To speak only for my own religion, some Christians have always given such arguments, although it's only fair to say that some Christians have always been suspicious of them. Those of us who want to use such arguments are fond of quoting Saint Paul's remark that "since the beginning of the world the invisible attributes of God, for example, His eternal power and divinity, have been plainly discernible through things which He has made and which are commonly seen and known." [4] For Roman Catholics the idea that God can be certainly known to exist by the use of our reason is actually defined as part of the faith. Other Christians wouldn't go as far as that, but the effort to give rational arguments for God's existence is certainly part of the Christian tradition. And, of course, this sort of proof is quite reasonable on the Christian view, since we regard the world as something made by God. Just as a book tells you something, although not everything, about its author, so we hope to know something, although not everything, about God by looking at the universe which we believe He has made.

I suppose that we could start at various points, but let's take a traditional one. When we look at the universe around us, one of the things that's very noticeable is that all of the things we have any experience of are *causally dependent* on other things. I exist because my parents

---

[4] Epistle to the Romans, Chap. 1, verse 20.

lived and met and married, and because of many other factors. This building exists because it was built by people, who existed before it did, and so on. And as we go back in history we find the same state of affairs, things coming into existence because of other things that existed before they did and brought them into existence. But now we can see that we're faced with three possibilities. If we push back far enough we come to a time when nothing at all existed; or we come to a time when there existed only something that always existed, without depending for its existence on something else—a *causally independent* something—or no matter how far back we go we always find things that depend for their existence on something else. The first view I think no one takes seriously, for reasons I'll come to in a minute. The second view is the one held by Christians—we believe that God is a causally independent being, that at one time only God existed, and that the universe as we know it was brought into existence by God. The third view is that held by many atheists and agnostics, but also by some theists, the view that something rather like the material universe we know has always existed. The atheists by and large think that *only* this sort of thing has ever existed. The theists think that in addition to this sort of thing some sort of God, who is a causally independent being, has also existed. Some theists of this kind think that the existence of the material universe depends on the existence of God, others have thought that only the form and arrangement of the universe, but not its existence, was due to God.

Now the major question which has to be settled once we've decided that something or other has always existed is whether *only* causally dependent beings have ever existed or whether the existing causally dependent beings don't in some way require the existence of a causally independent being. We'll come to that in a moment. But first we have to look at the possibility that I said no one really takes seriously. Could the universe have just popped into existence out of nothing? One minute nothing at all in existence, the next minute some existing things? I like to call that idea the "pop theory." It seems to me that we know that this could not have happened, and we know it because we know the truth of a metaphysical principle—"nothing begins to exist without a cause."

HOME: To clear up any confusion about this, perhaps you could say something about the "continuous creation" theory of the universe held by some scientists. Some people take this theory as showing that scientists can conceive of something beginning to exist without a cause, because in this view particles come into existence in empty space.

KIRK: Well, the scientists who hold the continuous creation, or "steady state," theory aren't, so far as I can see, saying that something begins to exist without a cause. What Professor Hoyle, the inventor and chief defender of the theory, says, for example, is that "the creation arises from a field, which you must think of as generated by the matter that exists already. We are well used to the idea of matter giving rise to a gravitational field. Now we must think of it also giving rise to a creation field. Matter that already exists causes new matter to appear." [5] And although other defenders of the theory wouldn't necessarily express it in that way, they also seem to have the idea that the universe as a whole, or the whole natural order, is the cause of the creation of matter. I might have philosophical objections to that as an explanation, but they wouldn't be the same as my objections to the pop theory. Far from favoring a pop theory view of the universe, the continuous creation theory says that there never was and never could be a state of nothingness or even a state of no matter. Both matter and energy have always existed and will always exist. There's lots more you can say about the steady state theory from a philosophical and scientific point of view, but the main point is that the theory doesn't at all contradict the metaphysical principle that "nothing begins to exist without a cause."

VENNER: I would have scientific objections to the steady state theory based on the fact that it violates the principle of conservation of matter-energy, which says that although matter can be changed to energy, the total amount of matter-energy in the universe remains constant. It seems to me that this principle is so basic that any theory that violates it must be rejected.

KIRK: Hoyle, as I understand him, denies that his theory violates that principle, [6] but I'll let you two fight that out. Let me add one point before going on: a traditional theist like myself wants to say that God brought matter into existence where no matter previously existed. He created the universe from nothing, or *"ex nihilo."* Sometimes you get people claiming that this idea is nonsensical or self-contradictory. But if it makes sense for Hoyle to envision matter bringing matter into existence, I don't see how it can be nonsensical or self-contradictory to envision God bringing matter into existence. Anyway, back to my first point; the continuous creation theory doesn't give us a counterexample to the metaphysical principle that "nothing begins to exist without a cause."

VENNER: Perhaps we could clarify what you mean by calling this a metaphysical principle. Do you mean that it is logically true?

[5] Fred Hoyle, *The Nature of the Universe* (New York: Harper and Row, 1950), pp. 123–24.
[6] Ibid., p. 130.

KIRK: Well, it seems to me that there is a narrower sense and a wider sense of "logically true." In the narrower sense a statement is logically true if it follows from the meaning of words and the ordinary rules of logic that the denial of that statement is self-contradictory. I don't think that "nothing begins to exist without a cause" is logically true in the narrow sense: I don't know of any way of deriving a self-contradiction from its denial. In the wider sense of logically true, a statement is logically true if we simply don't know what it would be like for its denial to be true, if its denial is inconceivable. I think that "nothing begins to exist without a cause" *is* logically true in this sense.

VENNER: But it seems to me that I can conceive of what you say is inconceivable.

KIRK: I grant that you can imagine, in the sense of making a mental picture, a sort of black void and then something suddenly appearing. But you haven't really made sense of something beginning to exist without a cause. In that case you've imagined, *you* were existing while you imagined the void and *you* "imagined" the object into existence.

VENNER: But now if inconceivable does not mean "unimaginable" and it does not mean "self-contradictory," I do not really know what you mean by it.

KIRK: Ah, but consider. Suppose I told you that this book on the table had simply popped into existence out of nothing a few moments before you came into the room, and that nothing at all had caused it to come into existence. You wouldn't take that possibility seriously for a moment. You would say that there must be a cause for its existence. But anyone who says that it's conceivable for a whole universe to pop into existence shouldn't boggle at a little thing like a book.

VENNER: Yes, I grant you that I would reject the possibility of the book popping into existence. But this is, I think, because I hold certain scientific views—for example, that the principle of conservation of matter-energy is well established.

KIRK: But wouldn't you grant that a principle like "nothing begins to exist without a cause" is not on the same level as an ordinary scientific law? Isn't it a demand that we bring *to* experience, not something that we learn *from* experience?

VENNER: I grant that it is not on the same level as an ordinary scientific law. I might even grant that it is a demand that we bring *to* experience. We do presuppose that things have causes. We do not admit the possibility of a thing coming into existence without cause. But the universe is not bound to meet the demands we put to it. We can only find whether it will meet our demand for simplicity, let us say, by experience.

KIRK: I wonder if you haven't already granted at least part of what I have said about this principle, and whether your reluctance to grant more isn't due to the ghost of the verification principle. You grant the principle is true; we agree that it isn't logically true in the narrow sense. So for you it can only be scientifically true. But that's just the verification principle: "any true statement is either logically true (in what I call the narrow sense), or verifiable by the methods of science."

VENNER: Ah yes, but although the verifiability theory will not do all that we hoped in the Vienna days, I think that it is still a very good methodological principle. So long as I can fit all the truths I know either into the "narrow" logical truths or into scientific truths, then I have no need for any other category. What more are you claiming for your principle than would be involved in claiming that it is a high-level, empirical generalization, or a methodological principle that has been successful so far?

KIRK: One important thing that would be involved is that whereas scientific laws hold only for this universe, metaphysical principles hold for all possible universes.

VENNER: But then I would want to know how you know this, and perhaps also what you mean by "possible universes," if you do not mean logically possible in your narrow sense. But perhaps we spend too much time on this point. I certainly grant that we need not take what you so amusingly call the pop theory seriously at all, and though I do not agree that there are such principles I quite understand what you mean by a metaphysical principle.

HOME: As moderator perhaps I should nudge you back toward your main point by noting that both of you reject the pop theory, Kirk for metaphysical reasons and Venner for scientific reasons. You also seem to have reached understanding, if not agreement, about what Kirk means by a metaphysical principle.[7] So perhaps you could get back to your main line of argument, Professor Kirk.

KIRK: Right. Taking it for granted that the pop theory is out, we come to the disagreement between those who hold that only causally dependent things have ever existed, and those who hold that at least one causally independent thing has existed. Since the theory that only caus-

---

[7] See Readings from Hospers' collection at the end of Chapter 10.

ally dependent things have existed supposes an endless chain of causes, let's call it the "endless chain theory." Let's call the theory that a causally independent being does exist the "God theory." It seems to a great many people, philosophers and nonphilosophers alike, that an endless chain theory, in which only causally dependent beings have ever existed, is just as inconceivable as the pop theory.

VENNER: That I will not grant you.

KIRK: Well then, let me begin on a quite simple and popular level, and we can pursue the question as far as time allows. Suppose that I want a copy of Kant's *Critique of Pure Reason* and I ask you to loan me one. Let us suppose that you say, "I don't have one but I'll ask my friend Oxmore to lend me one, and I'll lend it to you." But suppose Oxmore says, "I don't have one but I'll ask my friend Home to lend me one and I'll lend it to you to lend to Kirk." And so on into the night. Now in that situation two things are quite certain. If the process goes on to infinity— if everyone says "I don't have one, but I'll ask my friend . . ." then I'll never get the book. And, second, if I do get the book then the process has come to an end somewhere. Someone had the book without having to borrow it. Similarly, if I ask Home to give me my check for travel expenses for this colloquium early, and he says, "I can't give it to you but I'll ask my department chairman," and the chairman says, "I can't authorize it, but I'll ask the Bursar," and so on, then one of two things happens. The process goes on to infinity, in which case I never get my check, or I get my check, in which case someone was able to give permission to issue the check without getting permission.

All right, now take any existing thing. It received its existence from some other thing or things, which in turn received its existence or their existences from other things, and so on. Now it seems to me that the same two principles apply. If the process of everything getting its existence from something else went on to infinity, then the thing in question would never come into existence. And if the thing has come into existence then the process hasn't gone on to infinity. There was something that had existence without having to receive it from something else. In other words, a causally independent being. So it seems to me that if anything at all exists, as it obviously does, a causally independent being must exist also.

VENNER: Already I see a very serious objection—both of your examples go forward in time. I agree that if I must wait for an infinite number of people to borrow from each other before I can present you with the book you requested, then I, and you, will never get that book. And similarly with the check. But this is because each transaction takes time, and you and I are mortal. But in the other case, the case of existence, if we suppose that an infinite amount of time has elapsed, then there is time for all these "transactions" to have taken place and for the thing in question to come into existence.

KIRK: I disagree that time is of the essence here. The point about the book is that no one has it without borrowing it, so to put it crudely, where does the book *come from?* But if that feature of the examples bothers you, let's go on to other examples. First, imagine a case where you have a number of shining objects, and you're told that none of the objects shine by their own light, but each shines by light reflected from some other object. So far so good. But now imagine a situation in which nothing shines by its own light, but everything reflects light from something else. I submit that this just makes no sense—how does the light get into the system at all?

But I think there are even better examples. There are several arguments in Aristotle [8] which have basically this structure we've just been finding. One is the argument that not every word can be defined, another is the argument that not everything can be proved, and the third is the argument that something must be desired for its own sake and not everything can be desired for the sake of something else. Take the definition argument as typical. Not every word can have its meaning made clear by definition. Start with any word whose meaning you will not understand unless it is explained by a definition. If you understand the words in the definition, fine. But if not you must define them, and so on. Either you arrive at some words whose meaning is clear to you without definition, or the process goes on to infinity. But if the process goes on to infinity you never understand the word you started with, or any of the other words. Since we obviously do understand some words, not every word needs to have its meaning made clear by definition.

VENNER: About this argument I have some doubts; the conclusion is clearly true but I do not think that that particular argument establishes it. It seems to me that there are better arguments for that conclusion. I am also dubious as to the general principle which you seem to be trying to establish.

KIRK: Yes, well you do see that I'm trying to establish a general principle: one that I think could be stated in a general way. It seems to me that this is the only way in which a general principle of this kind can be established, by what Aristotle called induction, or one of the things which

---

[8] Aristotle, see Biography (Appendix A). For the arguments, see his *Posterior Analytics* I, 2–3 and *Ethics* I, 2 (in for example, R. McKeon, ed., *Basic Works of Aristotle* (New York: Random House, 1941).

he called induction. All you can do is give a number of instances of the principle, try to make clear what they have in common, and wait for the person to see the principle. It seems to me that in practice this is what we do when we explain logical principles and even mathematical principles to students.

VENNER: It may or may not be the way in which we in fact teach these principles, but it is not the way in which we justify them.

KIRK: I'm not so sure of that. Given certain axioms we can, of course, show that denying certain other propositions leads to self-contradiction. But it seems to me that when we justify the axioms themselves we depend on the "logical intuition" or "mathematical intuition" of our students or our colleagues.

VENNER: But even if this were so, there is very wide agreement in accepting logical or mathematical axioms, but not very wide agreement in accepting your metaphysical principles. Perhaps I might urge certain objections to your proposed principle?

KIRK: Certainly.

VENNER: One objection is that of Lord Russell,[9] who argued that the attempt to deny an infinite regress of causally dependent things depended on an irrational objection to a "backwards" infinity. Russell pointed out that we feel no such objection to an infinity in a forward direction; we object to "beginninglessness" but not to "endlessness." But in mathematics we find no conceptual difficulty in counting backward from zero: minus one, minus two, and so on. But this series seems to be a "beginningless" one.

KIRK: Russell's objection was based on ignoring the distinction between a "vicious," or dependent, infinite regress and a nonvicious, or non-dependent, regress. In a vicious regress each member depends on the previous member: I don't get the book unless you do; you don't get it unless Oxmore does; and so on. Word A is not understood unless defined by word B, which is not understood unless defined by word C, and so on. It's only this kind of infinite regress that the argument refers to. The mathematical example, of course, is not to the point. When you count minus one, minus two, and so on you start with zero. The negative natural numbers are no more "beginningless" than the positive ones. And, in general, any mathematical infinity has some starting point and some procedure for going on.

9 Bertrand Russell, see Biography (Appendix A) and Further Readings at the end of Chapter 9.

VENNER: Perhaps this answers Russell's point, although I would like to explore the matter of vicious and nonvicious regress further. Another objection that goes back at least to Hume is that in the case of things which are caused to come into existence, if there is an infinite regress each thing has its own cause, so where is the difficulty about the cause of the whole? Professor Edwards,[10] I know, used the example of a group of Eskimos in New York City. Once we know why each Eskimo is there, then there is no further question as to why the group is there.

HOME: Perhaps you could make the point of Edwards' story a bit clearer, Professor Venner.

VENNER: Of course. Some theologians I know take the following line. They admit, perhaps, that scientists can in principle explain the existence of each particular thing in the universe, but they argue that we still need an explanation for the universe *as a whole*. Edwards' story is an attempt to show that when we have an explanation for each particular thing in a group, there is no need for an explanation of the group as a whole. If I know why the first Eskimo is in New York, and why the second Eskimo is in New York, and so on for the whole group, then it makes no sense to ask why the group as a whole is in New York. I already have as much explanation as can be given.

Similarly if I can explain scientifically the existence of the earth and the sun and the stars, and so on for each object in the universe, then there is no remaining question as to why the universe exists—I already have an item-by-item explanation. But I do not know whether Professor Kirk would use the line of argument against which Edwards' story is directed.

KIRK: Well, I think that it's a misleading way of putting a valid point. But I'm quite willing to attack Edwards' argument on its own ground.

VENNER: I *would* be most interested to hear your criticisms.

KIRK: There are several points here. First let's undermine the slogan "each one has its own cause" by considering circular cases. If I define word A by word B, word B by word C, and word C by word A, "each has its own definition," but we still may not understand the words. If I borrow the Kant book from you, you borrow it from Oxmore, and she borrows it from me, there is a sense in which the possession of the book by each of us is explained, but we still want to know how the book got into this circle of borrowers in the first place. Similarly, if A is caused by

---

[10] Paul Edwards, "The Cosmological Argument" in D. Burril, ed., *The Cosmological Argument* (Garden City, N.Y.: Doubleday and Co., 1967.)

B, B is caused by C, and C is caused by A, "each one has its own cause," but we would not regard this as a satisfactory explanation. Edwards' Eskimos are a complete red herring, I fear. He gives an explanation that goes completely outside the group for the presence of one Eskimo, then explains the presence of the others in terms of that one's presence. One is married to the first Eskimo, one is a detective following another, and so on. I believe that Edwards also throws in an irrelevant Eskimo—one who is present for some reason quite unconnected with the rest. But none of this will do for the universe. If the claim is that only causally dependent things exist, then there's no question of going outside the class of causally dependent things to find an explanation for the existence of any of them. In the case of explaining why a group of people is in a place, you can have two basic situations. In one, all of the things in the group, and therefore the group, are there for one reason; for example, "All of these Eskimos (this group of Eskimos) are here for the exhibition of Eskimo art." Or you can explain the presence of some members of the group by the presence of others: for example, "Nanook is here to make a movie and the others are here because Nanook is here." But there's no question of explaining the presence of each of the group in terms of the presence of each of the others: "A is here because B is, B because C is, and C because A is." That would be absurd. But that's what Edwards seems to be saying in the case of the universe.

VENNER: But the Eskimos are a finite group. The universe, let us say, is composed of an infinite number of things.

KIRK: What difference does that make, would you say?

VENNER: In the case of our Eskimos we must end up in a circle, since there are only a finite number. But in the case of an infinite collection, for each new thing we have another, different, thing or set of things that causes it. We will never run out of things, since their number is infinite.

KIRK: Yes, but you never get any forwarder. You start with a thing which needs a cause; you supply the cause, but it is in turn a thing which needs a cause, and so on. At any stage you are no better off than you, were to begin with.

VENNER: But you *are* better off; you've explained the existence of a number of things. This is just the situation we find in science; we explain A by B, B by C, and so on. At any given time our highest explanatory theory is itself unexplained, but may be at some later date.

KIRK: But even in science we hope for some ultimate "unified field theory" that would explain everything else.

VENNER: But if there is such a theory it would, in the nature of the case, be itself unexplained.

KIRK: Unexplained in the sense of being self-explanatory or in the sense of simply as a matter of fact having no explanation?

VENNER: Certainly not self-explanatory. Science I think does not recognize any category of the self-explanatory.

KIRK: But in the case of causes this won't work. The parallel to your highest theory, which simply as a matter of fact is unexplained, would be a cause which simply as a matter of fact existed. But this seems to get us back to the pop theory.

VENNER: If this cause came into existence.

KIRK: But if it didn't then you have something not caused which didn't come into existence, and this seems to me to be just the causally independent being we were aiming for.

VENNER: But then this presumes that we do come to such an uncaused cause. It still seems to me that an infinite series of caused causes is a possible alternative. We may feel more comfortable with a series that has a beginning, but the universe is not bound to make us comfortable.

KIRK: We seem to be back where we started.

VENNER: Yes, perhaps we are at an impasse here. But let's explore the consequences if we do come to the conclusion that a causally independent being exists. Do you identify such a being with God? Why could the physical universe not be a causally independent thing?

KIRK: True, simply proving a causally independent being is not sufficient to prove the existence of God in the Christian sense. But it's an important step on the way, as I hope to show. The universe itself couldn't be a causally independent thing if it is simply a collection of causally dependent things. You don't get a causally independent being by simply piling up causally dependent things, any more than you get a credit by piling up debits.

VENNER: You get a thing that weighs a ton by piling up things that weigh less than a ton.

KIRK: Ah, but in that case each thing you add gets you closer to a ton. Whereas no matter how many debits you add you're no closer to a credit. Causal independence is what you might call a nonadditive property. You can't arrive at it by adding together things that lack it.

VENNER: This is perhaps plausible. But what if we say that the basic matter-energy of the universe is causally independent—that it always exists no matter what else exists or does not exist.

KIRK: I think there are objections to that view, but let me grant it for the sake of argument. Suppose that matter and energy are causally independent things. But now you still have to explain why the particular things that exist do exist. And it seems to me that you're faced with three possibilities. Either each particular thing exists because of some built-in force or tendency in matter to produce things of that kind; or it just happens to come into existence because of some chance shift or combination in the arrangement of matter; or it exists because of an order imposed on matter by something in some respects like a human mind. The first I call the "natural necessity view"; the second I call the "chance view"; and the third I call the "weak theistic view." The weak theistic view isn't entirely satisfactory to a Christian, since it makes God an architect or designer working with independently existing materials, rather than a creator. If you accept the weak theistic view, presumably you think of the designer as a causally independent being, and matter-energy also as causally independent. And if you've gone that far it seems reasonable to admit that you might as well simplify things to one causally independent being and grant that matter-energy is causally dependent on God—that is that God created it. That I call the "strong theistic view." But the argument between the weak and strong theistic views is in a way a family quarrel—presumably you don't want either.

VENNER: Yes, I reject both.

KIRK: Well then, you're presumably stuck with the chance view, the natural necessity view, or some combination of the two. And both seem to suffer from absolutely fatal objections. If the chance view is true, then the apparent order and understandability of the universe is a mere illusion, like a series of throws of a single die where you happen by pure chance to get 1, 2, 3, 4. . . . If this is merely a chance sequence then there's no reason at all to expect the sequence to continue, and the apparent regularity is a mere illusion. Similarly, if anything like the chance view is true, there is no reason at all to expect the regularities we've observed to continue even one second into the future, and furthermore all the regularities we think we've discovered are mere illusions. Suppose that I give you a jumble of letters and ask you to decode it. After a great deal of work you say, "I believe that the first three words are "Meet me at." I laugh and explain that it's a practical joke; the letters are a mere chance sequence. But if that's true you not only lose any confidence that the "message" will continue in an intelligible way, you lose any confidence that what you have decoded so far is right.

VENNER: Suppose that this is correct. I do not defend this view myself, although it seems close to a view like that of Hume.

KIRK: Yes, and Hume drew the proper consequence from it: complete skepticism.

VENNER: Yes, perhaps. But we are still faced with what you call the natural necessity view.

KIRK: The natural necessity view seems to lead to complete determinism, which has fatal drawbacks.

VENNER: Ah, but I do not find that determinism has fatal drawbacks.

HOME: If I may intervene: determinism will be the subject of the session after next and perhaps we might postpone discussion of it until then. I notice that Professor Oxmore has been champing at the bit. Perhaps we might allow her to get into the discussion.

OXMORE: No, honestly, I've been sitting here lost in admiration as Venner and Kirk slugged it out toe to toe in the time-honored fashion. My doubts are doubts as to whether the entire discussion they're engaged in makes any sense. I have minor doubts about the way in which they've been talking about causing things—it seems to me that events are what is caused—and about the way in which they talk about existence as if it were a sort of parcel that could be passed from one to another. But my major doubt is this: aren't we getting so far from our ordinary ways of talking and thinking that we no longer know what we're saying or how to settle the disputes that arise? I mean, we don't ordinarily ask, "What caused Professor Kirk?" or "Is this table causally dependent?"

KIRK: Well, it seems to me that we constantly do use words outside their most common and basic use—if that's what you mean by their "ordinary use"—and we understand perfectly well what we mean. In science we make one kind of extension of the meaning of words, in poetry another kind, in philosophy yet another kind. The kind of objection you're making seems to depend on a theory of meaning that couldn't be defended in any precise form. Try to make clear what you mean by the ordinary use of words. Try to reduce to a precise rule your misgivings about whether we understand what we mean when we don't use words in an ordinary way. It seems very likely that you'd either come up with something trivial or something false. Trivial if it just turned out by definition that philosophical use of words wasn't "ordinary." The proper answer to that would be "so what?" But if you then went on to try to insist that we didn't know what we meant when we used words in a "nonordinary" way, this just seems to be false. Venner and I disagree, but we understand each other. As to your specific examples, both questions sound odd but for different reasons. We don't ordinarily ask whether this table is causally dependent because "causally dependent" is a bit of technical terminology. But I can explain what I mean by it. I mean "Was this table brought into existence by something else?" The answer is obviously "Yes."

As to "What caused Professor Venner?" I grant that philosophers use "cause" a bit more widely than it's used in ordinary conversation. What we would mean here is, "What brought Professor Venner into existence?" And since he is a human being the answer is obviously "He was born, of certain parents at a certain time, and so on."

OXMORE: But if we learn how to use words in certain ways and in certain contexts, and then start using them in new ways, out of these contexts, we may believe we still know what we mean but we may have cut ourselves off from what gave those words any meaning.

KIRK: But using words we've learned in one way in one context, in new ways in new contexts, is practically what language is all about. If I couldn't use a word except in contexts exactly like those I first learned it in, I could hardly use it at all.

OXMORE: Yes, but we've learned a certain pattern or rule for using words that connects it up in certain ways with other words, and with kinds of cases and situations. For example: if I talk about making a decision, this is connected in essential ways with taking certain actions, in certain kinds of social contexts. Remove the possibility of action, or the appropriate kind of context, and so many of the ordinary connections of the word are broken that it loses its meaning. So it may not make sense to talk about making a decision in a dream or to talk about a disembodied spirit making a decision.

KIRK: I'll grant you that can happen. What I deny is that it happens in the philosophically interesting cases—including the one you've used as an example. I think that we can learn to use words like "cause" and "existence" in fairly everyday and humdrum contexts and still know what we mean by them in philosophical arguments. Again, I'd challenge you to make explicit the theory of meaning you're using or else apply what you're saying to the specific argument before us.

OXMORE: The first alternative would perhaps take us too far afield, but let me have a go at the second. Bertrand Russell, for example, objected that you can ask about the cause of individual things, just as you can ask who is the mother of individual persons. But to ask about the cause of the universe, the cause of everything, is just as illegitimate as it would be to ask who is the mother of everyone. "Everyone" isn't a person and doesn't have a mother, and the universe isn't an individual thing and doesn't have a cause.

KIRK: I'm afraid that's merely a bit of sophistry. There are two sources of confusion here. If we mean by "the universe" *everything* that exists, that would, of course, include a causally independent being if there were such a being. Then I'd want to say that one "part" of the universe so defined, one of the things that exists, is the cause of the other things that exist, in the sense that they wouldn't exist at all if it didn't. But this doesn't prevent some of the other things in the universe from causing yet others. Or we could talk in another way and mean by "the universe" only the physical universe, or all the causally dependent things considered together. In that case I would want to say that the universe so defined has a cause, which is outside the universe in the sense of being nonphysical or not causally dependent, and is the cause of the universe in the sense that if it hadn't existed the universe would not have existed. To make the analogy with the "mother" case, assume for the sake of argument the truth of the old Christian story of the descent of the whole human race from Adam and Eve. Now if you ask "Who is the mother of the human race?" you can mean by "the human race" either "all humans" or "the descendants of Adam and Eve." In the first case the answer to "Who is the mother of the human race?" is that one human being, Eve, is the mother of the rest of the human beings in the sense that she is a mother who does not herself have a mother, and if she had not been a mother no one else could have been. But this doesn't prevent other human beings being mothers in their turn. If you want to talk the other way, then "the human race," meaning "the descendents of Adam and Eve," has or have *a* mother, Eve, who is not herself a descendent of Adam and Eve, and who is the mother of the human race in the sense that if she hadn't been a mother there would have been no human race.

OXMORE: I believe I see your point. I'll have to think about that a bit, but you may be right.

KIRK: That's a very fair admission, but I'll take advantage of your fair-mindedness to this extent. We've been talking about causation in quite a general and abstract way—quite a philosophical way in fact. But we understood each other quite well. You put forward a point and I replied to it and perhaps convinced you. But we weren't using "cause" in an "ordinary" way, if you mean by that a nonphilosophical way. So according to what you said earlier we shouldn't have understood each other.

OXMORE: That's going a bit fast. Some nonordinary uses might be all right and others not.

KIRK: I'm quite content with that admission. It means we have to argue the point in particular cases, and I'm quite content to do that. But you originally seemed to be trying to pull the rug out from any discussion of this kind, and you've retreated from that position.

OXMORE: Well, perhaps it's only a strategic retreat. But I ought to make my own position clear, since you and Venner have been admirably forthright. I feel myself that there are some reasons for supposing that something like a God exists; not necessarily high metaphysical reasons like the arguments about causation, but perhaps more prosaic reasons about what you call the apparent order and understandability of the universe. These are usually thought of as separate arguments, of course.

KIRK: Yes, I think myself that that's a "divide-and-conquer" tactic. I want to run the traditionally separate arguments in harness, if not actually making them one argument.

OXMORE: Well, calling them one argument doesn't make them one. I'd want to look pretty carefully at the connections. But to go on, I would also want to say that there are some rather impressive arguments against the existence of anything like the traditional God. And there is really no way of deciding objectively whether the evidence for is stronger than the evidence against. It seems very much a matter of personal choice which side you feel is stronger, and therefore a decision on the matter is outside the realm of philosophy proper, or, if you like, "technical philosophy," and gets into the area of "philosophy of life" in the sense of attitude toward life. I'm bound to say that I myself have the attitude that the evidence against the existence of God is stronger, and therefore I would call myself an agnostic, while admitting that in practice agnosticism and atheism come to very much the same thing.

KIRK: Of course I'd deny that the evidence is evenly balanced or that it's only a matter of personal choice.

HOME: Since Professor Kirk has been arguing singlehanded with both Professor Venner and Professor Oxmore, it seems only fair to let him have the last word. As you can see, their discussion of the existence of God has raised a number of other philosophical issues. We haven't, I think, settled any of the issues that have been raised, except possibly some minor points that have come up in connection with other things. But you now have some idea of what three very able philosophers have to say for themselves on these issues. Many of these points will come up again in future sessions, and in our final session, on the meaning of life, we may very well want to come back to some of the issues we've been discussing today. I'd like to get my own words in on some of these issues, and perhaps I'll have a chance then.

I'm very sorry to have to call this session to a close but we've already run over our allotted time. The next session will be in a way a continuation of this one, since we'll discuss arguments against the existence of God, especially the argument from the existence of evil. Our title will be "God and Evil," but we'll also look briefly at some other problems about God's existence. I'll be chairman again, so that Professors Kirk, Venner, and Oxmore can continue their discussion.

QUESTIONS

Answer the following questions as you think they would be answered by the panelist to whom they are addressed.

1. Professor Kirk: You say God made the world. But who made God?
2. Professor Venner: You deny that God made the world. How do you think it got here?
3. Professor Oxmore: You say that whether or not to believe in God is a matter of personal choice. But isn't this just what Christians are saying when they say it's a matter of faith?

Did you find these answers to questions in the dialogue satisfactory? Why or why not?

4. Venner's answer as to whether he is using the verification principle?
5. Kirk's answer to Russell's objection?
6. Oxmore's answers to Kirk's challenge to her theory of meaning?

Write brief essays on the following:

7. Which answer to a question or challenge in the dialogue do you feel you could improve on? How?
8. Which panelist's position is closest to your own? Why?
9. What objections would you like to raise to something said in the dialogue?
10. What argument would you like to put forward that is not in the dialogue?

FURTHER READINGS

Hick, John, *Philosophy of Religion* (2nd ed.), Englewood Cliffs, N.J.: Prentice-Hall, Inc., 1973, Chaps. 1 and 2, pp. 4–30.

Hospers, John, *Readings in Introductory Philosophical Analysis,* Englewood Cliffs, N.J.: Prentice-Hall, Inc., 1968.

    Aquinas, St. Thomas, "Five Proofs of the Existence of God," pp. 231–32.

Taylor, Richard, *Metaphysics* (2nd ed.), Englewood Cliffs, N.J.: Prentice-Hall, Inc., 1947, Chap. 10, pp. 102–20.

Wilson, Margaret D., Dan W. Brock, and Richard F. Kuhns, *Philosophy, An Introduction,* New York: Appleton-Century-Crofts, 1972.

    Anselm, St., "The Ontological Argument," pp. 47–53.

    Aquinas, St. Thomas, "The Five Ways," pp. 57–61.

    Geach, Peter, "On Aquinas' 'Five Ways'," pp. 61–68.

    Paley, William, "The Teleological Argument," pp. 19–24.

    Taylor, A. E., "Design and Intelligence," pp. 37–46.

See also Readings from Hospers' collection at the end of Chapter 10.

Questions on the Reading

1. Critically discuss Anselm's version of the ontological argument. Would you agree with Kirk's statement of it? With his criticisms of it?

2. Give reasons for accepting or rejecting one of Aquinas' five arguments for the existence of God. Does Kirk's restatement of these arguments strengthen the argument?

3. Compare Paley's version of the design argument with A. E. Taylor's. Which version does Kirk seem to be using?

4. Compare Kirk's version of the design argument with Richard Taylor's. Which version seems to be stronger?

5. Do Hick's criticisms of the arguments for God's existence apply to Kirk's version of those arguments? On balance are you more convinced by the arguments or the criticisms?

2

God and Evil

HOME: As I said last time our main topic will be the argument from evil against the existence of God: thus our title of "God and Evil." But perhaps we might start by dealing with some of the minor arguments against God's existence, and let Professor Kirk comment on them briefly.

KIRK: That would be fine from my point of view.

HOME: If I could start out—one argument, if you can call it that, that I find students and other people bringing up is that the idea of a personal God arose when the universe seemed to be a much smaller and cozier affair, and that now that we have a real idea of the tremendous size and age of the universe, the idea has to be rejected.

KIRK: Yes, I've encountered that view, but as you say it can hardly be called an argument. There's no logical step that I can see from "the universe is very large and old" to "God doesn't exist." I think that it's largely a matter of mood or emotion.

OXMORE: I'd agree with Kirk on that, and it seems to me that the mood or emotion varies a great deal from individual to individual. Russell once made some rather rhetorical remarks about man's smallness in the face of the age and size of the universe and Frank Ramsey,[1] a brilliant English philosopher who died much too young, remarked later that he'd never felt that particular feeling of smallness. That was partly a joke about his size because Frank was both rather tall and rather stout, but I think that it's just partly a matter of temperament, too.

VENNER: There's perhaps some argument here in that the anthropomorphic God pictured by the early Jews and Christians would not seem adequate as an explanation of a universe as great as we now know the actual universe to be.

KIRK: Well, setting aside the question of how anthropomorphic the Judeo-Christian concept of God was, even at an early stage I can agree with the spirit of your remark. If we have inadequate ideas of God, the greatness of the universe may give us a better idea of the greatness of its creator.

VENNER: This point is, I think, too slender to pursue, but it leads to another. Would you not agree that the atmosphere of much religious thinking is quite unscientific, much closer to magic and legends?

KIRK: Well, a good deal may be packed into an accusation that religious thinking is unscientific. Partly the issue may be the verification principle again. You mention magic. I think that basically magic is much closer to science than to religion. Magic is an attempt to compel the universe to do what you want it to, like technology, and to understand the principles governing the behavior of things, like science. The magicians failed. Their "technology" of spells and potions and amulets didn't work. The principles they claimed to have discovered were nonsense. But they were failures at playing the same game that scientists and technologists played successfully. The religious attitude of prayer and worship is quite different from the magician's attitude of bringing about "operations" by spells and so on.

VENNER: Isn't prayer a sort of magic formula?

KIRK: Good heaven's, no! In prayer you're asking a person who may either grant your request or refuse it, and you think that this person knows better than you what you need. The magician tries to compel things or people to behave in certain ways.

VENNER: What about miracles?

KIRK: A theist may or may not find the evidence for particular miracles convincing. But since he believes that the universe and its laws were

[1] Frank Ramsey, see Biography (Appendix A) and Further Readings at the end of Chapter 10.

created by God, he doesn't find any objection in principle to the idea that miracles are possible.

OXMORE: By way of trying to pin down the accusation that religion is somehow unscientific, hasn't one science, Freudian Psychology, gone some way to show that belief in God is a projection of certain hopes and fears?

KIRK: Well, a good many real things can be explained as projections of our hopes and fears if we start out by assuming that they don't exist. It seems to me that the Freudians try to have it both ways; they try to explain other people's beliefs and ideas as rationalizations, but they make an exception in favor of their own theories. You can give Freudian arguments on both sides of almost any question; for example, you could explain atheism as a rejection of a heavenly father figure due to an Oedipus complex. But it seems that Freud himself, and most Freudians, simply assume what needs to be proved in their theories about religion—that there are no good arguments for God's existence. Both sides can accuse the other of rationalization. What needs to be done is to look at the arguments pro and con.

HOME: Perhaps then we should turn to the basic arguments against the existence of God that philosophers have found worthy of attention.

OXMORE: Yes, I'd like to get down to what seem to me to be the real objections.

KIRK: By the arguments against the existence of God, you mean primarily the problem of evil, I take it?

OXMORE: That seems to be the essential difficulty.

KIRK: And, Venner, is this also what you meant at the beginning about strong arguments against the existence of God?

VENNER: Yes, and I'm quite happy to have Professor Oxmore state the difficulty.

OXMORE: I suppose we ought to begin by stating the problem and making sure we agree on what the problem is. The traditional way of stating the difficulty is to point out an apparent incongruity between three propositions:

1. God is all-powerful and all-knowing.
2. God is perfectly good.
3. Evil exists in the world.

The argument goes this way: if God were perfectly good, He would prevent evil if He were able to. So either God isn't perfectly good, or He isn't able to prevent evil, or evil doesn't exist. But since evil obviously does exist in the world, then we have to give up at least part of the traditional idea of God. Either God can't prevent evil or He won't; either He's not all-powerful or He's not perfectly good.

Of course, some people, like Christian Scientists or members of some Eastern religions, deny the reality of evil. That seems to me immensely implausible. Even if evil is in some sense an illusion, to be so deluded is surely an evil. And cruelty and cancer, and so on, are just undeniable facts. Other people, like William James for example, want to say that God is finite and limited, and although He would like to prevent evil, He can't. I take it that Professor Kirk is staunchly traditional, and refuses to evade the problem in either of these two ways?

KIRK: Yes, you're quite right.

OXMORE: And you'd agree with the statement of the problem?

KIRK: It will do very well to start out with, but perhaps we should make an immediate distinction between two sorts of evil. Pain and suffering of all kinds we'll call physical evil; morally reprehensible choices by human beings we'll call moral evil. Professor Oxmore mentioned both kinds of evil in her statement of the problem: cruelty is a moral evil and the suffering caused by cancer is a physical evil. Moral evil we blame on some person; physical evil may or may not be anyone's fault, but is an evil anyway.

HOME: I wonder if some people may not find that terminology confusing, Professor Kirk. When you talk about physical evil in that way it almost sounds as if pain and suffering were wrongdoing on the part of some person, as if a cancer could have a desire to hurt someone, for example.

KIRK: I don't find that suggestion in the term at all, and it seems to me to be rather farfetched—I mean the cancer desiring to hurt. But I suppose you might be right about the general confusion regarding the terms moral and physical evils. The idea is partly that both wrongdoing on the part of someone and physical pain or suffering are bad or objectionable or undesirable.

HOME: But we don't usually use "evil" to mean just something undesirable. This chair I'm sitting on is an uncomfortable, badly designed chair; a bad chair perhaps, but it isn't an evil chair.

KIRK: I'm certainly sorry about the chair, but I do see your point, and I suppose that it's just a bit of philosopher's jargon. Or perhaps there is a suggestion that pain *is* wrongdoing on someone's part, that is, on God's part. In that case I suppose a theist ought to object to the term. But if you don't mind I'll keep on using the terms for convenience.

HOME: As long as we're clear about what we mean, the words aren't vital.

OXMORE: Again, that may need further refinement, but I'll agree that we do need such a distinction.

KIRK: Well, then, the fact that physical evil exists in the world does, I agree, seem to create a *prima facie* difficulty for believers in an all-powerful, perfectly good God. I'll say more about that in a moment. But the problem of moral evil seems to depend tremendously on what you say about two other very basic philosophical problems—the nature of morality and the freedom of the will. If there is no objective standard of morality, if right is what each person thinks is right, then I don't see how you could possibly have a problem of moral evil in relation to God. You'd have a lot of people doing as they thought best, and God doing as He thought best, and you couldn't make any judgments about any of them. There wouldn't be such a thing as moral evil.

OXMORE: Moral evil might consist in violating your own standards.

KIRK: Yes, but if that's the only thing you can blame people for, and if no comparison of standards is possible, then I don't see how you could mount a moral objection to God's permitting people to violate their own standards. It might be His standard to let others violate theirs—He might be super-tolerant or a noninterventionist. You can't really consistently be tolerant of everyone's moral standards except God's.

OXMORE: I see that, but you could still object to physical evil.

KIRK: I'm not sure that a pure subjectivist in ethics could object to moral evil. All he'd be saying is that it would violate his moral code. But if there's no right moral code, then God's moral code might just happen to be different from yours, and no question of blame could logically arise.

OXMORE: I do see that, and I'm not trying to defend ethical subjectivism or relativity.

VENNER: I, on the other hand, would defend a purely emotive theory of ethics, and I agree that I cannot consistently use moral evil as an argument against God's existence. But I can still protest that if there were a God, He would be a cruel and evil being to allow all of the disease and death and famine and hardships that exist in the world.

KIRK: You can protest, but if you really hold an emotive theory all that you're doing is expressing your own feelings about these things.

VENNER: And those of all decent men.

KIRK: But on your theory, "all decent men" simply means "all the men who feel as I do." But perhaps we can thresh this out when we talk about ethics.

OXMORE: Let's assume, at least for the sake of argument, some objective standard of morality. What would you say about moral evil then?

KIRK: We now come to the free will problem. If men are actually free and responsible, then moral evil is the fault of the free, responsible agent. It can't also be blamed on God. If telling a certain lie is my fault, it cannot also be God's fault.

OXMORE: Yes, but permitting you to tell that lie would be God's responsibility. God would be the great accomplice in all the moral evil He doesn't prevent.

KIRK: But this brings us back to freedom. It's no use telling me I'm free and then stopping me whenever I do something you don't like.

OXMORE: You're assuming, then, that God can't cause us to freely choose only to do what is right?

KIRK: That just doesn't make sense. If I'm caused to do it, I'm not doing it freely, and if I'm doing it freely, I'm not caused to do it.

OXMORE: Oh, that seems to me to be very doubtful.

KIRK: That's another thing we'll have to thresh out when we talk about determinism and free will. But you do see, don't you, that if giving someone real freedom means that he may misuse that freedom, then God can't both make men free and prevent moral evil?

OXMORE: You're assuming that freedom plus moral evil is a better state of affairs than no freedom and no moral evil?

KIRK: I haven't said so, but I'd be happy to argue for that, yes. Consider someone you're fond of. Would you rather have that person free to make moral choices, some of which were wrong, or would you rather have the person a sort of robot, unable to make wrong choices?

OXMORE: If the alternative were the person becoming a moral monster, I might prefer the robot.

KIRK: I wonder if you would, really. Moral monsters can repent; robots can only do what they're programmed to. How could you value loving behavior, for instance, from the robot, when you know that's just what it's programmed to do? If you had a son constantly getting into trouble, would you consent to have him lobotomized to make him a model citizen?

OXMORE: No, but then I don't know how he might turn out, and presumably God would.

KIRK: That raises some very deep problems, but you'll grant, won't you, that a great deal of moral evil, with an eventual free choice of good, is preferable to no free choice? Mary Magdalene is preferable to a "good little girl" robot?

OXMORE: Well, my own sympathies lie that way certainly. So you're saying that freedom without moral evil is impossible. . . .

KIRK: I'm not sure if it's impossible, but it hasn't happened.

OXMORE: And then you want to say that freedom with moral evil is preferable to no freedom with or without moral evil?

KIRK: Certainly to no freedom without moral evil. No freedom and moral evil is self-contradictory: you need freedom for responsibility and therefore for moral evil or good.

OXMORE: I'm not sure of that, but that's a matter for our discussion of free will. Would you grant that your preference for freedom plus moral evil over no freedom and no moral evil is a personal choice or preference?

KIRK: No, I'd say that it is a moral judgment, and one which reasonable people would agree with.

OXMORE: That, I think, makes your position clear and also shows that we can't examine it fully until we've explored some other areas. Venner, do you have any comments?

VENNER: Simply that I think that both freedom and responsibility are delusions, so that I cannot really enter into this discussion. For me, you see, this "problem of evil" is a matter of exposing inconsistencies in the theistic position. The major inconsistency seems to me to be the great suffering in the world on the one hand and the idea of a benevolent deity on the other.

OXMORE: Yes, the problem of physical evil still seems to be with us. What would you say about that, Kirk?

KIRK: I'd like to begin by seeing if I can get you to grant that some pains and sufferings are morally justified.

OXMORE: For instance?

KIRK: I suppose the easiest case is where pain produces moral improvement. Young Jones breaks a lot of girls' hearts, let's say. Then he falls in love with a girl who treats *him* badly and he comes to realize how badly he's behaved to the other girls, and winds up a much better person for the experience. Suppose that the pain was essential to the reformation; would you grant that it was morally justified?

OXMORE: That's a big "if," but yes, in that case I think I would.

KIRK: What about a case where someone brings pain on himself through his own bad moral choices? Someone loses the love of a girl by treating her badly, then is sorry that he can't have what he's lost through his own fault.

OXMORE: If the suffering doesn't do him any good, I'm not sure it's justified. To wish it would just be vengeful.

KIRK: What if someone else learns from his experience, and it does that person good?

OXMORE: I'm not sure about that case. Someone is done good, but it seems to make the suffering a sort of means to another person's end.

KIRK: Well, at least you grant that suffering is justified if it's for the person's own good?

OXMORE: If there's no other way of securing that good, yes.

KIRK: Well, the Christian position, which I think is philosophically defensible although not philosophically provable, is that all of the physical evil in the world is justified in some way, even perhaps ultimately in terms of the sufferers' own good. The Christian can very well agree with those who urge the problem of evil, in one respect. He agrees that if there is unjustified evil then there is not an all-powerful, perfectly good God. But that's logically equivalent to if there is an all-powerful, perfectly good God, then there is no unjustified evil. The Christian holds that there is an all-powerful, perfectly good God, so he concludes that there is no unjustified evil. The atheist holds that there is unjustified evil; therefore, there is not an all-powerful, perfectly good God. The major premise of both is the same: their logic is impeccable in both cases. The question for the philosopher is whether there is conclusive evidence on either side, and if not which side the balance of evidence is on.

OXMORE: That's a rather neat way of putting it. I'd say that there's no conclusive evidence either way, and therefore it's a matter of personal choice.

KIRK: That would satisfy some of my fellow Christians. Being an unreconstructed rationalist, I think that the balance of evidence is in favor of God's existence and that personal commitment, or faith if you like, plays a part only in the firmness of our assent. It doesn't tip a scale, which is perfectly evenly balanced, from one way to the other, as you seem to suggest.

OXMORE: Faith causes you to believe more firmly than the evidence warrants, then?

KIRK: No, that's misleading. It causes you to hold the thing in a different way. It becomes a matter of personal trust, not just of weighing evidence and proportioning belief to it. For example, Home has promised us travelling expenses for this colloquium. It's not logically or physically impossible for him to break that promise, and people have broken promises in like circumstances. But we trust Home. To say that we have a ninety percent probability that he will keep his promise and that we won't believe any more firmly than that would be to insult Home and to damage our personal relationship with him. A formula which C. S. Lewis [2] gave seems to fit very well both cases of personal trust and religious faith: "There is a psychological exclusion of doubt, though not a logical exclusion of the possibility of rebuttal."

OXMORE: In the case of Home, things *could* happen which would cause us to lose our trust in him.

KIRK: Oh, yes, but we don't believe that these things *will* happen.

OXMORE: But don't Christians say that nothing could happen that would cause them to lose their faith?

KIRK: Not that such things *logically* couldn't happen. I can imagine and consistently describe states of affairs that would cause me to reject my belief that an all-powerful, perfectly good God exists. What we believe is that such things *will not* happen because God in fact does exist and, therefore, there can't be evidence inconsistent with His existence.

OXMORE: Wait a minute—first you said there could be evidence, then you just said there couldn't.

KIRK: No, it's the old business of the necessity of the conditional and the necessity of the consequent. If I am alive today, then there can't be conclusive evidence that I'm dead today. I am in fact alive today, so it follows logically that there is no conclusive evidence I am dead. In that sense I can't be dead conditionally, because I am alive. But since it's possible that I could be dead today, it's *possible* that there could be conclusive evidence that I'm dead.

---

[2] C. S. Lewis, see Biography (Appendix A) and Bibliography (Appendix B), Part 10.

HOME: I think you'd better go over that a bit more slowly, Professor Kirk.

KIRK: Certainly. The necessity of the conditional case is where B follows necessarily from A, but neither A nor B are themselves necessary truths. If there are fifty people in this room it follows necessarily that there are more than twenty-five people in this room. But it isn't a necessary truth that there are fifty people in the room nor is it a necessary truth that there are more than twenty-five. If we had changed rooms there might be no one in this room today. Clear enough?

HOME: Yes, go ahead.

KIRK: But it's easy to confuse the case where B follows necessarily from A, but B *is not* itself necessary, with the other case where B *is* itself necessary. That's what I meant by the necessity of the consequent—of course in a statement like "If A then B," A is called the antecedent and B is called the consequent. Actually lots of bad arguments consist of confusing "B follows necessarily from A" with "B is necessarily true in case A is true." The difficulty is that both can be expressed by the same ambiguous form of words; for example, "If A then necessarily B."

OXMORE: I see the point, but do you want to say that it's possible God doesn't exist?

KIRK: Logically possible in the narrow sense, certainly. "God doesn't exist" can't be shown to be self-contradictory by the ordinary laws of logic and the meanings of words. So it's logically possible in the narrow sense that there could be evidence He doesn't exist; that is, I can imagine and consistently describe such evidence. Which is just what I said.

OXMORE: But you want to say that there is a sense in which God's existence is necessary.

KIRK: I've been avoiding that word, since it causes so many confusions. My term, remember, was "causally independent." God exists whether or not anything else exists. God exists, if you like, "no matter what happens." Since that's true, then "no matter what happens" there will never be con- clusive evidence that God doesn't exist. Or this may help: for me God not existing, there being evidence that God doesn't exist, and something coming from nothing, are all on the same level. Not logically impossible in the narrow sense, but inconceivable.

OXMORE: But there are consistently describable states of affairs in- compatible with God's existence?

KIRK: Yes, certainly. The existence of unjustified evil. Or if you want to be dramatic, all good men being sent to Hell.

OXMORE: This doesn't sound like what some of my Oxford friends who are Christians say about the matter.

KIRK: What some theologians, those influenced by Wittgenstein,[3] for example, say about the matter seems to me to be both immoral and contrary to what most Christians believe. So far as I can see they seem to want to put themselves into a state of complete logical impregnability, so that even if God *did* send all good men to Hell they could still say that their belief in God was not disproved. They seem to me to be perfectly open to the objection that a view which doesn't exclude any state of affairs is perfectly empty.

OXMORE: You don't think that your view is open to that objection?

KIRK: No, I don't think so. What I'm saying seems to me to be a stronger sort of case of what the scientist does when he rules out certain states of affairs as physically impossible. No matter what happens in this universe he doesn't expect to find a body exceeding the speed of light. No matter what happens in any conceivable universe I don't expect something to come from nothing. But the contrary is logically possible in the narrow sense.

VENNER: You want, then, to make religious belief disconfirmable in the sense that possible observations could disconfirm it?

KIRK: *Logically* possible observations, in the narrow sense of logically possible.

VENNER: But if it is then like a scientific theory, should we not make the same demands for confirmability that we make on scientific theories?

KIRK: The demands we make on very high-level scientific theories, and the demands we make on metaphysical theories, including those which form part of the content of religious belief, are very similar in my view. We ask that the theory be self-consistent, that it be consistent with all observed phenomena, and that it explain a wide variety of phenomena. I've been arguing that a belief in God is self-consistent, that it is not inconsistent with the existence of moral evil in the world, and that it explains such things as the order and understandability of the world. I'd also argue that God's existence explains our moral experience, but we seem to disagree quite a bit on what morality is all about, so I can't build on that foundation unless we can agree about morality.

[3] Ludwig Wittgenstein, see Biography (Appendix A).

VENNER: But a scientific theory predicts what will and will not be the case.

KIRK: One important consequence of belief in the creation of the universe by God is a sort of meta-prediction about science: the universe is understandable and we will be able to explain and predict phenomena by using our reason.

VENNER: Then what content does the belief in God have beyond that prediction?

KIRK: It provides a reason for that prediction. What content does the theory that Oswald shot President Kennedy have beyond the theory than Kennedy was hit by a bullet and died? It provides a reason.

VENNER: The cases, I think, are not similar. Also, it seems to me that you go too quickly over the matter of the consistency of the God theory. I find it extremely unlikely that all of the pain and suffering in the world can be justified.

KIRK: Well, we hardly have the data, do we? I don't know much beyond appearances in the cases of most suffering. I might find it extremely unlikely that most people in our society marry for love. But then what do I know of most marriages except my own and possibly a little about those of a few of my friends?

VENNER: But this is a mere argument from ignorance. That's saying we do not know it is unjustified, so it is justified.

KIRK: No, you're mistaking the burden of proof. I grant that unjustified evil would disprove the existence of a good God. If the atheist could produce an undoubted case of unjustified evil, I would concede that God is not good or not all-powerful. But I don't think that there are such cases. The burden is on the atheist to produce one.

VENNER: But this gives no positive reason to believe in God.

KIRK: No, my positive reasons are of the kind I've already tried to indicate. I argue to the existence of God from certain features of the universe, which the existence of a creator would explain. This in itself says nothing as to whether God is just or loving. I think I can argue for at least a just God if I can start with moral experience. But so far as we've gotten, I've given some positive reasons for believing in the existence of a creator, and I've defended the Christian belief that this creator is morally perfect against one line of attack. I haven't claimed to give any positive arguments for the idea that God is morally perfect at all, as yet.

HOME: That sounds like a good point to end the discussion for the time being. Some of the issues that have been raised can be dealt with again at the next session when we'll discuss free-will and determinism. Other things that were said can be clarified by our discussion of ethics in the session after that. But we've really run out of time for this session. Professor Kirk will be chairman for our next session. The title will be "Is Free Will an Illusion?" Now let's have questions from the floor.

QUESTIONS

Answer the following questions as you think they would be answered by the panelist to whom they are addressed.

1. Professor Kirk: How can you talk about philosophical justifications for suffering in the face of the suffering of innocent children?
2. Professor Venner: As an atheist don't you still have to face the problems of evil and suffering, without any partial understanding or explanation of them?
3. Professor Oxmore: If you admit that suffering may sometimes be good for people, how can you be sure that all suffering isn't beneficial in the long run?

Did you find these answers to questions in the dialogue satisfactory? Why or why not?

4. Kirk's answer to the Freudian objection?
5. Venner's answer to Kirk's point that an ethical relativist cannot use the argument from evil?
6. Oxmore's answer to Kirk's questions about free will?

Write brief essays on the following:

7. Which answer to a question or challenge in the dialogue do you feel you could improve on? How?
8. Which panelist's position is closest to your own? Why?
9. What objections would you like to raise to something said in the dialogue?
10. What argument would you like to put forward that is not in the dialogue?

FURTHER READINGS

Hick, John, *Philosophy of Religion* (2nd ed.), Englewood Cliffs, N.J.: Prentice-Hall, Inc., 1973, Chap. 3, pp. 31–47; Chaps. 5 & 6, pp. 68–96.

Hospers, John, *Readings in Introductory Philosophical Analysis*, Englewood Cliffs, N.J.: Prentice-Hall, Inc., 1968.

> Flew, Antony, R. M. Hare, and Basil Mitchell, "Theology and Falsification," pp. 255–63.

> Hick, John, "The Verification of Religious Hypotheses," pp. 263–66.

> Hume, David, "Evil and the Argument from Design," pp. 233–55.

Wilson, Margaret D., Dan W. Brock, and Richard F. Kuhns, *Philosophy, An Introduction*, New York: Appleton-Century-Crofts, 1972.

> Flew, Antony, and Basil Mitchell, "Theology and Falsification," pp. 83–88.

> Hume, David, "Refutation of the Teleological Argument," pp. 25–37.

> Kant, Immanuel, "The Impossibility of an Ontological Proof," pp. 53–57.

Questions on the Reading

1. What elements of Hume's criticisms of the design argument were not dealt with in the dialogue? Does reading the full version of Hume's arguments alter your opinion of the argument?

2. Do Venner or Oxmore seem to be using arguments like Flew's? Are Kirk's replies to the arguments satisfactory?

3. Are the replies to Flew by Mitchell, Hare, and Hick improvements on Kirk's replies to Venner and Oxmore? Why or why not?

4. In his book Hick concludes that arguments against God's existence are not conclusive. Do you agree? How would Venner reply?

5. How does Kant's criticism of the ontological argument compare with Kirk's in chapter one? Which criticism is stronger?

3

Is Free Will an Illusion?

KIRK: I've agreed to chair this session, on the understanding that the chairman is not forbidden to get into the discussion if the spirit moves him. I may not need to, however, since the three main positions on this subject are represented by Professors Home, Venner, and Oxmore. It might be useful to our audience if each of you briefly stated your own definition of free will and determinism and your position on them before going on to argument. Let's let Professor Home go first, for a change.

HOME: Right. By determinism I understand the position that every event, including every human action, has as a sufficient cause some preceding event. This may seem harmless enough, but recall that a sufficient cause is a cause such that its occurrence makes it *necessary* for the event of which it is the cause to occur. But if my actions now have a sufficient cause in events which took place earlier, and these in turn have their cause in events which took place still earlier, and so on, then we eventually come to events which occurred before I was even born. Now sufficient causes are transitive: if the sufficient cause of A is B, and the sufficient cause of B is C, then C is a sufficient cause of A. In other words, if A is bound to happen if B does, and B is bound to happen if C does, then once C has happened A is bound to happen. So if A represents my actions now and we trace back along the line of sufficient causes to some event, call it *W*, which occurred before I was born, then once *W* had occurred, *A* was bound to occur. This means that once some set of events, which occurred before I was even born, had occurred, I was bound to do what I am doing right now. If this is true, I just don't see what it could mean to speak of my actions now as free or as something that I'm responsible for.

The free will view, which is sometimes also called the libertarian view or the indeterminist view, can be put quite simply now that we've cleared the ground. The free will view is that at least some human decisions or actions have no sufficient cause. This is the view which I believe is true and which I will try to defend.

Many of the apparent reasons for rejecting this view are due to misunderstandings of it, so let me make two preliminary clarifications. First, the free will view does not deny that there are *necessary* conditions for all human actions and decisions. Second, the free will view does not deny that there are *reasons* for human actions and decisions, although it does deny that reasons are always sufficient causes. Finally, let me say that even though in theory one single event of any kind without a sufficient cause would be enough to disprove determinism, the important events for the free will view are human actions and decisions. Like most upholders of this view I believe that a great many human actions and decisions lack a sufficient cause, not just one or two or a very few.

KIRK: Professor Venner, you represent a determinist point of view. Since Home has already given us a definition of determinism, may I ask if you would agree with that definition?

VENNER: In general I would find it satisfactory. I would myself prefer to talk about laws of nature and antecedent conditions, and say that for every event there are some laws of nature and some description of antecedent conditions, such that a description of that event can be deduced from the laws of nature and the antecedent conditions. In other words, a "covering law" explanation of the sort explicated by Hempel[1] is available for every event, including human actions and decisions. If this were not so we could hardly hope that psychology could ever be a truly scientific enterprise, by the way.

HOME: Professor Venner, for the sake of some members of the audience perhaps you could briefly explain a bit more about "Hempel-type explanations."

VENNER: Of course, take, for example, a very simple case. Suppose that

---

[1] Carl Hempel, see Biography (Appendix A) and Further Readings at the end of Chapter 9.

a man drops an object, perhaps a camera, from a great height. Let it be for the sake of illustration a very high building, or a hovering helicopter. The camera of course would strike the ground with great force, perhaps sufficient force to go through an automobile that happened to be underneath it. Suppose now that someone asks for an explanation of why the camera was able to do so much damage. We can give a very full and adequate scientific explanation of this circumstance by looking at scientific laws and initial conditions. For example, we know that force equals mass times acceleration. We know that the acceleration of a falling body in earth's gravitational field is thirty-two feet per second, and so on. This sort of information is included in what I am calling "scientific laws" for the sake of brevity. But we also have certain information about the mass of this particular camera, the height from which it was dropped, and so on. This is what I am calling "initial conditions." Putting the laws together with the conditions, we could have predicted in advance the force with which the camera would strike. But since the camera has fallen, we can use this same information to explain why it fell with that degree of force. Carl Hempel has argued that all scientific explanation follows this pattern; with a combination of scientific laws and initial conditions we are able to deduce the event that needs to be explained.

HOME: And you want to say that there exist scientific laws from which, given certain initial-condition type of information, we could in principle deduce all human behavior?

VENNER: That is correct. I do not claim that we now know these laws, but I do claim that they can be discovered and will eventually be discovered. However, this view that every event has a Hempel-type explanation seems to me simply to be a clearer and more up-to-date version of the view that every event has a sufficient cause.

That is part of the view I wish to defend. But I also want to say that the fact that every event has a sufficient cause is inconsistent with the view that man is free or responsible, in the way in which these terms are commonly understood. Thus the view I hold is the view that I prefer to call "strict determinism," but which has also been called "hard determinism" or "incompatibilistic determinism." This view I would wish to defend.

KIRK: And, finally, Professor Oxmore.

OXMORE: Well, Professor Kirk chose the order in which he called on us very cannily, because now all that I have to say to state my own position is that, like Professor Venner, I deny that any event lacks a sufficient cause, but unlike him I want to say that this fact has no real effect on the question of whether people are free or responsible. Actually, perhaps that's a bit strong. To be more cautious, as far as I can see there are good reasons for holding that every event has a cause, but whether or not every event does have a cause, if you look at the way our concepts of freedom and responsibility actually work, you'll see that whatever answer we give to the question about every event having a cause won't affect our judgments about people being free or responsible. Of course, if you define freedom in the way that Home does, free will and determinism are incompatible, but in my view that's not at all the way we actually use the concept of freedom. In fact, as I'll argue later, when we hold someone responsible for his actions, we presume that he had a cause for doing what he did, and thus in a sense freedom and responsibility imply determinism. The view I'm defending is sometimes—rather offensively, I think—called "soft determinism," but I prefer "compatibilism" or "compatibilistic determinism," although I admit that's rather a mouthful. Or it might be an idea to call it "loose determinism" in contrast to Venner's "strict determinism." Actually I'm a little uneasy at calling it determinism at all, since this often seems to mean a view like Venner's.

KIRK: That gets the issues on the table, and now we'll see where we go from here. Perhaps if Professor Oxmore had a try at reconciling free will and determinism, it might bring out the conflict between Venner and Home.

OXMORE: I'll certainly try, but let me begin a bit obliquely. There's a well-known bad argument for determinism that goes roughly as follows. Take any action that has a cause. Now if the cause occurs, the action is bound to occur and if the cause doesn't occur, the action is bound not to occur.

HOME: Only if it's a necessary and sufficient cause.

OXMORE: Oh, yes; well, let's presume for the sake of argument that it is. Well then, the argument goes on to say that the cause is either bound to occur or not to occur, so the event is either bound to occur or bound not to occur.

KIRK: Yes, that's what the Stoics called the "lazy argument."

OXMORE: How delightful! But are we agreed that it's a bad argument?

HOME: Oh yes, it's a common fallacy in modal logic [2]—the logic that deals with necessity and possibility, and their interrelationships.

KIRK: Yes, just the fallacy of confusing the necessity of the conditional

---

[2] For a discussion of modal logic as applied to philosophical arguments, see R. L. Purtill, *Logic for Philosophers* (New York: Harper and Row, 1971), Chaps. 7 and 8.

with the necessity of its consequent which I mentioned during the last session.

VENNER: I would certainly not defend this argument, or rely on it as an argument for my position.

OXMORE: Well fine, if we're agreed on that then let me go ahead and ask Home if in his original statement he didn't commit the same fallacy. Didn't you argue from the fact that something was bound to happen *if* something else did to the statement that it was bound to happen? And isn't this just the same fallacy over again?

HOME: No, I was using the "master argument," not the "lazy argument." This would be fairly simple if I could use modal logic, but I don't know how many of the audience would follow me. Well, maybe it's not all that complicated, so let me have a stab at it. I'll write it out for the audience. The lazy argument is:

> Necessarily if A then B
> Necessarily if not-A then not-B
> Necessarily either A or not-A
> *Therefore* necessarily B or necessarily not-B.

That's just a plain fallacy. You can't, so to speak, get the "necessarily" from "outside" of the if statements and the either-or statement and apply it "inside" to the consequents of those conditionals.

But the master argument goes like this:

> Necessarily if A then B
> Necessarily A
> Necessarily B

and that's a valid argument.

VENNER: That's correct in its logic, but now you have to show us how it applies to what you said.

HOME: Right. The version of the master argument I'm using is this. Take the event A, which is my actions now, and some event W, back along the chain of sufficient causes that occurred before I was born. I can put down this way:

> It is beyond my power to change that if W then A.

That's because A follows from W as a consequence of natural laws, and it's beyond my power to change natural laws.

VENNER: That is satisfactory, yes.

HOME: Now I can put down:

It is beyond my power to change W.

That's because W happened before I was born, and I can't change what happened before I was born. So now I can conclude:

It is beyond my power to change A,

and that follows validly from my two premises.

VENNER: I agree, that is a good explication of the argument.

OXMORE: I'm still unhappy. Surely I *could* have changed W if I had been born earlier.

HOME: Yes, but if we go back far enough along the chain, I can get to a place before there were any humans or before the earth existed.

OXMORE: But these things could have been different too.

HOME: Oh yes, I grant that on the determinist view my actions *could* have been different *if* the whole history of the universe was different.

OXMORE: But then you grant that they could have been different.

HOME: "Could" in a very funny way. I'm quite willing to define determinism as the view that my actions could have been different only if the whole history of the universe had been different.

OXMORE: Surely not the *whole* history?

HOME: Well, I'm not sure that on a determinist kind of view you can alter parts without altering the whole, but let's say that the determinist view is the view that my actions could not be different now unless a number of things that happened before I was born had been different.

OXMORE: Your actions couldn't be different from what?

HOME: From what they are. For example, I'll touch my right eye with my little finger. According to the determinist view, for me to have touched my nose or my left eye, or used my index finger, would have meant that events that happened before I was born were different from what they in fact were.

VENNER: That is an odd way of putting it, but I agree. On the view I would defend, the history of the universe flows inevitably from the nature of matter and its laws. For any part to be different would require far-reaching changes in the whole.

OXMORE: Even if I concede that point, it seems to leave my main contention untouched. If whether or not an action is "free" depends on what happened before I was born, obviously you're not using the ordinary concept of freedom at all. Because we decide every day that such and such actions are free, or not, without ever inquiring as to what happened before the man in question was born.

HOME: Yes, but in ordinary life we make the presumption that a person has free will. Sometimes the presumption is defeated by some matter of concurrent fact, such as an electric current passing through a man's arm, which causes his finger to jerk convulsively and fire a gun, thus injuring someone. If the current was due to a chance lightning flash, we wouldn't say the man freely chose to pull the trigger. Sometimes we go back further into history: maybe the man was hypnotized or conditioned, say last year, to tighten that finger if he heard the word "atomic." If the hypnotism or conditioning left him no choice, we don't say he freely chose to pull the trigger. But sometimes we do go back beyond the man's birth. We may learn that one of his parents had a disease that always results in a certain kind of brain damage in the children, and that people with this type of brain damage always tighten their fingers when they hear a loud noise. Then if the man pulled the trigger when a chance sonic boom occurred, we don't say that he freely chose to do it.

OXMORE: I'll grant you those cases, but how do they help you?

HOME: Well, they're all cases where we exonerate a person from blame if the action was due to circumstances beyond his control. But if the determinist was right, *all* of our actions would be beyond our control. Thus we could never hold anyone responsible for anything. But we plainly do hold people responsible for things.

OXMORE: Yes, but what are we doing when we hold them responsible? I find Nowell-Smith's suggestion quite plausible: to hold a person responsible is to say that exhortation and reasoning and punishment will have an effect on his actions.[3] Plainly in all your cases these things would have no effect on the person's actions, and therefore they are not responsible.

HOME: That just won't work. There are some individuals who seem quite responsible, but are quite determined to do certain evil things—

[3] P. Nowell-Smith, *Ethics* (Baltimore, Md.: Penguin Books, 1954), Chaps. 19 and 20.

professional criminals for instance. In that case we hold them responsible even though we don't think exhortation or reasoning or punishment will have any effect on them. Then there is the other sort of case; abnormally gullible people who can be exhorted or "reasoned" into doing anything, abnormally timid people who will do anything if threatened by punishment. We often don't hold such people responsible. So, in fact we hold people responsible that we ought not to if Nowell-Smith is right, and don't hold people responsible that we ought to hold responsible, again if he's right. So his definition of responsibility can't be the one we ordinarily use.

OXMORE: I think both kinds of cases could do with further analysis. But suppose that I grant that there is a certain connection between freedom and absence of factors outside one's control forcing you to do a thing. Suppose that common sense or ordinary language supports such a connection. It seems to me that ordinary language or common sense supports just as strongly the idea that every event has a cause. And if ordinary language and common sense are not just inconsistent—and I don't think that they could be really—there must be some way of reconciling these two "common sense truisms."

VENNER: I myself have no difficulty with the idea that ordinary language or common sense could be inconsistent. It seems to me that often they are.

OXMORE: Well, that would get us into some wider issues. Home, do you agree that "every event has a cause" is a common sense truism?

HOME: I'm not sure that I do. In the form in which you quote it, I think it may be a philosopher's slogan rather than a common sense truism. What gives it its plausibility is just the confusion between necessary and sufficient causes and the confusion between causes and reasons. In ordinary life we try to explain events other than human actions by causes, but we don't always insist on sufficient causes. And in explaining human actions we usually give reasons. But reasons aren't regarded as sufficient causes. I can give my reasons for doing something, but if you ask me whether nevertheless I *might* have done something else, I'll say yes.

OXMORE: Might have if things had been different, you mean?

HOME: No, might have even if things had been just the same.

OXMORE: But if you had reasons for doing what you did, doing otherwise would be irrational.

HOME: Not at all. There might be reasons on both sides, as there often are.

OxMORE: But hang it all, there must be some reason for coming down on one side or another.

HOME: Only if reasons had to be sufficient causes. If you look at your own experience instead of your theory, you'll find that you often have the experience of looking at factors pro and con, and *deciding* to let one set of factors weigh more than the other. Not having the weight of the factors decide *for* you, but deciding to let one set weigh more with you than the other.

OxMORE: There must be a decisive factor, whether I recognize it or not.

HOME: Why must there be? You're not arguing, but simply repeating your position that every event has a sufficient cause.

OxMORE: But unless you show why this thing happened rather than another you haven't really explained it.

VENNER: I must agree. To explain you must give laws and antecedent conditions that together necessitate the thing to be explained.

HOME: Well, if you want to use "explain" in that way, then you'll have to say that human decisions which lack sufficient causes can't be explained, in your very strong sense of "explain." But that isn't the ordinary sense at all. I can explain perfectly well, in the ordinary sense of "explain," why I didn't take that job at another university I was offered last year. But I *might* have decided otherwise, things being precisely as they were. In almost any moral choice, we *could* have decided otherwise in *that* situation, just as it was. That's why it makes sense to praise or blame people for moral choices. If I snap at my wife, you blame me if you think in *that* situation I could have refrained from snapping. If you discover that I couldn't have refrained from snapping in that situation, or could not have not snapped unless previous factors had been different, you don't blame me.

OxMORE: But I think we do a great deal too much blaming.

HOME: That may be so, but if it is, it's a moral judgment about our overhastiness to condemn people. If no one is free no one is to blame for anything they do, including the blaming of other people that they do. You're trying to have your cake and eat it. You blame people for blaming people too much. But if determinism is true, they can't help blaming others any more than the others could help doing what they did. Determinism removes all point from all moral judgments.

OxMORE: But my blaming them for blaming too much might lead to a change in their behavior.

HOME: Now you're back to Nowell-Smith's theory that the point of praising and blaming, and so on, is to change behavior. And we saw that his theory was inconsistent with the facts of ordinary language.

OXMORE: I'm not convinced of that. A good deal of praising and blaming aims at changing behavior—look at schoolmasters.

HOME: Yes, but it aims at changing behavior voluntarily. If the schoolteacher somehow hypnotizes or brainwashes his pupils into doing what he or she wants them to, then there's no point to praising them for doing it. In that case they couldn't help doing it, and it makes no sense to praise people for doing what they can't help. It's no use praising you for being English or blaming Venner for being German; you can neither of you help being the nationality you are.

OXMORE: Well, it seems to me that people do just that—blame people for things they can't help.

HOME: But then we condemn those people as immoral or unreasonable.

OXMORE: Perhaps we do. But what about the case where the praise itself brings about the desired result?

HOME: There are two bits of praise here to keep straight. You seem to be thinking of a situation where a bit of praise in advance triggers a bit of behavior. But if the words of praise in advance just automatically trigger certain behavior, which then can't help but follow the praise, there's no point in praising that behavior.

OXMORE: It might ensure a repetition of that behavior.

HOME: But then it wouldn't really be praise, it would just be a sort of reward or reinforcement. Anything that would do the same trick would be just as good.

OXMORE: But I don't see what's wrong with that. Perhaps praising *is* just reinforcing; the behaviorists think so.

HOME: But again that involves a view of man that is essentially deterministic. If you look at your own experience you'll realize the difference between dealing with a person who may choose to do what you want him to and may not, and dealing with a machine or a perfectly trained animal, which will automatically do certain things if you trigger the right response.

OXMORE: But in the case of the person, we just may not know the right buttons yet.

HOME: That presumes the buttons exist. I maintain that we have no good reason to think that they do, and the whole way in which we ordinarily think and talk about human beings presumes that they don't have such automatic responses. Think of the word "please." We don't use it in training animals (except for those who regard animals as quasi-persons or pretend to) or to a machine (except in burlesque of our normal behavior to humans). We say "please" to other *persons*, because we know that they are free to do as we like or not. And, of course, saying "please" doesn't automatically get us what we want; the other person is entitled to say "no." In fact you can almost define a person as an entity to whom you can meaningfully say "please."

KIRK: That would make God a person.

HOME: Yes, of course. Prayer is a special form of saying "please." And God is not bound to say "yes."

OXMORE: Aren't we getting rather far from the point?

HOME: Right. I'd say the main point that I'm making now is that we all ordinarily assume—and this assumption is built into ordinary language—that other people have free choice and can't be manipulated like machines or trained animals.

VENNER: But many false ideas are widely held, and many false ideas are built into ordinary language. And science corrects these ideas.

HOME: Yes, of course. But we need an argument for rejecting an idea that is so widely held and that seems to rest on experiences we've all had.

VENNER: You do not think that science supplies such arguments?

HOME: No, so far as I can see there are no scientific arguments for determinism. It used to be, you know, that the claim was made that the whole scientific world view required a deterministic view. Science, it was said, gave us a view of the universe in which every event had a sufficient cause, and if we completely knew the state of the universe at any particular moment and knew all the laws of nature, we could predict its state at all future times.

VENNER: Yes, this is the view I myself hold.

HOME: But surely that view can no longer be taken seriously because of quantum indeterminism and Heisenberg's principle. If I may, let me explain for some of our audience that Heisenberg's uncertainty principle says that we cannot know the precise position *and* the precise momentum of a subatomic particle at a given time. There *must* be some uncertainty about one or both.

VENNER: What in my view is shown by the Heisenberg principle is that we cannot in fact know the complete state of the universe at any time, since we cannot simultaneously know the position and momentum of subatomic particles. But *if* we could and *if* we knew all the laws of nature, we could predict the future states of the universe.

HOME: But we now know that the laws themselves are probabilistic rather than deterministic. So the only predictions that can be given are in terms of probabilities.

VENNER: This seems to be the state of affairs at the moment. Like Einstein, I have not given up hope of finding deeper laws that are deterministic. But these probabilistic laws of quantum physics give no more room for free will than do the previous deterministic laws. The future state of the universe depends on laws that give some scope for chance, and on antecedent conditions that cannot be completely known. They say nothing about free will.

HOME: I'm quite content to say that the scientific evidence from physics favors neither free will nor determinism. But what the view of the world given by quantum physics *does* do, it seems to me, is to break the spell of the general argument from science. The older determinists told us that science depends entirely on a deterministic view, and the least bit of indeterminism was quite incompatible with science. But now we find that the most advanced area of science gets along quite well with indeterministic laws, and merely probabilistic predictions about future states. The old argument that "science" or the "scientific world view" depends on determinism simply can't be maintained in the face of quantum physics.

VENNER: This argument was perhaps always a somewhat metaphysical one. But the new scientific world view describes only for a framework of laws in which there is some room for chance. Is this any better a climate for free will than the previous picture?

HOME: I think perhaps it is. The old picture was monolithic, a world of unchangeable law. The new picture is pluralistic; there is both law and chance. If you open the back door to chance events, so to speak, then free will may come in the front door.

OXMORE: But look—on your view aren't free choices just chance events? This seems to be a terrific flaw in your kind of free will view, because it's caused events not chance events that we hold people responsible for. I may dislike the way that your eyebrows happen to grow, but I don't blame you for it.

HOME: Aha! Here we have, I think, one of the most deceptive bad arguments for determinism. First you make a dichotomy between determined events and chance events. Then you insist that free choices have to be one or the other. But in fact they're neither.

OXMORE: Neither chance events nor determined events? Then what are they?

HOME: They're free choices. The distinction is perfectly clear in experience. Doing something because of some sort of phobia that compels us to do it is one kind of experience. Making up our mind on the basis of chance—actually tossing a coin or letting our decision be made by some chance occurrence—is another thing. And choosing something for a reason is a third kind of experience, not the same as either of the others.

OXMORE: Then you would say the cases where our minds are made up by chance are not free choices.

HOME: They may in some sense be free, but they're not really choices. Notice that what we would praise or blame someone for is his or her decision to let chance decide the issue, not the actual decision. If I flip a coin to choose which of two girls to marry, you may blame me for deciding such an important thing so irresponsibly. If I flip a coin to see whether to give you or Venner the last life jacket on a sinking ship, you may praise me for my impartiality. But you don't praise or blame me for choosing Sally rather than Sue or you rather than Venner. *I* didn't do that; the coin did. What *I* did, for some reason, was to decide that chance was the appropriate way to decide the issue.

OXMORE: That sounds plausible. But aren't chance events themselves caused by other events? Doesn't the way you flip the coin, in fact, make sure that it will come up heads or tails as the case may be? We just don't know all the factors.

HOME: That's what the older type of determinism would say; for the classical determinist, chance events were simply events whose cause we didn't know. But Venner is trying to update determinism by leaving room for a real indeterminacy of the kind that quantum physics seems to call for.

OXMORE: I'm not sure we're allies after all, Venner. If you allow a real indeterminacy, how can you still have determinism?

VENNER: As a strict determinist I can restate my position in this way: all events, including human choices, are the results of antecedent conditions working within the framework of indeterministic laws to be sure, but beyond *our* control. Thus I reject free choice as an illusion. Our apparent free choices are the result of factors, some of them chance factors, beyond our control. I agree with the behaviorist psychologists that we are randomly programmed by chance factors, and that this accounts for many of the evils of the human condition. We should scientifically reprogram ourselves to avoid these evils.

HOME: But people who say that kind of thing talk as if *they* were free and responsible, and had a choice as to whether they would "reprogram" other people. But, in fact, if this version of determinism is true, then the people who are planning to do the reprogramming are no more free than the others. They can't *choose* to reprogram people, or say that they *ought* to; it's purely a matter of how they themselves are programmed whether they will do this or anything else.

VENNER: One must use the language that one has available. It would perhaps be more accurate to say that humans are to some extent self-adjusting feedback mechanisms, just as thermostats are in a very simple way. We can foresee that the next phase of this adjustment of the organism to its environment will be a mental reconditioning of some of these organic mechanisms by others.

OXMORE: I don't like the sound of that at all. I don't want to say that free actions have no causes, as Home does. . . .

HOME: Excuse me—no *sufficient* causes. It confuses things terribly if you don't keep that in mind.

OXMORE: Well, I don't want to say that free choices have no *sufficient* causes then. But I do want to say that a free action must come from reasons, and from the character of the person acting. Freedom is autonomy.

HOME: Yes, but where does a person's character come from, and what makes his reasons his reasons? If it's outside factors beyond his control, where's your autonomy? What does it matter whether your character is created by heredity and environment or by one of Venner's reprogrammers?

OXMORE: It matters to me. Surely you grant that character is something we're born with?

HOME: I grant that we are each born with *a* character that is modified by our parents and our environment. But when we reach the age of responsibility, we begin forming our own characters by the free choices we make. In many cases we alter our original characters drastically.

VENNER: But this I would say is an illusion.

HOME: But why would you say so? The general argument from science won't work, you agree.

VENNER: I see no need to use a very general argument of that kind. I would base my view on the increasing success of science in explaining actions that we previously thought were free.

HOME: Surely that kind of argument won't bear the weight you want to put on it. There's no conceivable way of getting from "Psychologists have explained some of our actions as the result of forces beyond our control" to "Psychologists will eventually explain all of our actions as the result of forces beyond our control."

VENNER: I do not see why we cannot extrapolate to eventual complete success from the considerable success already achieved. From our success in reaching the moon, we can extrapolate to our success in reaching other heavenly bodies.

HOME: That's not a very good example from your point of view. We don't expect to land on the sun, or to reach the planets of other stars by any methods remotely in view now. Nor would the present state of space exploration justify us in building much on a theory which presumed that *all* bodies in space would eventually be reached.

VENNER: This becomes partly a technical question—what confidence our present successes should give us.

HOME: My own answer would be "not much." It seems to me that to claim any considerable success in explaining behavior, you have to exaggerate the successes of behavioristic learning theory, claiming credit for it for technical advances like teaching machines, which could just as well have been thought up if learning theory had never been thought of. Then you have to claim the success of Freudian and related theories as somehow part of the successes of "psychology," although they're quite unlike the behavioristic theories and quite unlike your ideal of science. But none of these theories have much success in explaining everyday behavior of the kind we ordinarily think of as free in terms of factors beyond our control. Freudian and other theories may give us some insight into abnormal psychology, learning theory may make certain predictions about rote learning, and so on. But no theory I know of gives anything like an explanation of the kind of free choices we make every day—moral decisions, political decisions, artistic judgments, and so on.

VENNER: This again depends on how you interpret the available evidence.

HOME: Yes, but I'm suggesting that your conclusions aren't the only reasonable ones on the evidence. Furthermore, I'd say they were unreasonable on the evidence.

VENNER: The first I might grant, the second I would not.

HOME: Well, even that is a considerable weakening of your position. But it seems to me that there is an argument quite fatal to any form of determinism which applies quite well to your version of it.

VENNER: This, of course, I would be interested in hearing.

HOME: We might start with several possible views of the universe. On one view the basic stuff of the universe is just there somehow, and all the events in the universe are due simply to chance combinations of this basic material. We can call this the chance view, and Professor Kirk has already pointed out some of its difficulties. Then we have the pure determinist view, the view that all of the events in the universe are determined by antecedent conditions plus laws that are somehow inherent in the nature of matter. Then there's the "mixed view," which says that any event is the result of antecedent conditions and laws inherent in the nature of matter, but that these laws are probabilistic and allow a certain amount of play, a place for chance events. Professor Venner would prefer the "pure determinist view," but will settle for the mixed view. He rejects the chance view.

VENNER: That is a fair statement, yes.

HOME: But on any of these views, minds are comparative latecomers in the history of the universe. On the chance view, consciousness simply occurs by chance at a certain time. On the pure determinist view, the laws inherent in matter inevitably operate to bring forth minds at a certain stage of the universe. On the mixed view, presumably you want to say that the laws inherent in matter make conscious minds possible, but exactly where and how they appear may be due partly to chance factors.

VENNER: Something like that is my view, yes.

HOME: But now we have the fatal difficulty, a difficulty about human reason. If any of these three views is true, then human reason is totally the result of mindless forces. But if that were so, we'd have no reason to suppose that human reason is trustworthy at all, that it has any real application to the universe around us. Reason might *happen* to be trustworthy and applicable to the world, but we'd have no good reason to think so.

VENNER: That might be true for the chance view, but I cannot see that it is true for the others.

OXMORE: I can't even see that it's true for the chance view.

HOME: Well, let's do that first. On the chance view every event occurs only because of random movements of matter. So whatever thoughts we have, about determinism or anything else, are due to those random movements. These thoughts might happen to turn out to be true, but that would only be a fantastically improbable coincidence.

OXMORE: But might not chance bring into existence a thinking being, which could, so to speak, take it from there? That seems to me a plausible view of what has, in fact, happened.

HOME: Well, on a pure chance view, *everything* is caused by random movements of matter. There's no question of a bit of the chance universe having real laws—there are only random sequences that give the illusion of laws. Similarly there'd be no question of having a bit of the chance universe consisting of beings who think rationally—there would just be some random sequences that gave the illusion of connected thought. You may be thinking of something more like the mixed view.

OXMORE: That's random variation within a framework of probabilistic laws? And if I were?

HOME: That still doesn't get you out of the difficulty. If chance variation throws up intelligent minds, perhaps laws of development and heredity will keep such minds in existence in a mixed universe. But if the origin of the creatures was mere chance, then we can have no real confidence that they are really intelligent rather than being programmed in such a way that their thinking is completely unreliable.

VENNER: But if these minds are due to forces inherent in matter rather than to chance variation?

HOME: I don't think that really helps you. After all, these forces aren't intelligent, nor are they the result of intelligence. So they might happen to produce real intelligence, or they might happen to produce completely unreliable pseudo-intelligence.

VENNER: But if the forces are such that they necessarily produce intelligence?

HOME: Why should they be? Anyway, anything these supposed forces bring about they bring about necessarily, so saying they necessarily bring about something is just to say they bring it about.

OXMORE: But hang it all, surely we know that intelligence does exist and does apply to the universe. So whatever brought it about, chance or natural forces or whatever, *did* bring it off. It may have been very improbable, it may have been a terrific long shot, but the longshot *did* come off.

HOME: But did it? You determinists think of the mind as a sort of computer that is programmed. Now if you tell me that it's programmed by mere blind chance, or by totally mindless natural forces, what kind of confidence could I have that it's programmed correctly? The surer I am that reason is reliable, the surer I ought to be that reason is not just like a computer programmed by a monkey biting holes in IBM cards or a vine growing up in the machine and making a circuit. Oxmore's chance programming would be as random as the monkey bites, and Venner's forces would operate by their own laws, as the vine grows by its own laws. But the forces would have as little chance of producing intelligence as the vine would of producing a workable program for solving equations.

OXMORE: What do you see as the alternative?

HOME: Well, at a minimum, reason must somehow be independent of nonrational forces. If the mind is just a sort of channel through which random events pass, as on the chance view, or a mechanism through which mindless forces operate, as on Venner's view, then we can put no confidence in its operations.

VENNER: Are you claiming that to be caused by natural forces and to be rational are mutually exclusive? How about the computations of a computer—they are rational, but caused by natural forces such as electricity.

HOME: I'm not saying that they're incompatible, just that if we know something is caused by natural forces or by chance we can have no reason to believe that it's rational. Take Kirk's cipher message as an example. If we find an apparent cipher message that is really just letters scrambled together by chance or lines and whorls made by the growth of some plant, we immediately stop expecting it to be intelligible. We admit as a fantastically unlikely possibility that it *might* turn out to contain a message in English that contains true statements—for example a description of tomorrow's weather—but the chance is so remote that we don't even consider it.

OXMORE: But what if the long shot has come off?

HOME: We couldn't have any reason to think that it had. Suppose your supposed message seemed to say "Rain tomorrow." Then you learn it's just random letters, or just a curiously shaped vine. Would you have any reason at all to expect rain tomorrow?

OXMORE: Perhaps not, but how does that apply to reasoning?

HOME: Well, you have a number of beliefs, including a belief in determinism. But if those beliefs are merely the result in you of the operation of nonrational factors, you have no more reason to expect the beliefs to be true than you would to expect rain tomorrow on the basis of the supposed cipher.

OXMORE: But at least some of our beliefs have been tested by experience.

HOME: But think of that cipher again. It was just a jumble of letters, but you thought you'd worked it out. Certain regularities seemed to have worked so far. But when you find out it's only a jumble of letters, you not only discover that these regularities won't help you solve the *rest* of the supposed cipher, you find that what you thought were your results up to then were only an illusion.

VENNER: Professor Home, let me suggest a possible way in which nonrational forces could bring about rationality.

HOME: Certainly, go ahead.

VENNER: We know, do we not, that organisms have developed as the result of mutation and natural selection? Why could not the mind develop in a similar way?

HOME: There are two kinds of difficulties with that. The first kind is the general difficulty of using natural selection as an explanation—you have to have a certain amount of organization to start with, including inheritance of mutated characteristics. Then selection operates merely to fit the individual to the existing environment. If the environment changes, the adaptation may be undesirable in the new environment. So natural selection might account for some practical success in reasoning, since people who reasoned too badly in practical affairs might not survive. Actually I think there are all kinds of difficulties even there, but let's grant that much for the sake of argument. But surely this kind of theory as to why reason "works" would give us no confidence at all about rarefied theoretical employments of reason—about theories such as determinism itself.

VENNER: In my more pessimistic moments I sometimes wonder whether reason *can* be trusted beyond the practical.

HOME: We'll be arguing about that kind of problem in a later session. But surely you have to make up your mind. You can't be skeptical about the theoretical employment of reason and at the same time confidently assert the truth of a theory like determinism.

VENNER: My pessimistic moments never last long.

HOME: But to get back to what I was saying, the second kind of difficulty with a determinist explaining the validity of reason by natural selection is that if determinism does, in fact, undermine reason, as I've argued, it undermines our belief in such theories as the theory of natural selection itself. You can't simply assume some theories arrived at by reasoning are all right, and then use them to argue that reason itself is all right.

VENNER: But whether in this way or another, natural laws inherent in the nature of matter may operate in such a fashion as to produce in man's mind an understanding of these laws.

HOME: Well, there are lots of difficulties in that. In the first place, why should these laws operate so as to produce misunderstandings of themselves in so many minds at so many times and places? Producing such understanding can't be an invariable result of such laws, at any rate. And then if they produce misunderstandings of themselves sometimes, one wonders if they might not always do it. And it just doesn't seem to me that natural forces do have a tendency to produce understanding of themselves. As C. S. Lewis says somewhere, the Japanese Current produces all sorts of effects, but it doesn't produce maps of the Japanese Current.

VENNER: It does in the minds of some marine cartographers.

HOME: But then it's a question of what's producing what. The Japanese Current doesn't produce maps unless there are minds about.

VENNER: It does not produce temperature changes on land unless there is land about, either.

HOME: Yes, but we can understand the way in which a warm current produces temperature changes on land. But we don't see how a current can produce an understanding of itself or a theory about itself or a map of itself.

VENNER: It would not be *just* the current, of course, but a complex of factors. I agree that we do not yet understand the mechanisms involved in full, but we are gaining greater understanding of such things.

HOME: But again, unless you're smuggling some sort of plan or mind or rationality into the natural laws or forces themselves, why should we have any confidence that the programming that these forces do on our minds would produce what we'd call truth or correct theories?

OXMORE: But hang it all, we do know that reason can be trusted. We don't need an argument or a justification for that. An argument to prove that arguments are valid is silly.

HOME: I couldn't agree more. But even sillier is an argument to prove all arguments invalid. And that's what determinism turns out to be. If determinism were true, we couldn't know that it was true, or that anything else was true. So determinism is self-stultifying. You can have a sort of blind conviction in it, or take a chance on its being true, but if you try to justify it by argument you find that justifying determinism would show that no justification was any good. So, determinism is a theory that can't be argued for. The free will theory, on the other hand, is consistent with the way we ordinarily speak and think about other persons. It isn't inconsistent with a scientific view of the world and, most important of all, it provides the best explanation for experiences all of us have every day. Doctor Samuel Johnson, who was overimpressed by the arguments of some contemporary skeptics, told Boswell that all the arguments were against free will, but all experience was for it. I'd say myself that no good argument is against it and all experience is for it.

KIRK: Our time is just about up, and I'm going to allow Home the last word on the same grounds that he gave me the last word at the previous session. It's been two-to-one against him. I myself think that Home has done an excellent job in defending his position, but then I agree with that position. You must make up your own minds where the truth lies.

I'd like to use up one more bit of time to tie up a loose end from the last session. Remember I maintained that it makes no sense to talk about God causing us to do some action freely. I said that if the action were free God couldn't have caused us to do it, and if God caused us to do it it couldn't have been a free action. On the view just defended by Home, which as I've said I agree with, we can see why this is so. If God caused me to perform an action or make a choice, then God would be the sufficient cause of that action or choice. But Home and I would define a free action or choice as one with no sufficient cause. Thus the incompatibility I argued for follows from the view of free will we've been discussing.

I think that we'll find as we go on that many of our future discussions will reflect back on problems we've discussed earlier. Philosophical problems are very much interconnected, and a satisfactory answer to one may have to wait on satisfactory answers to others. At our next session we're going to discuss another problem which was raised briefly in the session last time: the problem of moral judgment. The title of the session is "What Do Philosophers Know about Morality?" I've consented to act as chairman again, though I'm rather sorry that I did, now I see what a hard time the chairman has getting a word in edgewise. Some of you want to get a word in I'm sure, so I'll declare the session open for questions from the floor.

QUESTIONS

Answer the following questions as you think they would be answered by the panelist to whom they are addressed.

1. Professor Home: What is the point of holding a person responsible for something if holding him responsible won't have any effect on his actions? And didn't you argue against Professor Oxmore that holding someone responsible won't necessarily have an effect on his actions?

2. Professor Oxmore: Isn't your view that freedom is autonomy inconsistent with your view that our actions are the result of sufficient causes beyond our control?

3. Professor Venner: If Home is right determinism undermines all arguments, including scientific arguments. How then can you call determinism a scientific view?

Do you find the following answers to questions satisfactory? Why or why not?

4. Home's answer to Oxmore's challenge.

5. Oxmore's answer to Home's analysis of the statement "every event has a cause."

6. Venner's answer to Home's objection from quantum theory.

Write brief essays on the following topics:

7. Which position do you most nearly agree with? Why?

8. What objection would you like to make that is not made in the dialogue? Why?

9. What argument concerning determinism and free will would you like to advance that is not considered (or not considered adequately) in the dialogue?

10. What argument or objection in the dialogue impressed you as very good or very bad? Why?

FURTHER READINGS

Hospers, John, *Readings in Introductory Philosophical Analysis*, Englewood Cliffs, N.J.: Prentice-Hall, Inc., 1968.

Hobart, R. E., "Free Will as Involving Determinism," pp. 152–74.

Mill, John Stuart, "The Nature of a Cause," pp. 139–45.

Taylor, Richard, "Freedom and Determinism," pp. 174–91.

TAYLOR, RICHARD, *Metaphysics*, (2nd ed.), Englewood Cliffs, N.J.: Prentice-Hall, Inc., 1974, Chaps. 5 and 6, pp. 38–71; Chap. 9, pp. 91–101.

WILSON, MARGARET D., DAN W. BROCK, and RICHARD F. KUHNS, *Philosophy, An Introduction*, New York: Appleton-Century-Crofts, 1972.

Campbell, C. A., "Has the Self 'Free Will'?", pp. 499–512.

Hospers, John, "What Means This Freedom?" pp. 512–22.

Mill, John Stuart, "Liberty and Necessity," pp. 493–98.

Questions on the Reading

1. Compare Mill's arguments with those in this chapter. Are there any substantial arguments in Mill that are not considered in the chapter? How might Home reply to Mill?

2. How does Campbell's defense of free will differ from Home's? What arguments does Campbell give that Home does not? How might Home and Campbell disagree?

3. Hospers gives a form of what Home calls the "specialized argument from science." Are Home's criticisms of the argument applicable to Hospers?

4. How does Hobart's claim relate to the arguments in this chapter? How might Home criticize Hobart?

5. How do Taylor's arguments against soft determinism differ from those in this chapter? How might Oxmore reply to these arguments? Would Home be likely to accept Taylor's "Theory of Agency"?

4

What Do Philosophers Know about Morality?

KIRK: The subject of our session today is moral philosophy, our title is "What Do Philosophers Know about Morality?" I think that besides providing a springboard for a discussion of moral philosophy the title, which Home tells me was suggested by the students, represents a certain disappointment on the part of our students. I don't think it's always the sort of disappointment we suppose—I think that sometimes students want to get moral advice from their teachers not so much so that they can follow it, but rather so that they can reject it. Or to put it in a better light, so that they can consider it and make up their own minds. But by and large they're more likely to get moral advice from their professor of English or political science than they are from their philosophy teacher. Perhaps as each of you state your own position you might make some comment on this. I think we'll go in order of seniority this time. Professor Venner?

VENNER: Yes. I can answer the question that is the title of the session, and also the question that Professor Kirk raises, very briefly. Philosophers do not know anything about morality, and I do not give moral advice to my students *because* I do not know anything about morality. But I would also want to say that the professors of English and political science also do not know anything about morality and should not be giving moral advice, and in fact no one knows anything about morality, and no one is in a position to tell another person what he ought morally to do. In other words, I hold the position in ethics that is called noncognitivism, the position that morality is not a subject of knowledge, that ethical statements are neither true or false.

In the Vienna days we held one particular variety of this view, the view called emotivism. We held that statements about right and wrong were expressions of emotion rather than factual statements. To say "stealing is wrong" is to say no more than "stealing, ugh!" This view was accurately stated by Ayer [1] in his book *Language, Truth and Logic*. Since those days I have somewhat modified my views. I can see considerable merit in later suggestions that statments about right or wrong are in some ways more like commands or pieces of advice; that to say "stealing is wrong" is to say "I regard stealing with disgust and I urge or direct you to regard it in the same way, and to avoid it." But I have not changed my essential view, that ethical statements are neither true nor false and are not subjects of knowledge. After all, a command or request such as "Open the door!" is not true or false any more than an expression of emotion is true or false.

KIRK: Thank you, Professor Venner. Professor Oxmore next.

OXMORE: Well, I can't be as succinct as Venner; I'll have to first explain what my view of ethics is and then say why I don't set up to give moral advice. Many of my Oxford colleagues take a line rather like Venner's, that moral statements are related closely to commands and requests. But some of us take a line which has a very long history in English philosophy, which is almost the English contribution to ethics. That, of course, is utilitarianism, the view that to say something is right is to say that on the whole it will do more good to more people than any of the alternatives. I've stated it in a very general way to give myself room to develop my view, but I think that most people will have a general idea of what I mean. I don't necessarily want to say that happiness is the only sort of good we need consider, so I don't use Mill's formula of "the greatest happiness of the greatest number." But certainly in a great many cases the right action will be the one that causes the greatest happiness to the greatest number of people.

Now I think that most people would agree with this more or less, and I think that it's important for philosophers to make it clear, and to defend it against misunderstandings. But I don't think that philosophers as philosophers have any special expertise as to what will bring the

---

[1] A. J. Ayer, see Biography (Appendix A) and Further Readings at the end of Chapter 10.

greatest good to the greatest number of people, and therefore I don't feel that as a philosopher I have any particular right or duty to give moral advice to my students. Of course, in particular cases where it seems to me that the rightness or wrongness of a particular thing is quite clear-cut, I might say something about it merely in my capacity as a concerned human being. But I don't think that I'm especially functioning as a philosopher when I do that. My response to "What do philosophers know about morality?" would be that they know what morality is in the sense of being able to analyze the concept of morality, but that as philosophers they don't necessarily know what is moral in particular cases.

KIRK: And, last but not least, Professor Home.

HOME: Right. The view I want to defend is unlike Professor Venner's in that I think that statements about right and wrong can be true or false and can be known, but it's also unlike one thing that might be meant by Professor Oxmore's view in that I don't think that it's only a matter of empirical fact—for example whether someone is made happy or unhappy—that makes something right or wrong. Actually, I think that there are some points of contact between Oxmore's view and mine; but I want to insist on the existence of moral facts as well as empirical facts, and to insist that you can't get moral conclusions from purely empirical premises.

The view that I want to defend is the view that by using our mind or reason we can know or discover moral facts as well as empirical facts. I don't mind if you label this view "moral intuitionism," but I don't want to be identified with Moore's [2] views, which are what most people think of when they hear that name. The view I'd defend would be much more like the views of W. D. Ross, [3] but modified and updated in the light of what's happened in ethics since Ross.

I don't usually give moral advice to my students or anyone else, because in my experience what people are generally looking for when they ask for advice is merely support in doing what they've made up their minds to do anyway. But I don't rule out the possibility of a philosopher being able to help people make moral decisions, for reasons I'll come to in a moment.

I think that people's own reason tells them, in general, what is right or wrong in clear-cut cases, just as their own reason tells them whether an argument is valid in clear-cut cases. But just as a logician can help us make up our minds about the validity of arguments in less clear-cut

[2] G. E. Moore, see Biography (Appendix A) and Further Readings at the end of Chapter 4.
[3] W. D. Ross, see Biography (Appendix A) and Further Readings at the end of Chapter 4. See also Bibliography (Appendix B, Part IV).

cases by showing us rules that valid arguments keep and invalid arguments break, so I think that moral philosophers can show us the patterns behind our moral reasoning and help us to apply these patterns in borderline cases.

So my answer to "What do philosophers know about morality?" is similar to the answer to "What do logicians know about validity?" Logic couldn't get started unless ordinary people could recognize validity in simple cases, but the logician organizes and systematizes those presystematic intuitions. Moral philosophy builds on the fact that ordinary people can recognize right and wrong in simple cases, but it organizes and systematizes our moral intuitions, and the rules it develops can help us to make up our minds in doubtful cases.

KIRK: Perhaps before going on we could say something briefly about a problem that almost always comes up in introductory ethics classes—the question of egoism. Is everyone basically selfish or if not, should they be? If we dealt with this now it might remove a stumbling block for some of the audience.

HOME: Well, of course, there are really two things to be considered here—psychological egoism and ethical egoism. Psychological egoism claims that everyone *in fact* always acts selfishly, while ethical egoism says that people *ought* to behave selfishly.

VENNER: Since psychological egoism makes a factual claim, it is possible to judge it by the same standards by which we judge any supposedly factual theory. By those standards it would seem to be false. The researches of psychologists, as well as our own experience, show that people do not always act for selfish motives. Some people act altruistically; some people act spitefully or maliciously or in a self-destructive fashion. The idea that people always act for their own satisfaction is simply an exploded piece of armchair psychology.

OXMORE: Often it's also a conceptual muddle. When you point out obvious cases of behavior contrary to the interests or desires of the person acting, the egoist often says, "But he must be getting something out of it or he wouldn't be doing it." It's easy enough to show that all sorts of things people do don't lead to their own satisfaction, in any ordinary sense of "satisfaction." The egoist has to admit this, but he then tries to claim that since the person chooses to behave in that way he must be "getting something."

Now it's perfectly true that most of our behavior has some end or purpose. But, of course, often this end or purpose is the good of someone else, or harm to someone else, or even harm to oneself, as in self-destructive behavior. The only sense in which this behavior is "self-interested" is that the person chooses that behavior. When you really press the psychological egoist, you either find him making false factual claims, or you find that he's trying to make his claim true by definition. And if you press him on that, you find that all you can really defend along those lines is some harmless truism such as "people act for reasons."

KIRK: What about ethical egoism, the view that we *ought* to be selfish?

VENNER: That, of course, is an ethical statement. As such it is, like all ethical statements, merely an expression of emotion or attitude. My own emotions or attitudes are opposed to selfishness, but the dispute between me and the ethical egoist is not a factual dispute and cannot be settled.

KIRK: Well, that's certainly consistent with your views as you've expressed them. What would a utilitarian say, Professor Oxmore?

OXMORE: Well, of course, some utilitarians have tried to base the principle of acting for the greatest happiness of the greatest number on considerations of self-interest. But I don't think that will really work. The utilitarian in my view has to show that we can act, and ought to act, for the good of others, even when this isn't to our personal advantage.

HOME: That's true in a sense but over-simple. Not all behavior supposedly directed toward the good of others is good, and certainly not all behavior directed toward our own good is bad. Sometimes doing the right thing is to our advantage, sometimes it isn't. The important thing is to do the right thing.

VENNER: But I would ask Professor Oxmore how she would show that we ought to act for the good of others, and Professor Home how he would decide what is right.

KIRK: Yes, perhaps we should get back to the question of how these theories are to be justified. Professor Venner, would you get the discussion going with a justification for your views?

VENNER: Yes. In the Vienna days what especially impressed us was the fact that in science you had interpersonal agreement and a way of settling disputes, whereas in ethics you did not. Polish and German scientists could agree about science and settle their disputes by reason. But Poles and Germans could not agree about what was right to do about the border question, and the only way that they could settle their dispute was by going to war with each other. I would make this the basis of a general argument: moral arguments cannot be factual disagreements because there is no interpersonal agreement and no decision procedure.

HOME: To make that a valid argument you need the premise that in matters of fact there is always interpersonal agreement and there is always a decision procedure.

VENNER: Yes, I would agree to that.

OXMORE: But look here, the fact that people disagree on moral questions can be explained in a number of ways. Very often there are differences in factual beliefs involved which account for the disagreement. You and I might be perfectly well agreed that each person has a right to his own property, but disagree about whether you or I had a right to that briefcase there, because we disagree over the factual question of whether it is yours or mine.

VENNER: But then the question could be settled.

OXMORE: Yes, of course, and moral disagreements frequently are settled. There are disagreements in the courts all the time, but that doesn't mean that these disagreements can't be settled and aren't settled.

VENNER: But if there is a procedure for settling them, then they were factual questions after all—you understand I use the word factual in a sense such that what is the law in America or Germany is a matter of fact.

OXMORE: But then you're simply making your position true by definition—if there's a way of settling a question you call it a factual question. But if you do that then you may have to call some moral questions factual.

VENNER: I think not, for in the moral questions there is no way of settling the matter if we disagree on principles. If you and I happen to agree that a man has a right to his own property, so good. But if an anarchist should say property is theft, we cannot convince him that he is wrong.

HOME: But I think we might. In my view every reasonable person would agree that institutions which serve the greatest good of the greatest number of people are right. The anarchist thinks that private property doesn't serve the general good; you and I think that it does. We may very well be able to convince him, if he'll listen to argument.

VENNER: But what if he is not reasonable, and will not listen to argument?

HOME: But you have no security against that in science either. If a philosophical skeptic refuses to accept scientific reasoning, and won't listen to argument, you won't get him to agree with you on matters of science. A theory only has to be proof against reasonable objections: if we allow unreasonable objections no theory is safe, scientific *or* ethical.

OXMORE: I'd prefer to put it another way—I'd say that a person who didn't agree that what was for the greatest good of the greatest number was right, didn't understand the concept of rightness, or if you prefer the English word "right." But I'm glad to see you coming over to utilitarianism, Home.

HOME: Oh, I don't deny that utilitarianism is part of the truth about right and wrong. I only deny that it's the whole truth. It's an over-simple view—like trying to reduce the whole of logic to the theory of syllogisms. And I'd disagree with you that we can justify utilitarianism simply as an analysis of moral language, even supposing that it's the right analysis.

OXMORE: Well, suppose for a moment that it is the right analysis. What's wrong with saying that actions which are for the greatest good of the greatest number are the sort of actions that our language, or our conceptual structure, describes as right?

HOME: Because saying something is right is saying that it ought to be done, and you can't get that out of an analysis of language.

OXMORE: Why not say that that's part of the meaning of the concept also?

HOME: Well, let me give you a comparison. Suppose that we're at a house party with some rather old-fashioned relatives of yours, and you and I want to argue philosophy. But our hostess tells us that we shouldn't argue, and that instead we ought to be out shooting or riding. We object, and she says that it's the "done" thing. Riding and shooting are "done"; sitting and arguing "aren't done." Or she might say that the one sort of activity is "well bred" or "gentlemanly" and the other isn't.

OXMORE: My dear fellow, I have an aunt just like that!

HOME: Well now, suppose that we analyze the conceptual structure of people like your aunt and we find that riding and shooting rather than arguing are the sort of actions that their language, their conceptual structure, describes as "done." And furthermore, suppose that we discover that if a thing is described as "done," this *means* that one ought to do it. But it seems to me that we might still feel no obligation at all to go riding or shooting. We might very well say "I know that's the sort of thing people regard as obligatory, but I disagree. I don't think that it is."

OXMORE: You just try saying that to my aunt!

HOME: Well, of course, there might be reasons of politeness—or prudence—for not saying it.

OXMORE: I do see what you mean. You want to maintain that it makes sense to say that a thing is correctly described in English as being right, and therefore obligatory, but that nevertheless it might not be obligatory. But would you want to say that a thing could be correctly described in English as black, and therefore not white, but still be white?

HOME: I think color words are a very special case, and also "correctly described" is ambiguous. A substance might be "correctly described" as a medicine, in the sense that people do call it a medicine, and it might be true by definition that medicines cure people. But the thing that was called a medicine might be completely worthless and never cure anyone. You can't settle what will cure you just by looking at language, and you can't settle what you ought to do just by looking at language.

OXMORE: You're using something like the "open question" test, aren't you? Arguing that no matter what nonethical definition of an ethical term like "right" we give, we can always raise the question "But is a thing which meets that definition really right?"

HOME: I'm arguing that you can't get a moral "ought" from an "is," can't get ethical conclusions from nonethical premises. I wouldn't necessarily want to be stuck with Moore's formulation of that argument.

OXMORE: But do you want to draw a conclusion like Moore's from this argument, that rightness or goodness is some sort of simple nonnatural property of actions or things?

HOME: I wouldn't want to claim that moral properties were simple properties. I'm completely convinced by Hare's argument that moral properties are "supervenient" or "consequential." [4] That is that they follow upon the possession of other properties. You can't have two actions which are alike in every way *except* that one is right and the other is wrong, as you could have two actions which were alike in every way except that one was done rapidly and the other was done slowly. I'm not sure just what Moore *meant* by a nonnatural property except just not following from the possession of empirical properties. I'd agree that moral properties are nonnatural in that sense.

OXMORE: Wait a minute, haven't you contradicted yourself? First you said that moral properties were supervenient, that they followed from other properties. Then you said they were nonnatural, that they didn't follow from other properties.

HOME: I think I said "followed upon" when I was talking about supervenience; if I didn't it was a slip of the tongue. It's a necessary versus

[4] R. M. Hare, *The Language of Morals* (Oxford: Oxford University Press, 1952).

sufficient conditions thing again. Possession of certain nonmoral properties is a *necessary* condition of something being right, but no set of nonmoral properties is a *sufficient* condition of something being right. There's no description of an action in purely nonmoral terms from which it follows that that action is right or that one ought to do it.

OXMORE: What about Searle's example—"I promised to do this and nothing has happened to release me from my promise, therefore I ought to do this"? [5]

HOME: That won't work. The conclusion obviously doesn't follow from the premise by any standard rule of logic. So either you have to add a premise like "One ought to keep one's promises," which is a moral rule, or else you need a rule of inference to get from "You promised to do it" to "You ought to do it." That's what Searle does; he talks about a "convention" that exists in the language to enable you to get from the one to the other. But Searle's convention is just the moral rule "One ought to keep one's promises" in disguise, made into a rule of inference instead of a premise. And if he says it's not a moral rule but a rule of English or a rule about our conceptual structure, I'd have the same objection as I did to your position a few minutes ago.

OXMORE: But to get back to that, I wouldn't want to say that rules based on our conceptual structure are just factual descriptions. They're inescapable and unavoidable; necessary if you like.

HOME: Ah, but if you're willing to talk about necessary principles that tell us what we ought and ought not to do, then you're getting very close to my view.

VENNER: Excuse me, but these necessary principles of morality—they sound quite medieval, quite like the idea of "natural law." How do we know such principles exist and which are true?

OXMORE: I'd say by the analysis of language, which leads to an understanding of our conceptual structure.

HOME: I'd say by generalizing from instances that are clearly instances of right or wrong.

VENNER: Well, I will deal with Professor Oxmore first. Is it not the case that other languages will have other conceptual structures?

OXMORE: No. The sort of principles I have in mind would be presuppositions of all languages. As Wittgenstein said, "Ethics must be a condition of the world, like logic."

[5] John R. Searle, "How to Derive 'Ought' from 'Is'," *Philosophical Review*, 73, 1964.

VENNER: Ah yes, in the Vienna days when we read the *Tractatus* with such admiration, we did not really attend to mystical remarks of that kind. But surely there are no ethical principles that are common to all languages. Surely there is no ethical principle that has not been denied by some culture.

OXMORE: I think that the ethical differences between cultures have been very much exaggerated.

KIRK: Just by way of comment, the differences have been exaggerated ever since the Greek skeptics tried to use the argument from divergence of moral practice to undermine moral laws. You should read some of the practices they attributed to the Persians and the barbarians!

HOME: I'd agree with Oxmore and Kirk; the basic similarities between moral codes at all places and times are much more striking than the differences. I think the explanation for a good many differences in practice, which can't be explained by differences in factual belief, can be laid to differences in who is to count as a person, differences of social institutions, and differences about who is responsible for what. In societies where the wife's brother is responsible for raising her children, for example, you can't expect the same attitude toward fathers as in our society. In societies where there are different ideas about social forms and politeness, something that we might regard from outside as a lie would be an accepted polite form. In societies where slaves are regarded as merely machines that can talk, behavior toward them will be outside of morality, just as in a society where some animals are regarded as persons or quasi-persons, killing them might be regarded as murder.

OXMORE: That's interesting, but I see an objection. Isn't the question of who is a person itself a moral question?

HOME: It's obviously related to moral questions on one side and to questions of one's whole world view on the other. But my point was that obligations of justice, mercy, and so on might be recognized toward people who are recognized as persons even in a society which behaved outrageously toward nonmembers not regarded as persons. Even in Nazi Germany there were ideas of loyalty and honor to members of the German race.

VENNER: There was at least much talk of German brotherhood, although it did not extend to German Jews or German political liberals. The Vienna Circle was soon dispersed by the rise of Hitler. I see that you are all against me on this matter of divergences in morality between cultures. But the anthropologists, I think, are on my side. On the other hand, I think I am perhaps on Professor Home's side over this matter of deriving an "ought" from an "is." It was the good Hume, was it not, who pointed out that one cannot do this?

HOME: Yes, noncognitivists and intuitionists can join together in belaboring the utilitarians for committing the "naturalistic fallacy" by trying to get "oughts" from "ises." In fact, positivists like Ayer often borrowed arguments against utilitarianism from intuitionists like Ross.

OXMORE: On the other hand, Venner and I are presumably agreed in being suspicious of Home's "moral facts" and "nonnatural properties." I'm still dissatisfied with your moral properties that depend on nonmoral properties but can't be defined in terms of them.

HOME: Well, I think that you get this in a number of areas, and there's nothing mysterious about it. A legal decision may depend on a number of nonlegal facts, and the decision couldn't be different in two cases where all of the nonlegal facts were the same.

OXMORE: But sometimes it is.

HOME: Excuse me, my "couldn't" wasn't a factual "couldn't"; such things do in fact happen. But according to the principles of consistency built into the law, this "legally can't" happen. If a later case is decided differently than an earlier one on the same facts, it's grounds for appeal because the law uses the principle of precedents to ensure consistency.

OXMORE: But the law can change.

HOME: Yes, there my analogy with law breaks down because in my view the principles of morality don't change, any more than the principles of logic do, although we can understand both sorts of principles better or see them in a new light. And I really think that Oxmore will have to admit at least one principle of this kind in order to get her utilitarianism started, and perhaps more than one. Because if you can't get an "is" out of an "ought," you need some principle such as "One ought to do what is for the greatest happiness of the greatest number" as a sort of major premise in all of your ethical arguments.

OXMORE: Yes, I can see that, if your argument is correct. But why perhaps more than one?

HOME: Well, there are these rather hoary objections to utilitarianism, which I'm sure you know as well as I do, that seem to show that you need a principle of justice in addition to the "greatest happiness" principle. For example, if we could make everyone in this city happy for a year by quietly torturing to death some anonymous drifter in the basement of city hall, it would still be immoral to do it, even though that action would seem to meet the "greatest good of the greatest number" criterion.

OXMORE: Well, of course there are several ways of handling that kind of case. I think there's something to be said for Nowell-Smith's objection that to make cases like that work you have to eliminate so many of the factors we'd ordinarily take into consideration that they're no longer possible cases.[6] And you can always hold that if it's really for the greatest good of the greatest number it really is right, regardless of what we'd usually say or think. But like Mill I do have the feeling that one ought to have some sort of principle of fairness or equal treatment. You recall that Mill's principle actually reads "The greatest happiness of the greatest number, each to count as one and no more than one."[7] And he tries to stretch the last clause to cover a sort of equal treatment.

HOME: Well, in my example we counted the drifter as one and no more than one, but his good was outweighed by the happiness of all those other people.

OXMORE: Yes, I agree that Mill's clause won't do the job, but I think that in some way justice or equal treatment can be regarded as a kind of good thing in itself, and therefore to be counted in distributing goods.

HOME: But let's say that in my example we weighed the drifter's right to equal treatment in with all the good done others, and he still lost out.

OXMORE: Yes, and to argue against myself I'm really uneasy about regarding things like justice and equal treatment as goods in themselves apart from happiness. It doesn't seem to me that if everyone is going to be very miserable it's awfully important that they be all equally miserable, for instance. I'm afraid that the best I can do with the kind of case you raise is to say that for civilized people knowing that they live in a society where that sort of thing doesn't happen is an important part of their own happiness. I happen to know, for instance, that Professor Venner could have had quite a prestigious chair at one of the German universities under Hitler, if he had kept quiet about politics. But he refused, and I think that at least part of the reason was that he didn't want to be one of the privileged members of a society that was built on the suffering of a minority. If you start altering your "drifter" case so no one knows that it's that sort of society except a few, and somehow they aren't damaged by the knowledge, and so on, then I think I'd give you an answer like Nowell-Smith's: such a state of affairs isn't really possible.

6 P. Nowell-Smith, *Ethics* (Baltimore, Md.: Penguin Books, 1954), Chap. 11, Sec. 3.

7 John Stuart Mill, see Biography (Appendix A) and Further Readings at the end of Chapter 4.

HOME: But look, why should it make you unhappy to live in an unjust society unless you recognize that injustice is a moral evil that shouldn't be allowed? After all, the Bentham type of utilitarian would live in such a society quite happily, so long as he was convinced that the balance of happiness over unhappiness was better in that society than in a just society.

OXMORE: My answer to that would involve talking about rules and institutions and societies. Living in a society with a rule of law, with institutions that enable people to obtain justice, is more likely to lead to happiness than living in a society with a rule that allows people to be tortured for the benefit of others, or with institutions that treat people unequally. I think that you can make quite a good case that the more just and more equal society is the happier society. That's true in practice, whatever may be the situation in imaginary cases.

VENNER: But this is all a matter of empirical fact.

HOME: Yes, but the principle that we *ought* to bring about happiness can't be a matter of empirical fact.

VENNER: With this I have agreed, no "oughts" from "ises." But now you want to get "oughts" from nothing at all, is it not?

HOME: No, I want to get "oughts" from our direct awareness of right and wrong in particular situations.

VENNER: But how does this work? Is it like an extra sense, this thing that tells us right and wrong?

HOME: No, I wouldn't say that it was like a sense at all. We do speak of "seeing" that an action is wrong, but then we speak of "seeing" that an argument is valid, too. No, I'd say that moral judgments are assessments on the basis of evidence, like the assessment of a historical or philosophical argument. I choose those two examples because I think that ethical judgments are dialectical, like philosophical, and to some extent historical, judgments. Certain considerations can give you a *prima facie* case, but it's possible for there to be considerations that count the other way. If there are such considerations, they need to be replied to, and so on. Your final judgment will be made after considering the pros and cons, but in principle it's always possible for new considerations to come up that might change your judgment.

VENNER: Can you give me an example?

HOME: Yes, of course. Consider a case where you see a large man twisting a child's arm and the child is screaming, obviously in great pain.

Prima facie you would say that what the man is doing is wrong. Then someone explains that the man is a doctor, and the boy dislocated his elbow. The doctor is trying to snap it back into place. If this is done immediately there's a good chance that damage to the muscles and so on will be minimized. But then another doctor in the crowd says that the first doctor could have minimized the pain by giving the boy a shot from his medical bag, which is right by his side. Furthermore, the first doctor is angry at the boy, who injured his arm by running into the doctor on a bicycle. If we stop there we might come to the conclusion that what the man is doing to the boy is wrong, although not quite in the way we thought at first.

VENNER: Now let me understand your view. Some of the points you mention are matters of fact—that the man is twisting the arm, that he is a doctor, and so on.

HOME: Yes, and this illustrates the point that moral judgments can depend in a way on empirical facts, and in another case where all the facts were the same, we ought to make the same moral judgment.

VENNER: Besides these facts, there are your own emotional reactions to the situation. But you do not identify these with the moral judgment?

HOME: Oh no, that's quite a different thing. I might feel very indignant if the boy looked very much like my son, or not very indignant if he was the nasty little neighborhood pest who just the other day had been tormenting my dog. But in either case I'd make my moral judgment on the basis of the facts.

VENNER: But now you must tell me what is this basis for decision if it is not just the facts, nor the facts plus your emotional reactions.

HOME: It would be my recognition of the moral aspects of the situation, which I *could* put in the form of general principles, although I don't always do so.

VENNER: And what would be the nature of these principles?

HOME: Well, one principle involved would be the principle that pain should not be inflicted where avoidable. Another would be the principle that pain may be inflicted for the good of the person concerned.

VENNER: This was not precisely what I meant. I wanted to know the justification of these principles, and whether they are supposed to be logically true or empirically true.

HOME: I wouldn't claim that they were logically true in what Kirk calls the narrow sense, but I would claim that they were necessarily true or logically true in what he calls the wider sense.

VENNER: In other words, they have the same status as Professor Kirk's metaphysical principles?

HOME: Yes, I'd say that they were very much that sort of thing.

VENNER: But his metaphysical principles he said were at least empirically true, so that I could agree that "Nothing begins to exist without a cause" would be scientifically verifiable without agreeing that it was any more than that.

HOME: Right. But in the nature of the case you can't get that kind of "at least empirically true" in the case of moral principles because they don't say what is, but what ought to be. I'd say that what corresponds to the "at least empirically true" kind of thing in the case of moral principles is a sort of hypothetical imperative. Let me explain. If someone says that he can't understand "Nothing comes from nothing" as being necessarily true, he may at least concede, as you did, that it's universally true in experience. If someone can't understand "Don't inflict pain when avoidable" as a necessary truth, he might still grant that "If you want to have a satisfying life, don't inflict pain when avoidable" is true in experience.

VENNER: This would be a matter of psychological fact?

HOME: Yes, the claim in a general form would be that a life lived according to moral principles is the most fully satisfactory life.

VENNER: You would claim this is true as a matter of experience?

HOME: Partly, yes. In addition, Kirk and I would want to say that moral rules are in effect God's instructions for running the human machine properly, and this gives us additional confidence that leading the moral life will lead to ultimate satisfaction.

VENNER: Well then, why not simply base morality on this claim of satisfaction?

HOME: There are both practical and theoretical reasons. Let's look at the practical reasons first. A term like "satisfaction" or "happiness" has several senses. There's a minimal sense in which satisfaction or happiness is simply having no unsatisfied desires. I call it a minimal sense because someone with no desires, someone totally apathetic, is satisfied in that sense. Then there's the sense of having pleasant experiences—joy or delight. I'm satisfied or happy when I'm enjoying something. And finally there's the sense of getting our own way. I can be unsatisfied or unhappy at not getting my own way even if I have no other unsatisfied desires and have the chance at joy or delight. Now the claim I'd make is that obeying the moral law will lead in the long run to the satisfaction of our deepest desires, that it leads toward joy and peace. And breaking the moral law leads ultimately to the frustration of our deepest desires, leads away from joy and peace to anger and bitterness and hatred. But, of course, to obey the moral law often involves leaving unsatisfied a particular desire at a particular time and can often lead to pain and suffering, rather than joy or delight, in the short run. Also, I can "set my heart," as we say, on a particular thing—a woman, a job, an honor— getting which involves breaking the moral law, and I can refuse to be satisfied with anything else. What satisfies us is partly a matter of what we allow to satisfy us. So in practice I can't promise anyone that living morally will satisfy him; all I can say is that it will satisfy him if he lets it satisfy him.

VENNER: But anything will satisfy us if we let it, is it not so?

HOME: Oh no, it has to be the sort of thing that's capable of satisfying us in the sense of giving us joy or delight. It's no use saying that torturing yourself half to death daily will satisfy us in the sense of giving us joy or delight if we let it—it won't, no matter how much we "let it."

VENNER: But we are somewhat off the point, are we not?

HOME: Yes. I was saying that the practical problem of basing morality merely on personal satisfaction was that what satisfies us is at least to some extent what we decide to let satisfy us. So, merely keeping moral rules can't be guaranteed to make us happy; this depends to a great extent on our attitude. And this leads us to the theoretical problem, because the attitude that is required by morality is an attitude of love or concern for others, and considering their interests as well as our own. Now we can see that a person who tries to be moral only for what he can get out of it, thinking only of his own interests, will never have the proper attitude. The kind of motives he has makes the attainment of his end impossible.

VENNER: His end being what?

HOME: Well, we're imagining a case where a man wants to be moral only because he thinks that this will be a source of happiness for him. But this very attitude makes it impossible for him to be moral, for what morality requires is a concern for others as well as for oneself.

VENNER: In what sense would morality require this?

OXMORE: I'd say that it was a matter of meaning; concern for others as well as for ourselves is what we mean by morality. Would you agree, Home?

HOME: Yes, that's at least part of the answer. Morality essentially involves doing to others as you'd have them do to you, just as logic essentially involves assessing arguments, judging their validity.

VENNER: Ah, but even if I grant you that this is what is meant by morality, there remains the question of why one should be moral.

HOME: The sort of answer you give to that depends a bit on what the questioner has in mind. If he means "What's in it for me," I would tell him that a moral life will in the long run lead to joy and peace, and an immoral one will in the long run lead to despair and frustration. But in order to get this joy and peace he has to stop worrying about himself and be concerned about others and about doing the right thing because it's right. If on the other hand he means to ask why the rightness of an action should be a motive for action, I'd try to show him that all normal people recognize that there are two general kinds of motive for action— one's own interests and what is morally right, or is in the interests of others. "I wanted to" is a perfectly good motive for action, but so is "I knew it would make him (or her) happy," or "I thought it was the right thing to do." Anyone who doesn't recognize this is not recognizing the moral experience almost all men share, and which is embodied in our ordinary thinking and ordinary language about action.

VENNER: You speak of "all normal people," and the moral experience *almost* all men share. What about those who do not share it?

HOME: There may be, and indeed there seem to be, people who entirely lack moral experience, who are completely *a*moral. But these people are very rare and are exceptions to the norm in the same way that color-blind people are exceptions to the norm. Far more common are *im*moral people, people who recognize their moral obligations, but freely choose to do wrong or sacrifice the interests of others to their own.

VENNER: But could you convince such a person that you were right and he was wrong?

HOME: Perhaps and perhaps not. It would depend on what sort of person he was. But this doesn't prove that the amoral person isn't abnormal and defective any more than a red-green color-blind man refusing to recognize that there is a distinction between red and green.

VENNER: But in the red-green case there is agreement among all people who are not color-blind, and there are ways of testing.

HOME: But there's considerable agreement about moral principles too. Not the same kind of agreement as about colors. I think that kind of comparison is misleading, and I'm sorry I slipped into it. It's more like the general agreement of historians that Napoleon lost the battle of Waterloo, or the general agreement of philosophers that Plato's Theory of Forms is unsatisfactory. Reasonable men could, in principle, dispute either of those things, but they would need powerful new evidence or arguments. Someone who simply denied the accepted view for no reason would be a defective historian or a defective philosopher.

VENNER: But again, widespread disagreement seems to be a fact.

HOME: Yes, because most actual cases are complex and can be interpreted in various ways. But those, for example, who defend the Vietnam war aren't denying that unnecessary suffering should be avoided, and those who attack it aren't denying that commitments to allies should be kept. The defenders would argue that the suffering is necessary; the attackers would deny that we have a commitment.

VENNER: But to the man who denies that it is wrong to inflict useless suffering, you have no reply.

HOME: No more, and no less than I have a reply to a man who denies some logical principle, for instance "If p and q are both true then p is true." I can see if he misunderstands the principle, I can try to illustrate it or convey it to him in some way, but if he still continues to refuse to admit the principle, I either conclude that he's insincere or that he is somehow abnormal mentally and lacks the ability to understand logical principles. But so far as I can see moral skeptics aren't usually amoral people; they're just people with a false theory about morals which causes them to distrust their moral experience. Similarly epistemological skeptics know the same things we all do, but they have a false theory which causes them to distrust their knowledge.

VENNER: You think the cases are parallel?

HOME: Oh yes, there are even similarities in arguments. Just as one kind of epistemological skeptic treats deductive reasoning as if it were the only type of reasoning, and therefore rejects other kinds of reasoning because they can't be justified deductively, so one kind of moral skeptic treats reasons of self-interest as if they were the only type of reason for action, and rejects moral reasons for actions because they can't be justified solely in terms of self-interest. In both cases, part of the argument against the skeptic consists in showing that there's no justification for treating their favored case as the only case.

VENNER: I look forward to going into this more deeply when we discuss the problem of knowledge in a later session. But perhaps it might help me to understand your position if you give me examples of a few of your moral rules.

HOME: I'll do that rather informally. Suppose we grant for the sake of argument that one's own happiness and satisfaction is *a* reason for action, and so is treating others in a fair and kind way. When these two reasons conflict in a particular case the immoral man puts self-interest first, even if he has to treat others in a cruel and unfair way. The moral man acknowledges his duty to, and makes some effort to, treat others fairly and kindly even where his own interests have to be sacrificed. One specific moral principle which has to do with this situation is the principle that one ought not to cause pain and suffering to others merely for one's own amusement. A cruel man is precisely a man who enjoys hurting others, and cruelty is one kind of immorality. Another principle in this area is that one ought not to treat others unjustly merely for one's own convenience or gratification. If I play favorites in grading my students, or assign grades at random to save myself the trouble of grading papers, I'd be violating this principle. Then there are principles that have to do with more general obligations—truth telling, for example.

VENNER: These principles are universal in form?

HOME: The kind of ethical view I'd be prepared to defend says that there are certain very general moral principles of which we can give an exhaustive list. My own list would be a revision of a list given by W. D. Ross, which goes roughly as follows: Don't harm others unless harming them is the lesser evil of the choices available to you. If you do harm others avoidably, make it up to them if you can. Keep promises and other commitments. Repay benefits done to you, if possible. Deal fairly with others. Sometimes do good to others even if they have no strict claim on you. Sometimes improve or benefit yourself. . . . I'd want to claim that all of our moral obligations come under one of those headings. When two of those rules conflict, I'd want to say that normally the one higher on the list takes precedence, but that sometimes an important or very important case of a rule lower on the list could override a less important case of a rule higher on the list.

VENNER: These principles seem plausible, and my own emotions and training incline me to accept them. But I can see no objective way to justify them.

HOME: Well, I'm afraid that we're being haunted by the ghost of the verification principle again. Moral principles aren't logically true in the narrow sense and can't be verified by the methods of the sciences. For you this means that they can't be justified at all. But that doesn't follow unless we accept the verification principle, and there seems no good reason to accept it.

KIRK: If I may tie up a loose end again, I'd like to point out that once we recognize the force of morality and the demands it makes on us, we then have a problem about its origins and foundations. I would argue that a universe without a just and righteous God, just a universe like the universe of the chance view or the natural necessity view, or the mixed view, can't really provide any foundation for the demands of morality. In any of these views our moral ideas are merely programmed into us by mindless and purposeless forces and can have no validity. Thus, as a brief sketch of the argument from moral experience, I'd argue that objective morality requires the existence of God. But objective morality does exist, so God exists. That's just a quick sketch of the argument, of course. But I'd argue that just as a universe without God undermines reason, it also undermines morality.

VENNER: Then you would acknowledge that I am at least consistent on this point: I reject both God and objective morality.

KIRK: Oh yes, that's just the contrapositive; no God, no objective morality.

VENNER: I should have thought though, that for you morality would be simply whatever God commanded.

KIRK: On no. I realize that some Christians have held that view, but that makes nonsense of the demand for repentance and the promise of salvation from sin directed toward those who become converts to Christianity. Unless we could recognize the demands of morality before we realize God existed and was the foundation of morality, we couldn't realize our need for forgiveness, or indeed be held responsible for breaking laws we didn't know about. Saint Paul, for example, makes it quite clear that the pagans knew right from wrong before they had a chance of knowing God.

VENNER: God could not, then, make cruelty right or kindness wrong?

KIRK: Oh no; the rightness or wrongness of things like that depend on the nature of God, who is Love. A being who commanded cruelty wouldn't be God, and would have no moral claim on our obedience. But of course God is a moral authority: he can give us commands that then become obligatory for those who are aware of them. Worshiping God once a week on the Sabbath is an example of a command which doesn't bind us until we know that God has commanded it. But respecting our parents is something we should know is right without having to be specifically commanded. Of course, God can reinforce such obligations, remind us of them, by making them part of His explicit commands.

VENNER: This is most interesting: I am no closer to agreeing with you and Home, but I feel that perhaps I understand your positions better.

KIRK: I think that's an excellent note on which to end the panel discussion and go on to questions from the floor. At our next session we'll discuss a particular moral problem, the morality of war. Professor Venner will be in the chair. The title of the session is "Curse This Stupid War!" which is, I believe, a quote from that famous World War I ace, Snoopy. Perhaps we'll find further enlightenment on the more general problems of morality by confining ourselves to a specific example. At least I hope so.

QUESTIONS

Answer the following questions as you think they would be answered by the panelist to whom they are addressed.

1. Professor Venner: How can you justify any action, such as opposing Hitler, which is not directly in your own interests, if moral judgments have no validity?
2. Professor Oxmore: Wouldn't a utilitarian have to agree that it was a good thing to raise the general average of happiness by killing off unhappy people?
3. Professor Home: Wouldn't any moral principle you could put forward have exceptions in some cases, and thus not be a reliable guide to action?

Do you find the following answers to questions satisfactory? Why or why not?

4. Venner's reply to the criticism of his argument from disagreement by Home and Oxmore.
5. Oxmore's reply to the point by Home that she needs at least one independent moral principle to make utilitarianism work.
6. Home's reply to the attacks on his theory of moral knowledge by Venner.

Write a brief essay on the following questions:

7. Which position do you most nearly agree with? Why?
8. What objection would you like to make to any position?
9. What alternative position or argument would you like to advance?
10. What argument or objection in the dialogue impressed you as very good or very bad? Why?

FURTHER READINGS

FRANKENA, WILLIAM, *Ethics* (2nd ed.), Englewood Cliffs, N.J.: Prentice-Hall, Inc., 1973, esp. Chaps. 1–3, pp. 1–60.

HOSPERS, JOHN, *Readings in Introductory Philosophical Analysis*, Englewood Cliffs, N.J.: Prentice-Hall, Inc., 1968.

Mill, John Stuart, "The Utilitarian Ethics," pp. 346–63.

Rand, Ayn, "Values and Rights," pp. 364–87.

Ross, Sir David, "Kant's Categorical Imperative," pp. 342–46.

RACHELS, JAMES, *Moral Problems*, New York: Harper and Row, 1973.

(Detailed discussions of particular ethical problems, e.g., abortion, civil disobedience, sex, etc.)

WILSON, MARGARET D., DAN W. BROCK, and RICHARD F. KUHNS, *Philosophy, An Introduction*, New York: Appleton-Century-Crofts, 1972.

Kant, Immanuel, "Duty and the Moral Law," pp. 563–73.

Mill, John Stuart, "Utilitarianism," pp. 573–80.

Stevenson, Charles L., "The Emotive Meaning of Ethical Terms," pp. 588–602.

Questions on the Reading

1. How does Kant's ethical theory differ from that defended by Home? What criticisms might Home make of Kant?
2. How does Mill's utilitarianism differ from Oxmore's? How might Home criticize Mill?
3. Is Rand's version of egoism open to the criticisms in this chapter? Why or why not?
4. How does Stevenson's theory differ from Venner's? How might Oxmore or Home criticize Stevenson?
5. How might Venner, Oxmore, or Home criticize Frankena's ethical theory?

5

Curse This Stupid War!

VENNER: For this session and the next I have agreed to be chairman, since the discussion will be on detailed points of ethics. As you know from what I said at the last session, I regard ethical statements as not a matter of knowledge, so I will have not much to say about these topics. With much of what the other panelists say about these matters I am sure that I will be in sympathy, but it will be, in my view, emotional sympathy rather than intellectual agreement, since what they say will not be provable or disprovable. Professor Home, already I find myself at a disadvantage as chairman, since I understand that there is a point to be made about the quotation which is the title of this session, but since I have never acquired the habit of reading comic strips, I am unable to explain the reference. Perhaps you will help me out?

HOME: Of course. The reference again is to the comic strip *Peanuts*. Snoopy the beagle, as most of you know, likes to imagine himself as a World War I flying ace, flying his Sopwith Camel against the Red Baron. But sometimes as he sips a root beer in the canteen, Snoopy says to himself, "Curse this stupid war!" I think that this expresses some of the ambivalence many of us feel about war. On the one hand, we feel that to go to war to defend our country against attack is justifiable, and we can admire the courage of those who defend their country. On the other hand, we feel that war is stupid and wasteful. The beagle who dreams of himself as a war hero and yet as part of that fantasy says "Curse this stupid war!" represents that ambivalence very well.

OXMORE: I don't feel that ambivalence. My feeling is that war is always a mistake. Not all utilitarians would agree with me, but I would argue for pacifism on utilitarian grounds. A war brings more unhappiness with it than almost any alternative to war. You really can't secure the greatest happiness of the greatest number by killing great numbers of people, maiming or injuring other great numbers, arousing feelings of hatred and contempt between two large groups of people, and so on.

HOME: Surely we have to make a distinction between, say, Genghis Khan and his Huns attacking a village to plunder it and wipe it out and the villagers who defend themselves against the invaders.

OXMORE: Even in that case I think that nonviolent resistance would be better than war.

HOME: But nonviolence wouldn't get you anywhere with Genghis Khan. He had the pleasant habit of killing everyone he could find in a village, pretending to go away, and then circling back to kill any survivors who had been hiding.

OXMORE: Well, I think again it's a matter of choosing an extreme case where considerations we'd normally use don't apply. Usually you'd lose far less by simply giving the aggressor what he wants than by fighting a war to resist him.

HOME: But suppose he wants you as a slave to work to death or abuse sexually? Suppose he wants your children to train as his mercenary killers?

OXMORE: But if you use violence against him, he's really defeated you. He's made you descend to his level.

HOME: I wouldn't agree. A man killing or wounding in self-defense against someone who's trying to kill or wound him is in a far different moral position than the person who is the aggressor.

OXMORE: But hang it all, isn't a prohibition of killing one of those moral principles whose existence you were arguing for last session?

HOME: I'd want to say "Thou shalt not kill" is a general principle to which people have always recognized exceptions. Among those would be killing in self-defense, in a justified war, or by the legal executioner.

OxMORE: What about you, Kirk? Don't your religious principles forbid war? What about the commandment?

KIRK: Well, that's a theological question rather than a philosophical one, but wearing my other hat as a theologian, I can tell you that arguing for unrestricted pacifism from the Old Testament isn't very promising. The Ten Commandments occur two places in Exodus. In the first place they're immediately followed by a list of crimes for which there is a death penalty—including cursing your parents! In the second occurrence they immediately follow an account of a war waged by the Jews at God's command.

OxMORE: What about Christianity? Turning the other cheek, and all that?

KIRK: There have always been two schools of thought on that within Christianity, with the pacifists decidedly in the minority. The non-pacificists argued that a slap on the cheek is a symbol for insult and humiliation which a Christian should accept cheerfully, and not for a threat to life or limb. After all a slap isn't the sort of thing that usually kills or injures someone. And as you know, later Christian philosophers like Augustine and Aquinas worked out a theory of "just war."

OxMORE: You'd defend that theory?

KIRK: Yes, I would. But I'd argue that if you apply that theory to modern war, you find that no war nowadays could meet the standards necessary for a just war. So I can agree with Home about the villagers and Genghis Khan, but agree with you that a modern nuclear war would be worse than any possible alternative.

OxMORE: That's cheering. What would you say to that, Home?

HOME: I'd agree with Kirk that a modified form of the just war theory provides a more reasonable answer to the problem of war than straight pacifism. But I think that even under today's conditions there can be wars that meet the conditions for a just war.

OxMORE: Perhaps you or Kirk could describe such conditions, and we can discuss them.

HOME: I'll let Kirk give us the traditional theory and then say something about the way in which I think it needs to be modified.

KIRK: Fair enough. Shall we discuss the conditions one by one, or shall I give them to you all at once?

OxMORE: Give them all, so we'll have some idea of the whole theory and then we'll discuss them one by one.

KIRK: Very well. I came prepared. Here's one version of the traditional list, which I'd be prepared to defend.

> Nation A is justified in waging war with Nation B if and only if (1) Nation A has been attacked by Nation B or is going to the aid of Nation C, which has been attacked by Nation B; (2) The war has been legally declared by the properly constituted authorities of Nation A; (3) The intentions of Nation A in waging the war are confined to repelling the attack by Nation B and establishing a peace fair to all; (4) Nation A has a reasonable hope of success in repelling the attack and establishing a just peace; (5) Nation A cannot secure these ends without waging war. It has considered or tried all other means and wages war only as a last resort; (6) The good done by Nation A waging war against Nation B can reasonably be expected to outweigh the evil done by waging war; and (7) Nation A does not use or anticipate using any means of waging war that are themselves immoral, for example, the avoidable killing of innocent persons.

Let's look at each condition in turn. The first condition, that Nation A has been attacked by Nation B, or is going to the aid of a country that has been attacked, is obviously one that we do take into consideration in deciding the justice of a war. "They started it" is a defense of the justice and necessity of a war that applies to my Genghis Khan example. It applies to Nazi Germany invading Poland and England and France going to the aid of Poland. It applies to the Japanese attacking at Pearl Harbor . . .

OXMORE: And the United States' invasion at the Bay of Pigs.

KIRK: I'm quite willing to admit that I don't think that that incident was justified. Whether we say it was the United States doing the invading or not is a different question.

HOME: What about the case of the Six-Day War, where Israel apparently struck just before the planned Arab attack, thus securing an advantage without which it might not have won, or won so completely?

KIRK: That's a very difficult case, but I'm inclined to think that the traditional criteria for a just war were violated in that case.

HOME: Then I'd say that this shows a weakness in those criteria. That, I should think, was plainly a defensive war, and the exact moment that the first bullet was fired doesn't seem to me to be crucial. If Dirty Jake tells you to get out of town and then starts to draw his gun, and you're quicker on the draw, it doesn't seem to me that you're obliged to let him shoot first.

KIRK: But you don't want to allow preemptive strikes on the grounds that you *think* your enemy will attack you sooner or later, do you?

HOME: No, that would be like shooting Dirty Jake without warning because you knew he would make a move against you sooner or later. What I'm saying is that the Six-Day War situation was like the situation where the man is actually drawing his gun.

OXMORE: But wouldn't it be a great deal better to get out of town when Dirty Jake tells you to, in order to save bloodshed?

HOME: Well, of course in the case of Israel that would involve getting out of a whole country which the Jewish people had claims to, although I'm quite willing to say that the Arab refugees had claims to it too, and that it's a case where conflicting claims are very hard to resolve. But in the imaginary case of Dirty Jake, notice what the effect would be. If Dirty Jake can tell anyone he wants to get out of town, and men of good will simply get out in order to avoid bloodshed, then Dirty Jake becomes in effect the dictator of that town, or any other town he comes to with his gun. As the old couplet goes,

> Pale Ebeneezer thought it wrong to fight
> But Roaring Bill, who killed him, thought it right.

OXMORE: I still think that there are ways of dealing with the Dirty Jakes and Roaring Bills nonviolently, and preventing future Dirty Jakes and Roaring Bills.

HOME: I don't really see how we can, unless we're willing to restrain them, using force if necessary. And if we use force to restrain them and they resist, this can lead to bloodshed.

KIRK: We seem to be wandering a bit from the first of the traditional conditions for a just war. My own comment about this condition would be that I don't see how it can possibly be fulfilled in modern war. Nowadays if your enemy strikes first, there isn't really anything left of your country. So we're faced with the terrible choice of allowing the enemy to strike first and destroy our cities and poison our country, or of striking first ourselves, which seems to be horribly immoral.

HOME: You're thinking of nuclear warfare, of course?

KIRK: Yes, but even the more limited conflicts, like that in the Middle East, run such a risk of setting off a nuclear war that my objection carries over to them. However, perhaps we could go on to the second condition— about properly constituted authorities declaring war. In a way it's relatively trivial; presumably it serves to rule out wars started by a group of generals, or by some hotheaded faction, without legal authority. But in the debates about Vietnam a good deal had been made by the critics of this sort of point. Whether the Gulf of Tonkin resolution really gave authority for the commitment of troops that President Johnson made, whether the Diem government was a legal government, and so on. And, of course, supporters of the war tried to establish the Thieu government as legitimate on the basis of elections, and so on.

OXMORE: But surely lots of wars you wouldn't approve of were legally declared.

KIRK: Yes, but remember that this is supposed to be a list of individually necessary and jointly sufficient conditions. A war is just only if it meets *all* the conditions and unjust if it breaks *any* of them.

HOME: That would be the grounds of my objection, the fact that each condition is supposed to be necessary. There are lots of cases in which a war could be quite justified without being legally declared. The villagers attacked by Genghis Khan might get no chance to declare war legally. In modern conditions a sneak attack might wipe out the legal government and yet leave lots of survivors who might be quite justified in carrying on the fight.

KIRK: But aren't you agreeing with me that the traditional conditions can't be met in modern times?

HOME: No, I'd say that this was never a reasonable condition—there are too many situations, even quite simple ones, where it doesn't apply.

KIRK: Well, how about the next condition, "The intentions of Nation A are confined to repelling the attack by Nation B and establishing a peace fair to all"?

HOME: I'd agree very much with the spirit of that, but I have my doubts about the way it's put. Certainly it's both reasonable and moral not to overreact. If you're defending yourself from attack and this is your excuse for going to war, then you should be content when you're safe from attack. But, of course, this doesn't necessarily mean that you stop fighting as soon as your enemy can't harm you at the moment. You may know that if you do, he'll simply retire to lick his wounds and regroup, and then attack again. In our Wild West example, our hero can't just shoot the gun out of Dirty Jake's hand and walk away. Dirty Jake would just get another gun and shoot him in the back. Or in the Six-Day War example, it's all very well to object to Israel keeping the captured territory, but if Israel is right in saying that only by keeping the West Bank and so on, can it be secure from future attacks, then surely if it has a right to self-defense it has some right to these territories.

KIRK: Yes, but we have the clause about a peace "fair to all."

HOME: I agree that that creates complications in the Arab-Israeli case. But in general that seems a very difficult condition to meet. Who's to decide what is a peace fair to all? If the victor decides, the vanquished will be bound to think it unfair. I really think that the United States tried its best to make a peace fair to all in Japan after World War II, for example. But I doubt that the Japanese were convinced of the fairness.

OXMORE: What about an international body to make decisions, like the United Nations, which incidentally has called on Israel to return to its former boundaries?

HOME: An international court, with the impartiality to make a fair decision, would be ideal. Even better in some ways would be an international peace-keeping force that would enforce such decisions. But such a court would have to be trusted as impartial by both sides, and I can't see that a group like the United Nations, consisting of competing pressure groups, can do the job. Or to take a more safely remote example, in the Middle Ages the papacy was in theory an impartial body that could adjudicate a fair peace. But when the papacy itself got involved in politics and began playing favorites, it soon lost its moral authority.

OXMORE: Wouldn't a perfectly impartial arbitrator render wars unnecessary?

HOME: Oh yes, in a perfect world you wouldn't need to go to war and then use your impartial arbitrator to make a just peace; you'd just have the impartial authority arbitrate the dispute in the first place. But in the world as it is, some people and groups will go to any lengths to get their own ways, and we must either let their victims defend themselves or have a really trustworthy system of judging disputes and enforcing decisions. In most civilized countries the court and the police provide an approach to such a system. But in the bigger, more problem-ridden countries people are beginning to lose their belief in the impartiality of the courts and the fairness and effectiveness of the police. Establishing such an authority on an international scale poses really staggering problems.

OXMORE: Well, we'd better set about it or we shall surely blow ourselves to pieces.

KIRK: I agree. Again, I think that in modern conditions it's nonsense to talk about establishing a just peace, or only repelling your enemy's attack, since we're forced to use weapons that will destroy our enemies, leaving no one to have a just peace with. I have similar doubts about the next condition, "Nation A has reasonable hope of repelling the attack and establishing a just peace." It seems to me that in a modern war neither side really has a hope of repelling the attacks of the other side; each will destroy the other. And as I said earlier, there will be no one left to make a just peace.

HOME: What about nonnuclear conflicts?

KIRK: There the condition perhaps still makes some sense. When Biafra rebelled against Nigeria or East Pakistan against West Pakistan, one thing that people took into consideration was the question of whether there was any real chance of success. I myself, for example, sympathized with the Biafrans at first, but later came to think that their leaders were causing great suffering by fighting on long after they had no real hope of success.

HOME: Again, I'd criticize this condition as too restrictive. There may be cases where you have no chance of winning, but you can secure a better situation for yourself by fighting and being defeated. For example, I think that one reason that race relations in New Zealand are relatively good is that the Maoris won the respect of the settlers by putting up a good stiff fight.

OXMORE: But is the result worth the price?

HOME: I think that it may be, even on strictly utilitarian grounds. After all, the unhappiness caused by being part of a despised race or group is very deep and widespread. I'd even justify to some extent the violent tactics of some minority groups insofar as they change the image of the group from one that can be safely pushed around. But I think that this kind of effect only occurs where the violence is plainly in self-defense. When the violence is seen as unnecessary or aggressive, it may lead to a worse attitude toward the group than the original one.

OXMORE: But doesn't nonviolent resistance gain even greater respect for the group?

HOME: Certainly. Ghandi, Martin Luther King, and others like them did great good. But that's only possible where you have relatively enlightened opponents or can reach over the heads of your immediate opponents to a wider public opinion. Tactics like those of Ghandi or King would have been completely ineffective against Hitler or Stalin. Anyone trying such tactics would simply have been annihilated without ever being heard of.

KIRK: I'm afraid you're right. Jewish nonviolence in Hitler's Germany didn't seem to gain Jews very great respect, and although there were some campaigns of nonviolent resistance by Christian groups in Stalinist Russia almost no one heard anything about them. Well, what about the "war only as a last resort" condition?

HOME: That seems to be reasonable. Using force only when forced to, and using the minimum amount of force necessary, seem to follow directly from the moral prohibition against causing unnecessary suffering.

OXMORE: I really don't see how you can have a war without unnecessary suffering.

HOME: Well, I don't think that it's merely jesuitical to make a distinction between what's directly intended and what's an unintentional result of what you do. After all, modern transportation causes a lot of suffering that in one sense is unnecessary, because of car accidents, plane crashes, and so on. But we still drive automobiles and support the airlines by flying on business and pleasure trips.

KIRK: But it doesn't seem to me that this can really justify the unnecessary suffering that is caused by modern warfare. Even ordinary bombing, let alone nuclear bombing, will cause terrible suffering to quite innocent people.

HOME: Yes, I'd agree that bombing civilians is an aspect of modern war that is very hard to defend morally. If it can be defended at all, it could only be as the lesser of two evils.

KIRK: Well, that seems to bring us to the last two traditional conditions, "The good done by Nation A waging war against Nation B can reasonably be expected to outweigh the evil done by waging war," and "Nation A does not use or anticipate using any means of waging war which are themselves immoral, for example, the avoidable killing of innocent persons." I think that Oxmore and I could agree that there's just no hope of satisfying those conditions in modern warfare.

OXMORE: Not just modern warfare. Think of the horrors at My Lai. That sort of thing is just bound to happen in any war. Think of the firebombing of Dresden by our side, or the robot bombs in London. Think of the American antipersonnel weapons dropped in North Vietnam.

HOME: I'd agree that these last two conditions are quite important. In fact, I'd be willing to abandon all of the others and keep only these two, which I think really include what is worthwhile in the others. Perhaps it would be only fair to say something about my own theory of just war, since I've been criticizing Kirk's.

KIRK: By all means.

HOME: I'd start by claiming that using force in self-defense is not immoral and neither is the use of force to defend others. I'd appeal to our ordinary moral judgments and intuitions to back me up on this. But if you allow the use of force, this will sometimes lead to bloodshed. The right to defense is one that we can give up, for religious or other reasons, just as we can give up the right to property or marriage. But we are giving up a right, not abstaining from something wrong in itself.

Then suppose we grant that for the sake of argument. I can state my theory of justifiable war or justifiable violence in defense quite simply. We must not, in exercising this right, do anything that is immoral, and we must not exercise the right if more harm than good will be done by exercising it. The same applies to any of our other rights, by the way. I have a property right to the apples on my apple tree, but no right to let a man starve rather than give him some of my surplus apples. I have a right to kiss my wife, but not if kissing her would for some reason kill her or cause terrible suffering to someone, which would far overbalance any pleasure I might get from kissing her.

Now applying this to war, I think that a nation has a right to defend itself against invasion. But I think that the Czechs were right not to resist the Russian invasion and the ouster of Dubchek, because the bad results of such resistance would have far outweighed any benefits secured by resistance. I think that we had a right to come to the aid of South Vietnam, but I think that our intervention led to terrible evils in Vietnamese society, and that we did far more harm than good by exercising that right. I think, on the other hand, that Israel had the right to defend itself against the Arabs and that more good than harm was done by that defense. I think that we had a right to go to the aid of England in World War II and that far more good than harm was done by that intervention.

KIRK: But you'll grant that many immoral things were done by our side during World War II.

HOME: Yes, and some of them were done as a matter of policy, and with the approval of the people, like the fire-bombing of Dresden and the atom-bombing of Japan. I certainly wouldn't say that World War II was a completely just war. But it was a war that was on the whole justifiable.

OXMORE: You think that World War II did more good than harm overall?

HOME: As opposed to a Europe dominated by Hitler? Certainly. By the way, those questions were very typical of your positions. It's just struck me that Kirk is by and large arguing that modern war can't be justified because it's bound to lead to immoral acts, and Oxmore is arguing that war can never be justified because it always leads to more harm than good. Each of you takes one of the principles that I want to use in judging whether a war is justifiable and, if I may say so, each exaggerates the principles you've chosen. For example, you, Professor Oxmore, seem not to face up to the fact that there can plainly be situations that are worse than waging war in self-defense.

OXMORE: I'm not so sure that I do. A good deal depends on the value you put on human life. A war always kills a lot of people who would still be alive if it hadn't been for the war. Life, even as a slave, is still life, and there are bound to be lots of things to enjoy, even if you've been conquered.

HOME: Well, in that case I think modern conditions count the other way. Being conquered by Alexander or Caesar or Napoleon might not have been so bad. They had an interest in keeping the conquered population reasonably content. But the modern tyrants have relied more on terror and repression and thought control. If we were conquered by China, we'd all have to parrot the thoughts of Mao, and there would be very effective pressures to make us do so. In fact the next great tyrant is likely to try to use behavioristic conditioning techniques to make us into reliable machines.

OXMORE: I must say that that's a very chilling prospect. Still, perhaps better a live machine than a dead body.

HOME: Here we're perhaps up against a fundamental difference in world view. If one rules out any hope of life after death, as I believe you do . . .

OXMORE: Yes, I do.

HOME: . . . then death for you is complete annihilation, and I can understand your attitude that anything is preferable to annihilation, even life in slavery.

OXMORE: Yes, I think that there's something to that. One's opinion about life after death is bound to make a great difference as to how one computes the utilities.

HOME: So our difference isn't really a moral one, but a metaphysical one.

OXMORE: I think you may be right.

HOME: On the other hand, Kirk and I are agreed in accepting the idea of life after death, so our difference can't lie there.

KIRK: No, there's nothing so terrible about *being* killed; it's having to kill others, and cause all the pain and suffering and corruption and evil that a war inevitably brings about, that bothers me.

HOME: Yes, but simply surrendering to evil causes pain and suffering and evil and corruption too. It's all very well to choose to remain morally pure by not resisting evil done to oneself, but can one remain morally pure by refusing to act when your action could save others from enslavement or corruption? Consider, for example, World War II, and compare England with some of the countries in Scandinavia that allowed themselves to be taken over by Germany without resistance. Don't you admire a man like Churchill, who resisted the Nazis with every means in his power, more than a man like Quisling, who cooperated with them?

KIRK: Well, certainly Quisling wasn't admirable, because he was acting in order to secure power and advantage for himself. But how about a ruler who surrendered to the enemy only in order to avoid death and suffering on both sides?

HOME: Well, the traditional just war standards take care of the situation where a ruler surrenders in order to avoid *useless* suffering, surrenders because he hasn't a chance of winning. We can admire a man like that. But if a ruler surrenders when he has a good chance of winning, just because he knows that to win he will have to injure his enemies and demand sacrifices from his people—would you really admire a man like that?

KIRK: I think I would.

HOME: But look what that leads to. Anyone who is willing to kill and hurt others to secure his objectives will become an absolute dictator, because good men will be unwilling to kill and injure in defense of others. You know, a few years ago radicals were talking about paralyzing or destroying the government of the United States. They seemed to assume that if they did that, the gentle, loving people could take over and do things their way. But, of course, that wouldn't happen. Destroy government and police authority, and groups like the Mafia would move in and start running things *their* way.

OXMORE: It sometimes seems that they *are* running things.

HOME: Yes, and in those places where they're effectively in control life is pretty unpleasant. It takes quite a bad government to be worse than the rule of warlords or bands of thugs. But unless we're willing to resist, we'll be ruled by those who are willing to bully.

KIRK: I agree with you to some extent. But you're really arguing against Oxmore's position, not mine. I'm saying that limited wars of the kind that we had in the past may have been justified, but nowadays going to war is different than it was in the past. It's not like two gunfighters fighting it out, which is a comparison you've used. It's more like a bank manager threatening to blow up the bank, or the whole town, if the bank robbers don't surrender. Surely in that case any injury that the bank robber could inflict on the bank or town would be less than the injury done to the bank or town by blowing it up.

HOME: Not necessarily. It would depend on what the bank robbers planned to do to the town. If they planned just to take the money and run, of course it would be better to let them go. If they planned to enslave the children, and kill or cripple all the adults to prevent pursuit, that might be a different thing.

KIRK: But wouldn't the act of blowing up everyone if the robbers didn't surrender be just as morally objectionable as anything the robbers might do?

HOME: In some cases, yes; in others, no. If the townsfolk were behind the bank manager and preferred to die rather than submit to the bandits, that would be one kind of situation. If they preferred to live at any cost, that would be another kind of situation.

OXMORE: But when we talk about an atomic war, isn't it the case that almost everyone *would* prefer to submit to the enemy rather than be blown up?

HOME: Well, if that's true then sooner or later they will have to submit to people who are willing to kill and die for what they believe in. But I see no real sign of that attitude in the world today. The North Vietnamese seemed to be willing to face annihilation rather than surrender to the United States. The Israelis seem willing to be wiped out rather than surrender their homeland, and so on.

KIRK: But again I'm not so concerned with the pain and suffering and death that might be caused to my side by losing a war. I'm more concerned with the great evil we might have to do to *win* a war.

HOME: Well, if it were true that we could only win a war by committing great moral evil, I'd have to agree with you that waging war would be unjust. The way I'd summarize the traditional just war requirements is that a war is unjust if waging it involves us in doing moral evil or if waging it would bring about more harm than good. I'd certainly agree that it's not allowable to do evil in order that good may come of it.

KIRK: But don't wars always involve moral evil of various kinds? Think of the use of spies, for example.

HOME: I wouldn't condemn every kind of spying. Some spies, it seems to me, are brave people who risk their lives to find information that may shorten a war or enable the right side to win. But the kind of spy presented in most modern fiction—ready to murder, corrupt, betray, so that some slight advantage may go to one side rather than another—that kind of spy I would certainly condemn. But my own view is that this kind of spy isn't really necessary or even very useful to a nation. All the Machiavellian maneuverings of the CIA and similar agencies have done us far more harm than they have our enemies. The worst harm in loss of information to our side has been done by sincere idealists like the Rosenbergs, and the worst harm in loss of information to our enemies has been through defectors who wanted to get away from intrigue and double cross.

OXMORE: It seems to me that I'm claiming that war always involves more harm than good, and that Kirk is claiming that modern war always involves us in doing moral evil.

HOME: I'd say that just isn't so. There's a great danger of moral evil in a war, but, of course, this varies tremendously with your position in the war. The anti-aircraft gunner shooting down planes that are bombing civilians seems to me to run little risk of moral evil, and the medic helping wounded men on the battlefield even less. The combat soldier, especially, who comes in contact with civilians runs a greater risk, and the flyer who delivers bombs on a city or the missile man who fires missiles at a city run the greatest risk.

KIRK: But doesn't even the medic run a moral risk by helping to keep the war machine going? He patches up men to go back and fight; after all . . .

HOME: That's always seemed to me to be sophistical. A war will probably go ahead whether there is any medical attention for the wounded or not—they did for centuries. If you don't patch up A to shoot the rifle, B will be available. And in my own experience the war protesters who spoke most effectively were people who were involved in this kind of activity—Quakers running Red Cross ambulances, conscientious objectors serving as medics, and so on.

KIRK: But even if that's true, you just can't fight a modern war without bombing civilians and that sort of thing.

HOME: I'm not sure that's true. The effect of bombing on civilian targets is always overrated by some militarists who belong to the "any-means-to-victory" school. It didn't stop the English during the Blitz or the Germans during our return bombing, or the North Vietnamese when we were bombing them.

KIRK: But nuclear bombing is quite different.

HOME: Yes, but nuclear bombs haven't been used since their first terrible misuse against Japan, which came at the *end* of a long and bitter war and before the horrible effects of such bombing were really realized. There really are some hopeful signs, you know—nuclear disarmament talks, the renunciation of chemical and biological warfare, and so on.

KIRK: But once a war starts, surely such weapons will be used sooner or later.

HOME: I don't think that's inevitable. But I think that we're really getting away from philosophy here and into prediction. I agree with you that if war couldn't be waged without terrible moral evil, we shouldn't wage it. But I deny that war, even today, necessarily involves terrible moral evil. I agree with Oxmore that if war couldn't be waged without doing more harm than good we shouldn't wage it. But I deny that war always does more harm than good.

OXMORE: I take it that we are all agreed that the kind of war that many people seem to find acceptable—simply destroying all your enemy's cities with nuclear bombs in order to win—I take it that *that* sort of war would be condemned by all of us.

KIRK: Yes, certainly.

HOME: Of course.

OXMORE: But Kirk would say that the villagers defending themselves against Genghis Khan, and similar cases were cases of just war . . .

KIRK: Yes.

OXMORE: And Home would defend some modern wars. Do you mind giving examples?

HOME: Not at all. I think that World War II was on the whole justifiable, although many unjust things were done in it and many evil consequences came from it. I'd say that Israel's continuing war with the

Arabs is on the whole justifiable, despite some bad consequences and some great injustices to innocent parties. I'd say that many people on both sides in the Vietnam War were morally justified in fighting because of their beliefs about what they were doing. At one time I thought that the Vietnam War was justifiable on our side, but I changed my opinion, partly because of increasing evidence that our "help" to South Vietnam actually did that country far more harm than good.

KIRK: I could agree with that to some extent. Even though I disagree that any modern war can be justifiable on the whole, in many cases I'd agree that the actions of particular persons in a war are morally justifiable.

OXMORE: Well, no doubt there are thieves and murderers whom we don't condemn morally because they are acting on the basis of ignorance or false beliefs. But we don't talk about "just theft" or "just murder."

HOME: But we do, in fact, talk about justifiable homicide in some cases and don't regard it as murder. And in other cases we regard taking of goods as justifiable, and therefore not theft. "Murder" and "theft" are words with built-in unfavorable moral judgments. But although war *may* involve moral evil, it isn't itself morally evil, in the view of most reasonable men.

OXMORE: But war is just widescale murder and theft.

HOME: That begs the question again. The legal system does take away goods from people sometimes, puts people to death sometimes. But it would be silly to say that our system of law and government "is just" theft and murder.

OXMORE: The legal system involves compensating advantages. I don't see that war does.

HOME: But that's just the issue between us, isn't it? Anyway, winning a war is like surviving a hurricane—you're glad that you've come through alive and have saved what you could. You don't expect the result of surviving the hurricane to be better than what you had before, just to be better than death or total loss.

OXMORE: Anyway, in your legal comparison I don't grant that legal execution *isn't* murder.

HOME: That's one of the things we'll be debating at our next session on punishment.

VENNER: This is perhaps a good opportunity to close this part of the discussion. In listening to our panelists I do not know what the audience's reaction was, but I was torn many ways. When Professor Home spoke of World War II, I remembered how glad I was to see Hitler overthrown, and that even my relatives who stayed in Germany were glad after the first shock of defeat. But when Professors Kirk and Oxmore spoke of the horrors of nuclear war, I was certainly also moved. However, I see no way to resolve this dispute between them in any rational way, and this is my objection to this kind of argument as a part of philosophy. Because I feel similar misgivings about our next topic, crime and punishment, I will again be chairman—so as to leave the discussion to the other panelists.

QUESTIONS

Answer the following questions as you think they would be answered by the panelist to whom they are addressed.

1. Professor Oxmore: If you were convinced that some war *did* do more good than harm, wouldn't you have to call it justified? And mustn't there have been at least one such war?
2. Professor Kirk: May there not be some cases where it is more immoral *not* to wage war than it is to wage war?
3. Professor Home: How can you defend World War II in view of the fire-bombing of Dresden, the atom-bombing of Hiroshima and Nagasaki, and so on? And how can you defend Israel in light of their policies toward the Arab refugees?

Are you satisfied with the answers given to the following questions or objections?

4. Oxmore's answer to the "Ghenghis Khan" case.
5. Kirk's answer to Home's objections.
6. Home's answer to Kirk's points about modern warfare.

Write brief essays on the following:

7. Describe some of the consequences that would result if pacifism were accepted by most people.
8. Apply the classical theory of the "just war" to some historical war. Was this war just or unjust by those standards?
9. Give your own views about war and justify them.

10. Which position in the dialogue is the weakest? How could it be strengthened?

FURTHER READINGS

BEAUCHAMP, TOM L., *Ethics and Public Policy*, Englewood Cliffs, N.J.: Prentice-Hall, Inc., 1975.

Nagel, Thomas, "War and Massacre," p. 213.

Purtill, Richard, "On the Just War," p. 190.

Wells, Donald, "How Much Can 'The Just War' Justify?" p. 180.

FEINBERG, JOEL, *Social Philosophy*, Englewood Cliffs, N.J.: Prentice-Hall, Inc., 1973.

RACHELS, JAMES, *Moral Problems*, New York: Harper and Row, 1971.

Anscombe, G. E. M., "War and Murder," pp. 269–83.

Narveson, Jan, "Pacifism, a Philosophical Analysis," pp. 241–49.

Wasserstrom, Richard, "On the Morality of War," pp. 284–322.

Questions on the Reading

1. What is the main point of Narveson's paper? Which position discussed in this chapter is Narveson closest to?
2. How does Anscombe's position resemble and differ from the traditional "just war" theory?
3. Which of Wasserstrom's points are philosophical and which are legal or historical or sociological?
4. In what ways do Anscombe and Wasserstrom disagree? In each case which, in your view, is right? Why?
5. What points raised in the readings are relevant to the discussion in the chapter? In what way?

6

Is Punishment a Crime?

VENNER: Again I am chairman and again I have reservations about our topic. Certainly when we hear of the things that go on in prisons, recall recent riots and disturbances in prison, we may feel a profound disgust at our treatment of those in prisons. But if we ask how society could survive without law and punishment we find it hard to give an answer. And most of us would prefer that society survive. Again I see no rational basis for taking us beyond these conflicting emotional attitudes, but this is what my colleagues will attempt to do. Perhaps it will be useful if we take a leaf from Professor Kirk's book and ask each of you to state the position which he will defend. Perhaps Professor Oxmore will begin.

OXMORE: Well, my position on the matter of punishment is again an outgrowth of my utilitarian position in ethics. I think that Venner hit on the basic justification for punishment when he said that society would be impossible without law and punishment, and that it is desirable that society survive. Punishing an individual who has broken the law deters other people from breaking the law, and ideally the punishment has the effect of reforming the individual. But even if it doesn't achieve the purpose of reform, punishment is justifiable if it serves the good of the community. I'm very dissatisfied with our present system of punishment because it seems to me that it doesn't serve the good of the community very well. Some of our worst criminals don't get punished at all, and many people come out of prison more dangerous to society than when they went in. However, I imagine that none of us would defend the present system.

KIRK: I certainly wouldn't, but perhaps my objections would be of a somewhat different kind than Professor Oxmore's. I'd defend punishment as something that is sometimes deserved, and I think that an important part of morality is seeing that people get what they deserve. My objections to the present system are that it is unjust in many ways—unjust to the prisoner, unjust to those injured by crime, unjust to those who have to administer the system.

HOME: I agree. I'm in the rather uninteresting position of agreeing with both of you to a large extent. I'd agree with Kirk that we are not entitled to punish anyone unless he deserves punishment through actions that he does freely. But I'd agree with Oxmore that the social dimension of punishment is very important. We don't punish every action that we think is morally wrong but only those actions that we want to prevent in the interests of society. I'm sure that we'll find plenty of grounds for disagreement in due course, but it might be useful if I played devil's advocate to start and present a point of view that doesn't seem to be represented here, but is very common nowadays. This is the view that criminal actions are due to a sort of disease or insanity and our whole aim should be to "cure" the criminal, or in older fashioned language, to reform him.

OXMORE: I wouldn't necessarily disagree with that point of view entirely. My only point is that we should protect society first. If a man has a dangerous contagious disease, we first isolate him so he can't infect others, then we try to cure him if possible.

KIRK: Of course, I wouldn't be opposed to efforts to reform people who commit crimes. But I'd object very strongly to identifying crime and disease or insanity. Certainly some people who break the law are mentally ill, and people of that kind shouldn't be punished, but should be restrained and given therapy. But many other people who break the law are quite able to keep it and freely choose to break it. Can we agree on that?

HOME: I'd agree myself, but supporters of the view I'm representing at the moment probably wouldn't.

OXMORE: I'd agree that many people who break the law might in other circumstances choose to keep it. In fact, in my view the main purpose of legal machinery is to make it true that respecting the interests of others is to the interest of the individual. In other words, if people won't respect the rights of others because it is moral to do so, the law with its punishments comes in to assure that they will suffer if they disregard other's rights.

KIRK: I don't think that's the whole story, but it's at least part of it. The insane person is often precisely the person whose behavior can't be influenced by legal threats. But I think that there's a more basic issue. It sounds very tolerant and merciful to say that all the people who steal and kill and so on must "really" be "sick" or "insane" or something of that kind. In saying that you remove responsibility from their shoulders. But removing responsibility is a two-edged thing. Someone who isn't responsible isn't fully a person. Other people have the right to make decisions for him, because he can't make them himself. He has to be taken care of, guided, controlled. His desires and opinions aren't seriously considered. Ideally, of course, everything that's done to a person of diminished responsibility is done in his own interest. But that doesn't mean that it's what the person himself would like or want.

OXMORE: But on the old theories, things were done to criminals that they didn't like or want.

KIRK: Yes, but these things were done to them just because they had freely chosen to break the law and just to the extent that they had broken the law. If a man had broken the law he could be punished, but if he hadn't, he could not. He could be punished to a certain extent and then he had "payed his debt to society," and nothing more could be done to him.

OXMORE: You're talking as if this were a thing of the past.

KIRK: In many places it *is* a thing of the past. Indeterminate sentences, which are used in California and many other places, mean in effect that people are sent to prison until the authorities are satisfied that they're "cured." If the authorities don't like your religious or political views—for example in California if you're a Black Muslim or a Black Panther—then you may not be declared "cured." Even where indeterminate sentences as such don't exist, parole boards and judicial discretion as to length of sentence often have very much the same effect.

OXMORE: But surely you're not opposed to parole or to a certain amount of judicial discretion?

KIRK: On the whole, no. But both of them have serious dangers. Judicial discretion can mean that you get five years for a crime if you come before a softhearted judge, and ten if you come before a hardhearted one, without regard to the merits of the case. Parole boards are sometimes taken in by plausible hypocrites, and are often biased in favor of the more articulate or the seemingly more respectable. The thing I'm objecting to, you understand, is the unfairness involved. Ideally the criminal should receive no *more* than the punishment he deserves.

OXMORE: Would you also want to say no less?

KIRK: No, I know that some retributivists have talked as if punishing the guilty was the exact correlative of not punishing the innocent, but I don't agree. I think that we have a very strong obligation never to punish the innocent, and that this overrides just about every other obligation. But our obligation to see that the guilty are punished is much less stringent. In setting up a legal system, for example, we are willing to let some guilty people get off if by doing so we can lessen the likelihood that any innocent person will be punished.

OXMORE: When you talk of one obligation being more stringent than others, you're thinking of something like Ross' *prima facie* obligations? [1]

KIRK: Yes. Perhaps I might make that clearer in order to help you understand my views about punishment. I think that we have to distinguish between what *would be* our obligation, other things being equal, and what *is* our obligation, all things considered. The first are Ross' *prima facie* obligations, the second are what I'd call *strict* obligations. Take the usual sort of case: I promise to come to dinner at your house tonight. Other things being equal, I'm bound to keep that promise. But on the way over my wife has a heart attack and needs to be rushed to the hospital. In that case I'm obliged to put my wife first. To go on calmly to your dinner party and let her die would be ridiculous and immoral. If my promise to you and my wife's need are the only *prima facie* obligations involved in the situation, then I'm strictly obliged to help my wife and strictly permitted to break my promise. I might apologize for any inconvenience I caused you, but if you blamed me for taking care of my wife instead of coming to dinner you'd be entirely unreasonable.

OXMORE: I'd agree, of course, but I'd say that this was an excellent case of applying the utilitarian principle. Helping your wife is right because it brings about more good than coming to my dinner.

KIRK: That's plausible in this case, but not in all cases. You certainly would have a right to blame me if I broke a promise to come to dinner with you just because I decided that doing something else that night

---

[1] W. D. Ross, see Biography (Appendix A) and Further Readings at the end of Chapter 4.

would give me more pleasure, and I figured that my increased pleasure would overbalance your annoyance.

OXMORE: I'm always struck by the extent to which people like Ross and yourself use promises as examples for anti-utilitarian arguments. Do you really find the obligation to keep promises that important?

KIRK: My ranking would be about the same as Home's: the most important moral principle is not to injure others in any way. The next most important is to make reparation for any injuries you have done. The next is to keep commitments of all kinds, including promises. The next is the obligation to repay benefits, next is the obligation to help or do good to others when we can, and finally the obligation of self-improvement.

OXMORE: And how do you justify this sort of ranking of principles?

KIRK: It seems to me that any reasonable person would agree to a ranking at least roughly equivalent to that one. Take a man with an extra ten dollars a week to dispose of, and the following possibilities of spending it: he can bribe a fairly honest but weak man who needs ten dollars badly to do something illegal in his favor; he can repay ten dollars he stole some time ago; he can give ten dollars to someone he promised that amount to; he can loan ten dollars to a man who has helped him in the past and now needs a loan; he can help a poor man in need. Now suppose all of the needs for the ten dollars are roughly equal: the man from whom he stole the ten dollars needs it about as badly as the benefactor, the benefactor about as badly as the poor man, and so on. It seems quite clear that he should not bribe the weak man, that he should repay his theft before making the promised loan, give the promised loan before giving the unpromised loan to his benefactor, and help the benefactor before just any person in need. The people involved would, I think, in most cases recognize that order of obligations. If the benefactor says, "I've helped you in the past, can you loan me ten dollars?" he should be satisfied with the reply, "My only spare money this week is already promised. I'll gladly loan you ten dollars next week."

OXMORE: But suppose that the needs aren't equal. Suppose the benefactor needs the money desparately; the man from whom it was stolen needs it only moderately.

KIRK: I'd agree that in that case the greater need might override the normal order of principles.

OXMORE: Then you're right back to utilitarianism.

KIRK: No, I think not, and the punishment case is a good example of the drawbacks of pure utilitarianism. There are many people who come before the courts on minor charges for whom a long criminal career can be predicted with a very high probability. It would be a great gain to society and perhaps even to themselves if they were immediately executed. But it would be immoral to do so, because they haven't done anything for which they deserve death.

OXMORE: I wouldn't say that any crime deserves death.

KIRK: That's a separate question which we may very well get into. But if you like we can vary the example: keeping the person under perpetual restraint instead of killing him.

OXMORE: Well, if the person was really almost certain to cause great unhappiness to society and to himself . . . some sort of preventative detention really might be justified.

KIRK: If I may say so, Oxmore, that's an excellent example of the way that a mistaken moral theory can lead a fundamentally decent person like yourself to conclusions that are really immoral. I won't raise the possibility of reformation, or anything of that sort, because by hypothesis the person is one for whom we can quite confidently predict a long career of crime. But even so, at the time we're imagining, he has only committed one minor crime. To imprison him for life on the basis of that minor crime would be immoral, and to imprison him for life because of the probability that he will commit further crimes is immoral too. Both go against the fundamental moral principle which forbids inflicting undeserved injury.

OXMORE: You'd be opposed then even to "habitual criminal" laws that impose a life sentence after a third felony?

KIRK: Yes, indeed. I think that it's quite clear that prisons are no good at reforming people—quite the reverse in fact—but even if they were we only have the right to attempt to reform people if they lay themselves open to punishment by deserving it.

OXMORE: You don't object to reform or deterrence as purposes of punishment?

KIRK: No, provided that the necessary condition of punishment is satisfied; provided, that is, that the man is guilty, then if we can make the punishment reformative or deterrent so much the better. But we don't do awfully well at either reforming or deterring.

OXMORE: The thing that bothers me most about your view is this idea of retribution—of a person deserving punishment whether or not it does him or anyone else any good.

KIRK: Well, it's the other side of the coin from deserving something good. There are probably cases where you feel that you ought to give praise or acknowledgment to someone even though he won't benefit from it—a dead teacher or a philosopher in the past, for example. And in some of those cases perhaps no one else benefits from your praise or acknowledgment of this man either.

OXMORE: Or it might have a beneficial effect, you know.

KIRK: Yes, but that's not why you do it—you feel you owe it to the dead man. Otherwise you'd just be being "edifying."

OXMORE: Yes, I see that. But I'd feel that it would do *me* good to acknowledge a debt like that.

KIRK: But how could you think so unless you think that what you're doing is a good thing to do—which comes back to the man you're praising deserving the praise.

HOME: I wonder if I could suggest an idea that's helped me on this point?

KIRK: Certainly.

OXMORE: Yes, go ahead.

HOME: Well, I presume that any moral theory has to take account of promises, contracts, and so on, by which we create obligations—that is, we make obligatory things that wouldn't otherwise be obligatory. For example, you weren't obliged to take part in this colloquium but then you promised to take part, putting yourself under an obligation.

OXMORE: Yes, I think that utilitarianism can give an adequate account of promises. I think that the practice or institution of promise keeping is extremely useful to society and therefore that many actions which can't be directly justified in terms of their consequences can be justified in terms of the practice or institution.

HOME: Do you feel that this amounts to a different theory from the classical kind of Mill-Bentham utilitarianism? Rule-utilitarianism rather than act-utilitarianism?

OXMORE: Not really, no. What's sometimes described as act-utilitarianism seems to me a mere caricature of utilitarianism. For example, one sort of case that intuitionists like Ross urged against utilitarianism was a case where a promise was given to a dying man; for example, to educate the man's son. According to the intuitionists, a utilitarian might consider the consequences of keeping the promise and the consequences of breaking it and decide to break it because of the greater good accomplished by breaking it. But, of course, a utilitarian would consider all the consequences, not just the obvious or immediate ones. The case was supposed to rule out any general weakening of confidence in promise keeping because no one but the promiser and the dead man knew of the promise. Now, of course, the case was a rather farfetched one . . .

KIRK: Not at all. It was based on a real incident that happened in the course of one of the Arctic expeditions, Scott's I think.

OXMORE: Oh? Well, at least it's not the sort of thing that happens very often. But the point I want to make is that this ignores the *strengthening* of public confidence in promise keeping when it becomes known that a man kept a promise at some sacrifice to himself when no one knew that he'd made it but himself.

HOME: That's a shrewd point about that particular case. But surely in many cases the effect on public confidence in promise keeping would be negligible?

OXMORE: Not necessarily. But aren't we getting a little far from the point you were going to make?

HOME: Yes, perhaps I'd better finish what I started to say. But I think some of the points about promising may become relevant later, because the theory I want to put forward is that laws function very much like promises. In fact, a law is like a sort of double-edged promise: if you do so-and-so you'll be punished, but if you don't do it you will be free from the threat of punishment, under this law at any rate. For example, if the law says that the speed limit on a certain road is 35 miles an hour and you go 45, you can be punished. But if you go under 35 you can't be punished for *speeding*, at any rate, although of course, you may break some other law.

Now it seems to me that this takes care of Kirk's point that it's unjust to punish a man who isn't guilty of anything. It's unjust because it breaks the implicit promise made by the laws, the promise that if you don't break any law you won't be punished. But this view also takes care of Oxmore's point that the main reason for punishment is the good of society. Laws are necessary for society, but laws would be ineffective if people weren't punished for breaking them. Actually, a good many people can be counted on to keep laws that are reasonable, and to go along with the majority even if they find some rules and regulations unreasonable. But there are always some people who refuse to consider the interests of others, and will do anything to get their own way. These people have to be restrained by the threat of punishment.

OxMORE: I think I see what you're doing, and how our digression about promising was relevant to all this. You want to justify the institution, "laws with punishments attached for noncompliance," on utilitarian grounds, then justify punishing the guilty and not punishing the innocent in terms of that institution.

HOME: That's roughly the idea.

OxMORE: Is this very much different from what some utilitarians have said about punishment?

HOME: Yes, I think that the point about the law being a double promise —punishment if guilty, no punishment if not guilty—is new to the discussion of the topic. It's not my point, by the way, but only my version of a suggestion put forward by J. R. Lucas in a paper read to the Aristotelian Society.[2]

KIRK: It's a very ingenious suggestion, as one would expect from Lucas, but I have misgivings about it. How, for example, do you distinguish a law from a conditional threat—"Do this and I'll clobber you"—that kind of thing.

HOME: I've simplified Lucas' theory a bit, and now I'll have to add the necessary qualifications. Lucas argues that we can only be punished, properly speaking, for wrongdoing. To say "This is not wrong, but I am punishing you for doing it," is to misuse the notion of punishment.

KIRK: How about "If you insult my sister, I'll break every bone in your body."

HOME: Surely that's *logically* all right; the speaker regards insulting his sister as wrongdoing, and is threatening you *with punishment*, not *just* threatening you. It's not legal punishment, because he has no legal right to punish you. The threat of punishment would probably be immoral both because the punishment seems excessive and because there are legal remedies available. But it would fit Lucas' formula all right.

KIRK: But there are no laws involved.

HOME: The business about laws was my version, not Lucas'. His formula is roughly that punishment is infliction of unpleasantness, because of wrongdoing that is prohibited and known to be prohibited.

[2] J. R. Lucas, see Biography (Appendix A) and Further Readings at the end of this chapter. See also Bibliography (Appendix B, Part III).

The form of the prohibition is something like "Either abstain from wrongdoing or be punished." Revenge is a special subcase where the wrong is done to the person who carries out the punishment. Legal punishment will then be the case where the prohibition is a legal one. But of course, as Lucas points out, parents, for example, can punish their children; not every punishment is a legal punishment. I started out talking about legal punishment because that's what we've mainly been discussing.

KIRK: This sounds like a rather complicated version of the deterrence theory of punishment—that the purpose of punishment is to prevent the same action being done again.

HOME: No, the deterrent theory looks to the present and says that the reason for punishing this man now is to prevent him and others from repeating the action. That's open to the objection that punishing an innocent man might be very effective as a deterrent, so if deterrence is the only purpose of punishment we might be justified in punishing innocent people. Actually some utilitarians have reached this conclusion and defend "strict liability" laws where if you do X you get punished whether doing X was your fault or not. You and I, Professor Kirk, would agree that that would be quite immoral.

KIRK: Yes, certainly.

OXMORE: I'm not sure I would.

HOME: Let's come back to that in a moment then. But on Lucas' theory you don't look at the situation at the time you're punishing the man and afterward in order to justify punishing him. You look back and ask, "What *was* the justification for saying to this man among others that if he did X he was going to be punished?"

OXMORE: I see, yes. The answer to that would be to justify the law that he broke and the necessity of punishments to make people observe the law.

HOME: That's the general idea. And, of course, the same general pattern applies to a parent punishing a child for coming home very late, or a teacher punishing a student for cheating or anything of the sort. You show that the rule is justifiable, that punishments are necessary to make people observe the rule, and that the person being punished has broken the rule. That's all you need to show to justify punishing him. You don't need to make any calculations about future deterrent effect, although, of course, if you can deter others or reform the person who broke the rule, so much the better.

OxMORE: This implies that the person must know the rule.

HOME: Yes, I think that that's a desirable consequence of the theory. Why do we object to after-the-fact laws? Just because no one could have known what the law was going to be and therefore no one could have avoided punishment by keeping the law.

KIRK: What about the Nüremberg trials?

HOME: There I think that it's quite reasonable to say that even though there were no written laws that could be applied, the Nazis knew very well that what they were doing was wrong and that they would certainly be punished for it if they lost the war. In the same way a family may never have discussed with the children a prohibition against torturing the cat or breaking every window in the house, but a child who does this sort of thing knows it's wrong and that it will be punished for it if caught.

OxMORE: Of course, that raises some rather large issues about knowing what's right and wrong.

KIRK: Before we get into those, I'd like to express one kind of discomfort I have with this theory. It seems to me that there are many cases where we want to say that a punishment is unjust, for various reasons. The law itself may be unjust, or the punishment may be grossly disproportionate to the crime, or something of that kind. But now on this Lucas theory, it's simply a matter of a law or rule which says, "Do this, or else."

HOME: Yes, the title of Lucas' paper was "Or Else."

KIRK: But this promise or threat that the law makes may be in support of a law that's quite unjust, or the threat may be out of proportion to the wrongdoing, or the person may not be able to refrain from doing what the law forbids. Some of the Nazi laws, for example, almost amounted to "Don't be Jewish, or else."

HOME: The first two points I think Lucas can take care of easily enough. In the first place, he's concerned to give a theory about what constitutes punishment. An unjust punishment is still a punishment, because it's an unpleasant experience inflicted for wrongdoing, or alleged wrongdoing at any rate, which is prohibited and known to be prohibited. Then I think Lucas says enough about how punishment is to be justified to enable us to see that unjust punishments couldn't be justified. In his view you have to show that the law was justified, which would seem to rule out punishments based on unjust laws being justifiable. Then you have to show that the law wouldn't be kept unless punishments were imposed. Stretching that condition a bit should take care of excessive punishments—

it seems clear that what you need to show is that punishments of this kind, or of this degree of severity, are necessary if the law is to be kept. I think Lucas implies this if he doesn't actually say it.

Your point about cases in which the person can't help doing what the law forbids is a little trickier. If that's an actual physical inability, then I think we run into the meaning of terms like "wrongdoing" and "prohibition." I think that an action which you can't help doing can't be morally right or wrong—the "ought implies can" principle. And to prohibit what people can't help doing or being seems to go against the logic of prohibiting.

But, of course, "I couldn't help it" may mean lots of things other than physical inability. We lessen responsibility but don't remove it entirely if people let their emotions run away with them and "can't help it" in that sense. Often the reply to "I couldn't help it" is, quite reasonably, "Well, you'd better learn to help it."

KIRK: In many ways this theory of Lucas' seems to give all the right answers to problems about punishment, but I still feel uneasy about it. Consider the case of deserving a reward, which is the other side of the coin from deserving punishment. It would sound very odd to say that there was any sort of implied promise in the case of rewards.

HOME: But consider the case where we'd say that someone has a right to a reward or a right to expect a reward. In that case talking about an implied or explicit promise seems quite all right. We could even make the two cases fit under one formula: "If you do A, you can reasonably expect B." The reward case is "If you do this good thing A, you can reasonably expect this good thing B." The punishment case is "If you do this bad thing A, you can reasonably expect this bad thing B."

KIRK: That formula would fit bad and good consequences which aren't rewards or punishments.

HOME: If it would, it seems to me that those are precisely the cases where we used "reward" and "punishment" somewhat metaphorically. "Good health is the reward of regular exercise." "Liver disease is the punishment of excessive drinking." But if we make our formulas "If you do this morally good thing A, you may reasonably expect some person to give you desirable thing B" and "if you do this morally bad thing A, you may reasonably expect some person to give you undesirable thing B." This seems to narrow down the cases to those that are unmetaphorically cases of reward and punishment.

KIRK: "You may reasonably expect" seems rather weak.

HOME: It's weak because it's general. I'm trying to span "you have a right to" in the case of rewards and "you are warned that you will receive" in the case of punishments. Perhaps "be advised that you will receive" might work as a general formula.

KIRK: Of course, we aren't always rewarded for good deeds or punished for bad ones.

HOME: Yes, that's all right. Doing good without hope of reward is just doing good where there is no explicit or implicit promise that you will receive something desirable for doing it. Avoiding evil without fear of punishment is just avoiding evil where there is no explicit or implicit promise that you'll receive something undesirable if you do it.

OXMORE: Would you say that doing good for the sake of reward or avoiding evil for fear of punishment was always mercenary or self-interested?

HOME: Oh, no. Being honest to collect a money prize would be mercenary; being honest so people would respect or trust you wouldn't be. Avoiding theft just for fear of the law would be self-interested; avoiding theft because it hurt people and you regard hurting people as undesirable wouldn't be self-interested at all.

OXMORE: That was another digression, I fear, but I was interested in what you'd say on that point. Well, I don't know that I might not find objections to your theory, or rather Lucas' theory, on further reflection, but at the moment it strikes me as rather reasonable. It also strikes me as quite utilitarian.

KIRK: I'm out of objections for the moment also, but I really do feel quite uneasy about this theory. You seem to be reducing one moral category—good and bad or merit and demerit—to another moral category, roughly the category of commitment. And I'm generally suspicious of such attempts at reduction.

HOME: I'm not claiming that there are no flaws in Lucas' theory, only that I haven't found any. But my confidence in it has grown as I've been able to meet objections to it. Well, we seem fairly well agreed about Lucas' theory, perhaps we should explore some of our areas of disagreement. What about this business of "strict liability" theories? Oxmore, do you want to claim that punishing people regardless of fault could ever be justified?

OXMORE: "Punishing people regardless of fault" doesn't seem to be a very fair way of putting it. But let's try that formulation for the moment. You intuitionists are very fond of giving us utilitarians hypothetical cases to worry about—let me try one on you.

KIRK: Fair enough.

OXMORE: Well, suppose that we had some way of knowing—this is the implausible part—but suppose we did have some way of knowing that by enacting "strict liability" laws we could practically eliminate automobile accidents. Let me put a rather extreme case. Suppose that the law said that both parties involved in an automobile accident of a certain degree of seriousness would have to go to prison. That's giving away rather a great deal to you, because I think that much more intelligent laws than that could be devised. But it would certainly make people "drive defensively" if they knew they would face prison if they had an accident and couldn't get out of it by claiming that it wasn't their fault.

Now, of course, this would result in the punishment of some genuinely innocent people. But it would also, on my hypothesis, prevent a tremendous amount of killing, maiming, orphaning, widowing, suffering of all kinds. Wouldn't you agree that if the facts were as I've imagined them, we'd be justified in enacting such laws and therefore punishing innocent people?

HOME: Let's be clear about the case. I'm driving along with all possible care and a car crosses the center line before I can even react and smashes into me. I go to prison as well as the other driver, right?

OXMORE: Yes, that's the way I've imagined it. But by taking this risk of injustice you prevent all sorts of deaths and injuries.

HOME: Even so, I wouldn't agree that such a law would be justified. Deliberate, institutionalized injustice on that scale would seem to me to be a worse thing than the present suffering from automobile accidents.

OXMORE: Well, let's now make the case more favorable to me. Let's say that the same crystal ball or whatever I used before to tell me that the accident rate would go down drastically also tells me that only a few innocent people will be punished—perhaps even only one.

HOME: I'd still disagree with the supposed laws. It now becomes very much like our earlier case of torturing the drifter to death to make the city happy.

OXMORE: What if the innocent people didn't suffer, because the thought of the deaths and injuries that the new laws prevent cheers them up?

HOME: But that alters the case. If you have some way of knowing that any person, or any reasonable person even, would consent to a sacrifice, for good and sufficient reasons, then you're no longer punishing innocent people, you're accepting the voluntary sacrifices of heroes or martyrs. That's why, although it would ordinarily be unjust punishment to destroy my home when I hadn't done anything to deserve it, it's not unjust to dynamite my home without consulting me if it's necessary to prevent a fire spreading to engulf the whole city. If I'm a reasonable man I see that my rights have to give way to the rights of others in a case like that. But that's not punishing me, it's asking me to make a reasonable sacrifice to ensure a definite good for others.

KIRK: It's on those very grounds that I'm wondering whether we shouldn't allow that if the facts were as Oxmore has imagined them, such a law would be justifiable.

HOME: I'd need a great deal of convincing about that. It seems to me that treating a man unjustly is doing him a considerable injury, just the kind of injury that may lead him to bitterness and frustration, may damage him physically and morally. Even if the traditionalist southerners had been right about blacks in the South being better off under slavery—which of course I don't admit—the injustice done these men and women would have inevitably led to bitterness and anger. It's not simply suffering that embitters people—in a natural disaster people often respond magnificently. It's injustice that causes bitterness. And bitterness can have a terrible effect on the mind and soul of a man or woman.

OXMORE: So you're arguing, in what seems to me to be a rather utilitarian way, that the bad effects of injustice done to even a few people to whom injustice would be done under "strict liability" laws would outweigh the good done.

HOME: Yes, that's about it. Injustice is a worse evil than suffering. A little injustice outweighs a lot of suffering. If it didn't, you'd be justified in doing all sorts of things—exterminating a minority group who disturbed society for example, if only this led to a great increase in general happiness.

OXMORE: What if injustice didn't have this embittering effect you describe?

HOME: Well, what if pulling out fingernails and toenails by the roots didn't cause great pain? I mean, you have to work with human nature as it is. If damaging our bodies didn't hurt us, then lots of things we now regard as wrong wouldn't be wrong. If we were all Franciscans who hated possessions and loved poverty, then theft wouldn't be a crime—or rather theft as we know it now wouldn't exist.

OXMORE: What about a case where people are so dedicated to a cause or organization that they don't care about their rights?

HOME: In that kind of case it might be true to say that you couldn't act unjustly toward such persons, just as you couldn't steal from Saint Francis; he'd gladly give you anything that was in his power to give you. But there are two points here to be careful about. The first is that if someone fools people into giving up their rights voluntarily he may still be doing them an injustice even though they in fact don't protest. If they knew the true state of affairs, they *would* protest. The second point is that you can give up your own rights, but not anyone else's. If Saint Francis had seen a thief stealing a poor woman's cow, I'm sure he would have tried to prevent the theft.

KIRK: If I may change the subject slightly, I agree with Home that injustice is a much worse evil than simple suffering, and that's why I'd want to say that our present prison system is in such a terrible state. The actual effect of prison on many people is to corrupt them morally and make lifelong criminals out of them. We just have to be doing something wrong!

OXMORE: I'm not sure that this is a properly philosophical question, but how could we do better?

KIRK: Well, after all, any utilitarian, any inheritor of the tradition of Jeremy Bentham and John Stuart Mill, ought to regard prison reform as an important part of practical ethics!

OXMORE: Touché. I'd forgotten how interested Bentham was in the subject.

KIRK: But to answer your question, I think that there are all kinds of things that could be done, from simple measures like separating first offenders from experienced criminals . . .

HOME: Isn't that done to some extent?

KIRK: Not nearly as much as it should be, and some places not at all, especially in facilities where men are held before trial. And that raises all sorts of questions about bail practices and inequities in our legal system. Lots of people are in jail precisely because they're poor. If they were even moderately well off, they'd be out on bail or could have got off entirely by hiring an expensive lawyer.

OXMORE: There's been some progress there, surely.

KIRK: Only a drop in the bucket compared to what's needed. Then there's the whole question of our attitude toward ex-convicts, which often drives them back to crime. Actually, I think this is tied up with the so-called "humanitarian" theory of punishment that Home mentioned at the beginning of this session. On the older theory a man was responsible for what he did, but his punishment wiped out the offense. He'd "paid his debt to society," in the old phrase. But nowadays when we regard the criminal as "sick" or insane this makes him somewhat less than human. We don't blame him, but we don't really regard him as we regard other people either.

HOME: I might mention that Professor Kirk speaks from knowledge on these points. He's been a prison visitor and worked with the John Howard Society for ex-prisoners. I learned this quite accidentally—he's quite close-mouthed about his good works.

KIRK: Well, that's beside the point except that it does give me a little inside knowledge. But that's nothing to brag of—some of the most stupid remarks about prisons I've ever heard have been made by experienced "penologists." Prisons may be a necessity, but they're certainly a necessary evil. They have a bad effect on so many people associated with them.

VENNER: We seem again to have returned to the point where we began, the inadequacies of our present system of punishment and yet at the same time its necessity. Perhaps I might, as chairman, take a moment, as Professor Kirk has done once or twice, to make my own position clear. I do not want to present myself to you as a person with no opinions or feelings on matters of morality or public policy. I applaud Professor Kirk's concern with prison reform, Professor Home's concern that our laws be just, Professor Oxmore's concern for the public welfare. I am happy to join with men of good will to make our society a better one. What I reject is the idea that there can be any certainty or any objectivity in matters of this kind. I cannot share even Professor Oxmore's certainty that right is what is for the public good, much less the moral certainties of Professor Kirk and Professor Home. But although I cannot agree with them intellectually, I often sympathize with them emotionally.

Part of our disagreement is no doubt a fundamental disagreement about man and his nature. This will be dealt with in the next session, where our title is "Is There a Ghost in Our Machine?" a reference to Professor Gilbert Ryle's characterization of a dualistic view of man as "the doctrine of the ghost in the machine." [3] By mere mechanical rotation it would be Professor Oxmore's turn to be chairman, but we do not want to be deprived of her views on this subject by her duties as chairman, especially as she is a friend and colleague of Professor Ryle. Both Professor Home and Professor Kirk have generously offered to be chairman

[3] Gilbert Ryle, see Biography (Appendix A) and Further Readings at the end of Chapter 7.

for this next session therefore, and we will probably toss a coin or something of that sort. At any rate it will appear at tomorrow's session who was chosen.

QUESTIONS

Answer the following questions as you think they would be answered by the panelist to whom they are addressed.

1. Professor Home: Do you regard it as just when your Israeli friends burn down Arab homes in retaliation for the raids against the Israeli occupying force by Arab freedom fighters?

2. Professor Kirk: Wouldn't we quite rationally distrust a person who had chosen to commit a crime of his own free will much more than a criminal who we regarded as having been sick, but as being now cured?

3. Professor Oxmore: If we regard anything which lessens suffering as good, even if it's unjust, shouldn't we admire a person who went around murdering people who were suffering greatly, or who caused great suffering to others by no fault of their own?

Are you satisfied with the following replies? If not, why not?

4. Home's reply to Oxmore's hypothetical case.

5. Oxmore's reply to Home's accusation that putting happiness ahead of justice would lead to morally undesirable consequences.

6. Kirk's reply to Oxmore's question as to whether prison reform is a philosophical question.

Write a brief essay on the following questions.

7. What major criticism would you have to make of this session or any of the participant's contributions to it?

8. What point, if any, especially impressed you in this session? Why?

9. Give your own view of punishment and attempt to justify it.

10. Give your own suggestions about the reform of our system of punishment and justify them. Be specific.

FURTHER READINGS

BEAUCHAMP, TOM L., *Ethics and Public Policy*, Englewood Cliffs, N.J.: Prentice-Hall, Inc., 1975.

    Bedau, Hugo Adam, "Deterrence and the Death Penalty: A Reconsideration," p. 106.

    Brandt, Richard B., "Retributive Justice and Criminal Law," p. 66.

    Hart, H. L. A., "Prolegomenon to the Principles of Punishment," p. 85.

FEINBERG, JOEL, *Social Philosophy*, Englewood Cliffs, N.J.: Prentice-Hall, Inc., 1973.

RACHEL, JAMES, *Moral Problems*, New York: Harper and Row, 1971.

    Hart, H. L. A., "Murder and the Principles of Punishment," pp. 188–221.

    Kneale, William, "The Responsibility of Criminals," pp. 161–87.

    Lucas, J. R., "Or Else," pp. 222–37.

Questions on the Reading

1. How does Kneale apply philosophical arguments to the legal issues of punishment?
2. Distinguish the legal and philosophical issues in Hart's paper.
3. How is Hart's discussion related to Kneale's?
4. What arguments used by Lucas are not discussed in the chapter?
5. What view of society seems to underlie Lucas' argument?

7

Is There a Ghost in Our Machine?

KIRK: By the luck of the toss, I'm chairman today. Our topic could be described as "mind and body," or "the nature of man," and our specific question is "Is there a ghost in our machine?" The phrase "ghost in the machine" goes back to Gilbert Ryle,[1] who used it as what he himself called "a deliberately abusive description" of the "traditional doctrine" about mind and body. Ryle identified the traditional doctrine with Descartes,[2] but I don't necessarily agree with his statement of it. So it seems to me that it might be useful for me to give my version of that traditional doctrine, and then for Oxmore to give Ryle's criticisms of that doctrine. Since I largely agree with the traditional idea, and Oxmore tells me that she largely agrees with Ryle, we'll be giving our own positions as well. After that, Venner and Home can give their views. Is that agreeable to everyone?

OXMORE: I don't entirely agree with Ryle, you know, but I'll be glad to develop first his view and then my own.

---

[1] Gilbert Ryle, see Biography (Appendix A) and Further Readings at the end of this chapter.

[2] René Descartes, see Biography (Appendix A).

VENNER: I am quite satisfied to begin with the traditional doctrine and Ryle's criticisms.

HOME: Yes, certainly.

KIRK: Well then, I take it that the traditional idea of man is that he consists in part of a material body which occupies space and has weight, which comes into existence, last eighty or a hundred years and then goes out of existence. But man also exists in part of a nonmaterial mind or soul which does not occupy space or have weight, which came into existence, but will never go out of existence. Neither of these *by itself* is a whole person, a whole human being, but the soul or mind is, so to speak, the dominant partner. The soul can exist without the body, but without a soul the body simply decays and decomposes. The separation of soul and body is what we call death, but religion tells us that soul and body will be reunited at the end of the world and that we will live eternally with soul *and* body. Philosophy can't prove this, but can explore its consequences. The disembodied soul, for example, can have certain experiences but not those for which a body is essential, whatever those may be. One would expect that hunger or enjoyment of food, sexual desire or sexual pleasure, the need for sleep or the experience of sleep would all be ruled out for a disembodied soul.

As to how we know that we have a nonmaterial soul, and what reasons we have to think the soul immortal, I'll reserve my comments until we hear Oxmore's version of Ryle's criticisms of the doctrine.

OXMORE: I'm very much afraid that in trying to present Ryle's criticisms briefly I may simply caricature them, but let me have a stab at it. Briefly, I think that Ryle's main criticism is that there is simply no *need* for the traditional idea of man as soul and body. On the traditional doctrine, when a man makes a decision a certain interior mental process goes on inaccessible in principle to other people, but entirely transparent to the man himself. But if we look at our knowledge about ourselves and other people instead of the theory, we find that a decision can be made without any interior musing or debating at all, and that a person's decisions are often far more understandable to other people than they are to himself. Again, when we say that a person is intelligent, we don't refer to certain interior processes that can't be known to anyone—we refer to the person himself. We mean that he would behave in certain ways in certain situations. The whole idea of an interior stage, on which ghostly dramas are played, as an explanation of our publicly observable behavior is unnecessary and confused. In broad outline, that's the line that Ryle took.

KIRK: Let's make this absolutely clear for the benefit of our audience, if not for our own benefit. Did Ryle really want to say that being intelligent just consisted of behaving in certain ways, or that making a decision just consisted of acting in one way rather than another? If so, that would be open to certain fatal objections. A very intelligent man who suffers a stroke and becomes totally paralyzed can't show his intelligence any longer, but he may still be intelligent. I can make a decision about which person in this room I would save in an emergency, and if the emergency never arises there may never be any action corresponding to that decision.

OXMORE: Well, each of those cases may be a bit more complex than you suggest—for example, if you never have a chance to carry out your decision about whom to save, how do you know that it was a real decision and not just idle musing? But because of cases like these we do need to be careful and make it clear that we're talking about *potential* behavior and not necessarily about *actual* behavior. To say that your paralyzed man is still intelligent is to say that if he were cured he would behave in such a way as to show that he had understood things he heard during his paralysis and had thought about them. To say that you really made a decision about whom to save in an emergency is to say that if that emergency occurred you'd do your best to save that person. It's just like saying that a piece of glass is fragile. By that we mean that if struck it would shatter. If it's never struck it will never shatter, but we can still say that it's fragile because we have ways of knowing that the "if" statement is true.

KIRK: Once again let's be quite clear. The reduction of mental goings on to overt behavior means only that for any mental state we can describe some piece of behavior which *would* result from being in that mental state, *if* certain circumstances were to occur. And to take care of tricky cases, like deciding I prefer Caesar to Pompey, this behavior might sometimes just consist of sincere answers to questions, truthfully speaking or writing an opinion, and so on.

OXMORE: That's at least roughly it.

KIRK: But that seems quite harmless in one way and quite misleading in another. It's like "reducing" spoken English to written English. It may be quite true that everything that can be said in spoken English *could* be written down *if* the circumstances were appropriate—someone present who was able to hear it and write it down, for example. But that doesn't show that spoken English and written English are the same, or that we don't often speak things without writing them.

OXMORE: I don't quite see the force of the analogy.

KIRK: Well, I'd say that it's quite important to realize that thinking is not the same as overtly behaving in various ways, and that we often think without ever overtly behaving in any corresponding way.

OXMORE: Ah, I think I see what you're driving at. But it makes sense to talk about saying words that for some reason couldn't be written down, whereas I don't think that it makes sense to talk about making a decision that couldn't possibly be carried out.

KIRK: I don't see why the cases aren't quite parallel. Any spoken utterance could in principle be written down. If an utterance could not be written down, it would be because of some special circumstance. Suppose I grant for the sake of argument that any decision could in principle be acted out in behavior. Then if some particular decision couldn't be acted out, it would just be due to some special circumstance also. For instance, suppose the last man on earth is illiterate. He decides to be kind to the next person he sees, and he says this aloud. His words can never be written down, since there's no one who could write them. His decision could never be carried out, since there are no other people.

OXMORE: But if he knew that there were no other people, he couldn't really make that decision; whereas he could still speak words, knowing that they couldn't be written down.

KIRK: Yes, I agree that a decision to behave in certain overt ways depends on the courses of action being open to you. But that's more or less accidental. Our last man on earth might decide to spend his life searching for survivors to help, which he could do whether survivors existed or not. Or if he knew there were no survivors, he might resolve to spend the rest of his life in prayer, or in getting drunk, or whatever he thought appropriate.

OXMORE: Yes, but my point is that "I know that X is impossible to do" implies that I can't intelligibly decide to *do* X; whereas, "I know that X is impossible to write" doesn't imply that I can't intelligibly *say* X.

KIRK: I think that I could quibble about the way you've phrased that, but I'm quite willing to grant that the connection between deciding and doing is more intimate than the connection between saying and writing. I'm not sure, on the other hand, that the connection between thinking in general and overt action is any more intimate than the connection between saying and writing. But perhaps the analogy is proving more confusing than enlightening.

OXMORE: Yes, we may have got tangled in a side issue. What I'm claiming is that any talk of interior mental states can be analyzed in terms of potential actions.

KIRK: And I'd say that "analyzed in terms of" is ambiguous. If you mean "totally reduced to" or "analyzed *away* in terms of," I'd say that's just false. Surely you don't want to say that there's some list of actual or potential pieces of behavior that is equivalent to, say, a state of admiration for Aristotle.

OXMORE: Oh no, any such list would be open-ended and would do no more than give you an idea of typical kinds of behavior appropriate to admiring Aristotle

KIRK: Then I can't see that you've in any sense succeeded in analyzing away mental states into overt behavior. I'd say that it's your understanding of what admiring Aristotle is like that tells you what to put on the list, not the list that explains what it means to admire Aristotle.

OXMORE: Yes, but look—the list gives you something observable, something that can be taught and learned. An idea inside someone's head, in the traditional view, is completely unobservable. How could it be a basis for teaching and learning?

KIRK: Aha! I think I've caught you using a trick that Ryle constantly uses to make his view plausible. An idea inside my head is not directly accessible to you. But it is directly accessible to me and is indirectly accessible to you.

OXMORE: What do you mean by "indirectly accessible"?

KIRK: I can talk to you about my idea, for instance, and you can understand me.

OXMORE: But what's the basis of my understanding, if we're talking about something that is in your head and not accessible to me?

KIRK: You may very well have had ideas that were the same in some respects, or at least similar.

OXMORE: But how do we know this if we can't compare our ideas?

KIRK: But we can compare our ideas; we do it all the time. The assumption that seems to be behind what you're saying is that people can only communicate about things which are directly accessible to both of them.

OXMORE: Yes, of course.

KIRK: But there's no "of course" about it; that's just plain false.

OXMORE: How could we communicate about something if we have no way of being sure we're talking about the same thing?

KIRK: In all sorts of indirect and complicated ways. For example, we use metaphors and analogies drawn from our experiences with material things. A doctor can ask you if the pain is like a knife stabbing you and you can answer yes, telling him quite a bit about the pain, even though neither of you have ever been stabbed with a knife. Talking about the floating or flying sensation we sometimes get in dreams, you can describe it as "effortless," "slow motion," "floating"—all terms drawn from physical experiences.

OXMORE: But if there's no way of making a direct comparison, it makes no sense to talk about making an indirect comparison.

KIRK: I'm sorry, but that's just not so. It seems to me that that assumption is just the kind of thing that the Wittgensteinians are always taking as true without any argument. But so far as I can see, it just isn't true, and there's no argument for it at all.

OXMORE: I just don't know what to say if you deny that.

KIRK: Of course not, you've had one of your basic assumptions challenged. We metaphysicians are quite used to having that happen, and have at least some idea of what to do about it. But many of the Wittgensteinians and ordinary language people don't seem even to be aware that they have basic assumptions, much less that they're open to challenge. It all goes back to what I said in the first session about the rather "inside" nature of many arguments among contemporary philosophers. You're all arguing about the cut of the lapel on the emperor's new clothes, and I come along and suggest that he's actually naked.

OXMORE: Well, we seem to be at an impasse here. Perhaps we could explore a related area. You claim that you have direct knowledge of your own ideas?

KIRK: Direct access to them, yes. "Direct knowledge" isn't ordinary English, and unless we give it some specific technical sense I'd rather not use it.

OXMORE: Well, is your direct access what Ryle calls "privileged access?"

KIRK: Yes and no. Sometimes by privileged access Ryle means just the sort of access that we have to our own ideas rather than the ideas of other people. But then he builds into the idea of privileged access the notion of infallibility—the idea that we can't be wrong about our ideas just because we have direct access to them.

OXMORE: You wouldn't agree to that?

KIRK: Good heavens, no! We can be quite wrong about things we have direct access to, and often are. And of course Ryle has no difficulty in showing that we're often mistaken about our own thoughts, feelings, motives, and so on. So if privileged access means no possibility of being mistaken, then Ryle can easily show something wrong with the idea that we have privileged access to all of our own thoughts. But, of course, the difficulty is based on a false assumption—the assumption that direct access means no possibility of error.

OXMORE: Yes, I do see that your position puts a spoke in the wheel of Ryle's argument. But what distinguishes direct access from indirect access, if not the impossibility of error?

KIRK: Well, there's nothing very complex about it. I'm aware of my own sensations, emotions, ideas, and so on, but not aware of yours unless you tell me about them or give them away by your actions. I need evidence for your thoughts, but no evidence for mine.

OXMORE: Then how could you be mistaken about your own thoughts? I can misinterpret evidence but if I have this direct awareness, how can I check to see whether I'm right or wrong? And if I can't check, what sense can I make of saying that I'm right or wrong?

KIRK: Yes, but I *can* check, in all sorts of ways. I can compare my thoughts at one time with my thoughts at another, compare notes with other people, and so on.

OXMORE: But in the absence of any objective checking procedure . . .

KIRK: But what do you mean by an objective checking procedure?

OXMORE: One that could be generally agreed on, at least.

KIRK: Yes, but anyone would agree on the general reasonableness of the kind of procedures I'm describing.

OXMORE: No, what I mean is some sort of procedure involving checking by more than one person.

KIRK: Ah, that's what I thought you might be driving at. In other words, what you insist on is a procedure involving checking by more than one person.

OXMORE: Yes.

KIRK: And these people must all have access to the thing being checked?

OXMORE: Of course.

KIRK: Direct or indirect?

OXMORE: I thought you were sounding rather Socratic. If I say direct access, you'll say I've gone back to the position you challenged, about the necessity of direct access.

KIRK: Right.

OXMORE: And if I say that some of those doing the checking can have indirect access, you'll argue that other people can have indirect access to my thoughts, and that therefore my "checking" requirement can be met.

KIRK: It's a pleasure to argue with an intelligent person.

OXMORE: Well, at least it's instructive. Let me try another angle. This business of the survival of the disembodied soul is quite important to the traditional view, I take it?

KIRK: Oh yes.

OXMORE: Well, I wonder whether we can really make sense of the idea of disembodied survival.

KIRK: Why not?

OXMORE: You'll grant, won't you, that the normal way we check on whether someone is the same person that we've met previously is by checking on whether his body is the same body—whether it's continuous with the body we met previously.

KIRK: Not necessarily. We look at physical appearance, memories, lots of things.

OXMORE: Yes, but all of these things are subordinate to bodily continuity. We've both met Home before, and we use various means to identify him. But if we meet someone who looks just like Home, but has never left Australia, we would agree he can't be Home, who we've met here in America. Or similarly, if we meet someone who seems to remember all the things that Home should remember, but has never left Australia, we wouldn't say that he was Home.

KIRK: I agree in the first case—physical resemblance isn't decisive. But I'm not so sure in the second case. If the person sitting at the table here began looking wildly about him, wondering how on earth he's been suddenly snatched from Australia, and soon after we get a frantic phone call from Australia from someone who seems to have all of Home's memories, mightn't we decide that the man in Australia is really Home, and that some kind of psychic transfer has taken place?

OXMORE: I agree that a case like that might give us pause, and if it happened often it might even cause us to change our criteria of personal identity. But our criteria as they presently exist make bodily identity decisive.

KIRK: Suppose I grant that for the sake of argument. As things are, bodily continuity is the decisive test of personal identity, and any other tests depend on it.

OXMORE: Well, if you grant me that, I think I have enough to make my point. In a disembodied soul, of course, there's no body for the bodily continuity test to operate on. Memory depends on bodily continuity, so that won't provide a test of personal identity. So we have no test of personal identity for a disembodied soul at all. Therefore, it's hard to see what can be meant by talking about a disembodied soul being the same person as a dead man or by talking about a number of disembodied souls at all, since we can't distinguish them.

KIRK: Wait a minute! You're going too fast. I agreed that in a conflict between bodily continuity and memory, bodily continuity is decisive, as things are now. But this isn't saying that if things were different memory might not be decisive. If a soul has no body but has all the memories of a certain dead man, why not identify it as the soul of that dead man?

OXMORE: There are a number of reasons. First, you'll grant that there could be two souls with the memory of a dead man.

KIRK: Well, it's logically possible, but I don't think that it's metaphysically possible for such a thing to happen. For God to create a duplicate soul would be irrational, and in my view such a soul couldn't just pop into existence. And how else could such a soul come to exist?

OXMORE: I don't pretend to know; the logical possibility is enough for my purposes. The point is that a soul could have the memories of a dead man without being that man, so having the memories can't be decisive.

KIRK: But if you're going to Xerox souls, I can Xerox bodies. Suppose a scientist discovers a way to make an exact duplicate of any object, including living things. Then Home walks into the machine and out walk Home 1 and Home 2. Now both Home 1 and Home 2 can be traced back to the original Home; both bodies have the same history up to the time of duplication. We can't say that both of them are the same as the original Home, since things the same as a third thing are the same as each other, and Home 1 and Home 2 obviously aren't the same. They occupy different spaces, begin to have different histories, and so on. So neither of them would be the same as the original Home, which I presume is what you want me to say about the two souls with duplicate memories.

OXMORE: Yes, I suppose so.

KIRK: But now this duplication of bodies is logically possible in the same way as duplication of souls with the same memories. The conclusion you drew in the case of the souls was "Therefore, memory can't be decisive; a soul could have the memories of a dead man without being the dead man." Why can't I argue just as well, "Therefore, bodily continuity can't be decisive; the body of Home 2 can be continuous with the body of the original Home without Home 2 being the same person as the original Home." Aren't the cases parallel?

OXMORE: Not really. In the case of bodily continuity it's possible in principle to keep the body under continuous observation. But you can't keep a soul under continuous observation.

KIRK: Well, perhaps God can. But that doesn't really meet my point. Obviously bodily continuity and memory are quite different sorts of things. But your duplication argument didn't depend on those differences and neither did my parallel duplication argument.

OXMORE: Well, let's concentrate on the differences then. Bodily continuity is a criterion that can be objectively applied, can be taught and learned. Anything that could serve as a criterion of personal identity would have to have those characteristics.

KIRK: I rather suspect that when you say "objectively applied" you're getting right back to the disputed principle that it's necessary to have something we can observe directly. Let's do a little science fiction and suppose that the disembodied souls are telepathic. Why can't they sort themselves out by seeing who remembers what?

OXMORE: Ah, but the point is are these really memories or just illusory pseudo-memories? The only way we can be sure of that is seeing if the person claiming to remember doing a thing was, in fact, the person who did the thing. And to settle that we need a criterion of personal identity all ready. So memory presupposes some criterion of personal identity and, therefore, can't be the standard.

KIRK: That's very ingenious. There may be something wrong with it, but it's the best argument you've produced so far. But all you've proved, even if your argument is successful, is that memory must depend on some other criterion of personal identity. You haven't shown at all that the other criterion must be bodily continuity.

OXMORE: What else would you suggest?

KIRK: There are two traditional suggestions. One is that each soul is uniquely fitted to animate a certain body and that a disembodied soul is distinguished by having a capacity to animate the body it once had. Of course, with the Christian doctrine of bodily resurrection the soul will someday *re*-animate its body.

OXMORE: Yes, but surely that depends on rather primitive ideas—bodies rising out of the same graves they were buried in, and so forth. Whereas, in fact, the same atoms would have been part of many human bodies, and most bodies would no longer exist as separate parcels of matter.

KIRK: Oh, the people who put forward this criterion were quite aware of that kind of difficulty. I think Aquinas discussed it somewhere.[3] The point is that the soul will re-animate a body which recognizably resembles the body it once had, has the same mannerisms, and so on. There'd be no question about recognizing a person you'd known in his resurrection body.

OXMORE: What about twins?

KIRK: Still troubled by duplication problems? People who know twins well have no real difficulty in telling them apart as things are now. I see no reason why they should have any difficulty with their resurrection bodies.

OXMORE: But again, if there was any real question about which of the twins I'd met, it would be possible in principle to check back on their spatial location during the interval.

KIRK: It seems to me that you're insisting that any criterion of identity be just like the bodily continuity criterion.

OXMORE: Only in the sense that it must pick out an individual uniquely. Spatial position does that because nothing can occupy the same space at the same time.

KIRK: That's very illuminating. I think the second criterion I meant to discuss, what I call the "unique personality pattern" criterion, might be relevant here. In this view each individual has a unique personality, shared by no other person.

OXMORE: Don't we sometimes speak of a son having just exactly his father's personality?

KIRK: Only in a very broad way. Have you ever met two individuals who were really exactly alike? The better you know people the less they seem alike.

OXMORE: That may be true as a matter of fact. But still it's logically possible to have two people with the same personality at the same time,

[3] *Summa Contra Gentiles,* Book IV, Chaps. 80–81.

whereas it isn't possible to have two people in the same place at the same time.

KIRK: What kind of fact would you say the impossibility of two things being in the same place at the same time is?

OXMORE: How do you mean?

KIRK: Is it logically possible for space to be constituted differently?

OXMORE: Well, I suppose so—I wouldn't want to take a Kantian view of space.

KIRK: Then the fact about space you're using is presumably the same sort of thing as natural laws—a fact about the way this universe is constituted, but not about how any possible universe would be constituted. But the uniqueness of each personality might be a fact of just the same sort.

OXMORE: But as long as space existed at all, that would have to be a feature of space.

KIRK: I'm not even sure of that. Imagine gaseous intelligences that could completely interpenetrate, for instance. If all we have to establish is a logical possibility, it's perfectly legitimate to use science fiction cases.

OXMORE: Then you want to claim that any condition that, in fact, establishes uniqueness would do as a criterion for personal identity.

KIRK: Not just any matter of accidental fact, but certainly anything that has the same kind of reliability or necessity as natural law. It seems to me that that's all you have with bodily continuity, and that you could get similar uniqueness in other ways.

OXMORE: Possibly you could, but, in fact, that's not our criterion.

KIRK: But how could you show that the criterion we use now must be the criterion we'd use in other circumstances?

OXMORE: I don't insist that it be the same; I just insist that it be a genuine criterion.

KIRK: Again it seems to me that you won't allow anything as a genuine criterion unless it's exactly like the bodily continuity criterion. Since no other criterion is *exactly* like the bodily continuity criterion, you eliminate all other possibilities. It's like deciding to give your brother-in-law a certain job and then saying that you'll consider all genuine candidates for the job, with the proviso that any genuine candidate must be exactly like your brother-in-law.

VENNER: I wonder if I might interject here.

KIRK: Good heavens, yes. As chairman I really should have restrained myself and given you and Home a chance.

VENNER: No, the discussion between you and Oxmore was quite illuminating. Perhaps you can repel Oxmore's criticisms even. But my question has to do with what positive reasons you have for accepting a nonmaterial soul.

KIRK: Well, I've already taken more than my share of the time, but very briefly I'll try to give you some reasons. If you consider something like a thought or a memory or a feeling, you'll realize that it doesn't have weight or occupy space. It's nonmaterial, in other words. Starting with that I'd argue that the mind in which these thoughts exist must be nonmaterial also.

VENNER: But a frown or a smile does not have weight or occupy space, does it?

KIRK: It doesn't have weight certainly, but it's a change or process in something that does. And it occupies space all right; it can be localized.

VENNER: But I would argue that a thought or memory or feeling is just a process in our brains and, therefore, like the smile or frown, it is a change in something that has weight and occupies a certain portion of space.

OXMORE: Then you want to say that "Where is my memory of Aunt Millie?" or "Where is my idea of going to town tomorrow?" are questions that make sense?

VENNER: I grant that these questions do not make sense in ordinary usage; I will concede that ordinary language is on Kirk's side. But that is because ordinary language is pre-scientific. The scientific answer to your questions is that both the memory and the idea are located in your brain, and eventually neurophysiology will be able to pinpoint the exact location in your brain. Even now we can evoke memories by electrically stimulating certain areas of the brain.

OXMORE: You can stimulate memories by letting me smell certain scents, too, but that doesn't mean that my memory is in my nose.

KIRK: I think we have to be fair to Venner. As a materialist he has to say that everything real is material. Since thoughts are obviously not physical objects, he has to make them changes or processes in physical objects. And of course there's some plausibility to this because our thoughts affect our body and what happens to our body affects our thoughts. I can't see Venner unless light reflected from him strikes my eyes, and when I decide to say certain words my decision affects my brain, then my nerves, then my vocal cords; then sound waves affect your ears, your nerves, your brain. Bodily changes are a necessary condition of the mind affecting other things or being affected by them. So it's possible to treat the bodily changes as if they were the whole story, like talking about the changes in a piano while it's playing and ignoring the fact that these changes are brought about only by a human being playing the piano. The piano player can't produce piano notes without a piano, and the kind of notes he can produce are conditioned by the state of the piano. But a theory of piano music that ignores the player and talks only of the piano would be unsuccessful, and a theory of thought that ignores the mind and talks only of the brain and body will be unsuccessful too.

VENNER: Ah, but what if the piano is a player piano, driven by a motor? Then the mechanism itself accounts for the production of the music.

KIRK: In your view then, men are just "player pianos," mechanisms that can be completely explained in mechanical terms.

VENNER: Yes, and to continue the metaphor, the activity of the player piano is completely determined by the structure of the piano and the program rolls on it. Similarly, man is completely determined by his inherited structure and the programs that are put into him by the environment.

KIRK: It seems to me that there's just no good evidence that we can explain human behavior in this way.

VENNER: Again this depends on the interpretation of the scientific evidence, what hope we have of complete success in explaining human behavior in this way.

HOME: Yes, but we've been over that in our discussion of determinism. The evidence just isn't there.

VENNER: Consider then such a machine as an electronic computer. It carries on activities just like human thinking, but we explain its activities without resorting to the hypothesis of a ghost in the computer.

HOME: I'd deny that what the computer does is just like human thinking. And although the computer doesn't have a mind or soul, the man who programs it does.

VENNER: Let us consider your denial that computers carry on an activity like human thinking. Professor Alan Turing once proposed that we make this question more precise by asking whether a computer could play what he called the "imitation game," succeeding in deceiving a human being into believing that the computer was a human being.[4]

HOME: Right. A questioner would ask questions of human being A and computer B, communicating by teletype to avoid physical clues. The point of the game was to see if the computer could give answers so deceptive that the questioner would pick B rather than A as the human being.

VENNER: Yes. Turing predicted, I recall, that such a computer could be constructed within fifty years. He wrote in the 1950s, so it could be available around the turn of the century.

HOME: Speaking as someone who's done a certain amount of computer programming, I'm afraid that's just science fiction. There's just no way within the foreseeable future that a computer can be constructed to answer relevantly any arbitrary question anyone might put to it. And that's what Turing's imitation game would require.

VENNER: How about if we restrict the number of questions that can be asked?

HOME: In that case you might be able to program a real computer to play the game. It would be extremely complex, but it might be fun to try. But actually all that would be happening would be a sort of duel of wits between the programmer and the questioner. The answers given by the computer wouldn't be answers given by a machine in the sense of being originated by a machine. They'd be originated by a man and transmitted by a computer. If the questioner chose B rather than A, he'd have been fooled into thinking that answers transmitted via computer and presumably thought up in advance were spontaneous answers. But of course if you know the allowable questions in advance, this kind of deception might not be too hard to bring off.

VENNER: But suppose the computer is programmed to program itself? After all, this is what we do in training a child.

HOME: A computer can be programmed to modify its own program, although this gets very complicated technically. I see no way at all in which it could be brought off for anything like the imitation game set-up. And I'd deny emphatically that teaching a child is anything like programming a computer.

[4] A. N. Turing, "Computing Machinery and Intelligence," *Mind*, Vol. LIX, 1950.

VENNER: In what way are these things unlike?

HOME: The essential difference is that anything the computer does can be explained in terms of its structure and its program, whereas the child originates behavior.

VENNER: But computers also can originate, can they not?

HOME: Not really. What you're thinking of, probably, is the sort of program where a random element is built into the program—the computer "reads" from a table of random numbers, for instance, and takes different paths depending on what number comes up.

VENNER: But I would say that human "originality" is no worse than the result of structure and programming plus random inputs.

HOME: That's enormously implausible as an explanation of any reasonably complex bit of behavior—our discussion here and now for example. And if it were true that our behavior here and now was simply a result of structure and programming plus random inputs, it couldn't be what we know it to be—a genuine argument, a search for truth. We'd simply be buzzing along on our preset tracks, not really thinking or arguing.

VENNER: Perhaps we are.

HOME: Then how could we hope to convince one another or reach the truth?

VENNER: We could modify each other's behavior.

HOME: Well, if it's just a matter of modifying behavior, you might just as well do that with brainwashing drugs. On your principles, I don't see what's wrong with that. But as usual, you're better than your principles— you show a commendable reluctance to bring out your syringes, as Lucas says. Speaking of Lucas, he's put forward a most interesting argument to show that man can't be explained simply as a machine.[5]

VENNER: I would be most interested to hear it.

HOME: My only hesitation is that the argument is rather technical. This may be no obstacle for you, Professor Venner, but I hope we don't lose the audience.

KIRK: Do a bit of explaining for the audience as you go on, Home. I'd like to hear what you have to say about that argument. I think I understood Lucas' book, but I'm not entirely sure.

HOME: I'll have a try at it then. Perhaps the best place to start is with

[5] J. R. Lucas, *The Freedom of the Will* (Oxford: Oxford University Press, 1970).

self-reference paradoxes, things like "The statement I am now making is false." That's paradoxical because if the statement is true then what it says is true, and what it says is that it itself is false. But if it's false then what it says is true, and therefore it's true. So if it's true it's false, and if it's false it's true. So we have an apparent contradiction. Now there are various ways of dealing with this in ordinary language, but in a formal system such as logic or mathematics we eliminate such paradoxes by saying that "true" and "false" can't be terms *within* the system, but must be terms of a language we use to talk *about* the system—what's called a *metalanguage*.

VENNER: You should perhaps note that there can be a meta-metalanguage to talk about the metalanguage, a meta-meta-metalanguage to talk about the meta-metalanguage, and in each of these there is a concept of true or false that applies to the next lower language.

HOME: Right—I'm trying not to be too complex, but that may be relevant later. Now consider terms like "provable in this system" and "not provable in this system." We can't leave such terms out of any reasonably complex formal system in the way in which we can leave out true and false. We need to be able to say within the system what's provable and what isn't. But now consider the statement "This statement is not provable within the system." That can't be both true and provable within the system, because if it were true it would be unprovable. It can't be false and not provable in the system, because if it were not provable, it would be true. But it can't be false and provable within the system because then your system would have false statements in it, and besides it would be provable that the statement *wasn't* provable. Thus it *has* to be true and unprovable. And any formal system of a certain degree of complexity will have such statements in them—true but unprovable in the system.

VENNER: This is the Gödel incompleteness proof.[6]

HOME: Yes—I'm just trying to present it simply enough for the students in the audience. For you, of course, I could just say "Consider the Gödel incompleteness proof."

OXMORE: But now why not say, as Ryle does in his paper "Heterologicity," that the statement in question isn't a genuine statement? For any genuine statement, we have to be able to specify what it's about. We have to be able to say "This statement, namely that Napoleon was fat . . ." or "This statement, namely that 256 is even. . . ." But with paradoxical statements there's no way of specifying them with such a "namely rider," as Ryle called it.

[6] See "Gödel's Theorem," *Encyclopedia of Philosophy* (New York: Macmillan, 1967), Vol. 3, 348–57.

HOME: That's where the Gödel numbering business comes in. A namely rider isn't the only way of specifying a statement. Specifically, Gödel showed that there's a certain numbering procedure by which we can give a unique number to each statement that can be made in a formal system. We can, that is, if our system is rich enough to contain numbers or some equivalent. Thus our "Gödel sentence" can refer to itself by means of its unique Gödel number, getting around the difficulty of specifying what sentence we're talking about without using a namely rider.

KIRK: Then all of that complex business about Gödel numbers is just to get a unique reference to the Gödel sentence?

HOME: Essentially, yes. This is an awfully rough explanation, but it will have to do. Those who know more can make their own corrections and those who don't won't be too badly misled.

VENNER: It may be sufficient for our purposes now.

HOME: Well then, I'll simply have to tell you that a complete description of any machine program, any computer program, can just be regarded as equivalent to a formal system. The program by which the machine works is equivalent to the axioms and rules of inference; the theorems are like possible operations of the machine, and so on. So for any machine program there's a formal system that is equivalent.

VENNER: Yes, this is proved in the mathematical theory of computability.

HOME: Right. Now suppose a materialist like Professor Venner says that *I* am a machine. Well, if I am, then I must be some specific machine and have some specific program. Then there's a formal system equivalent to the machine program which is me, which is my thinking. But in that formal system there's some statement, the Gödel sentence for that system which is true but unprovable in that system. Thus if I am a machine, there's no way I can "reach" that sentence, no way in which I can know that it's true. But I can know that that sentence is true, by following Gödel's argument.

OXMORE: You mean you have no way of *proving* that it's true. That doesn't prevent you from knowing it is.

HOME: It does if I'm a machine. If I'm a machine the only way I have of arriving at truths is following out my program. Some of these "following outs" would be what we'd ordinarily call proofs, some wouldn't. But from the point of view in which my program becomes a formal system, all operations according to program are proofs.

OXMORE: What about the programs with random inputs?

HOME: No problem on the theory of computability. The instruction is just "Do A *or* B *or* C . . ." and that can be translated into the formal system. The Gödel argument still goes through.

VENNER: That is correct. But what if we insert instructions for constructing a Gödel sentence into your program?

HOME: Then we can get a sort of meta-Gödel-sentence for the augmented system. Think about Gödel's original proof—you can never augment your system so that there isnt *a* Gödel sentence in it.

VENNER: Ah yes, I see. But now what is the basis of your confidence that you will always be able to know the truth of the Gödel sentence?

HOME: Just my ability to understand Gödel's argument. Once you've grasped the principle, applying it to particular cases presents no theoretical difficulties.

VENNER: We can always construct a new machine, or augment our old machine to do what you have just done. Turing, I remember, discusses this point.

HOME: "You will have your petty triumph over particular machines, but there is no question of triumphing over all machines simultaneously" is what he says. But I don't need to triumph over all machines simultaneously. You're claiming that I'm a machine and that you could in principle specify or build a machine that does everything I can do. But this argument shows that for any definitely specified machine I can do something that *that* machine can't do. Thus you can never specify a machine equivalent to me.

KIRK: That's fascinating, but I somehow feel that there's a trick to it.

HOME: The Gödel principle is as well established as anything in the foundations of mathematics, and Lucas' application of it is, I think, unassailable if properly understood. You just can't get around it. You can cheat on what you mean by "machine," but if you do then it's quite harmless to say man is a machine. You could simply say that anything a machine can't do I can't do, but that flies in the face of the evidence that I can understand and apply the Gödel argument. I grant you that the argument may seem trivial. But Lucas claims that it's just an especially clear case of the argument I used against determinism—what he calls the "presupposition" argument—freedom, and therefore nonmechanism, as a presupposition of reason. Then the argument is connected on the other hand to our awareness of ourselves as beings who are self-conscious, able to reflect on our own thinking and our own abilities.

KIRK: Yes, both of those points are certainly vital to our understanding of ourselves. In fact, I'd use our ability to reflect on ourselves and our own thinking as another starting point for an argument for the nonmaterial nature of mind. There's nothing in the merely material universe that corresponds to this self-reflexiveness of mind.

HOME: Right. There is, of course, a great deal of work still to be done on the connection between the Lucas argument and the presupposition argument on the one side and self-consciousness on the other. But a breakthrough has been made.

VENNER: Have you similarly ingenious arguments for the immortality of the soul?

HOME: No, I've never been greatly impressed by the traditional arguments for the immortality of the soul. So far as I can see the most that philosophy can do is defend the religious doctrine of the immortality of the soul from objections. I don't know if Kirk would agree.

KIRK: I'd put the traditional arguments somewhat higher than that. One point that's always impressed me is that whereas my body has parts that can come to pieces and I know the sort of things it can change into, my soul doesn't seem to have parts in the same way and I don't know what a soul could decay into or turn into. And if the soul is real, for it simply to vanish, simply to be annihilated, would be totally unlike anything that we see in any other part of nature. But I wouldn't put arguments for the immortality of the soul on anything like the level of convincingness as the arguments for the existence of God. Once that's established though, there may be indirect arguments *via* God's justice.

I see that our time has more than run out. I'm sorry for monopolizing the early part of the discussion, but we did agree that chairmen could get into the argument. The chairman for the next session will be Oxmore, and our topic is knowledge. The title is "How Do We Know?" Now let's take questions from the floor.

QUESTIONS

Answer the following questions as you think they would be answered by the panelist to whom they are addressed.

1. Professor Venner: If man is only a machine programmed by natural

forces, how do you account for great works of human genius, such as the plays of Shakespeare or the symphonies of Beethoven?

2. Professor Oxmore: You seem to be saying that it's logically necessary to have a body to carry on human activities. But surely this is true only of some activities, like laughing or kissing, and isn't true of others, like thinking or loving.

3. Professor Home: You say that injuries to the body only inhibit our mental activities in the way that injuring a piano can inhibit a pianist from playing certain notes. But don't we have conclusive evidence that memory consists of traces on the brain, and can be destroyed by destroying parts of the brain? And wouldn't this mean that your supposed disembodied spirits would have no memory?

Criticize the following replies to questions or challenges by the panelists:

4. Venner's reply to the criticism of his "player piano" view of man.
5. Oxmore's reply to the criticism of Ryle's view of man.
6. Kirk's reply to the criticism of his dualistic view of man.

Write short essays on the following topics:

7. Which view presented in the dialogue do you most nearly agree with? Why?
8. What criticism would you like to make which is not presented in the dialogue?
9. What argument would you like to present which is not dealt with or not adequately dealt with in the dialogue?
10. What sort of question is the question of whether we survive death? How might it be settled?

FURTHER READINGS

Hospers, John, *Readings in Introductory Philosophical Analysis*, Englewood Cliffs, N.J.: Prentice-Hall, Inc., 1968.

Fullerton, George J., "The Insufficience of Materialism," pp. 195–206.

Shafler, Jerome, "Could Mental States Be Brain Processes?" pp. 219–27.

Smart, J. J. C., "Sensations and Brain Processes," pp. 207–19.

TAYLOR, RICHARD, *Metaphysics* (2nd ed.), Englewood Cliffs, N.J.: Prentice-Hall, Inc. 1974, Chaps. 2 and 3, pp. 10–26.

WILSON, MARGARET D., DAN W. BROCK, and RICHARD F. KUHNS, *Philosophy, An Introduction,* New York: Appleton-Century-Crofts, 1972.

Ryle, Gilbert, "Descartes' Myth," pp. 186–200.

Smart, J. J. C., "Sensations and Brain Processes," pp. 209–20.

Strawson, P. F., "Persons," pp. 200–209.

Questions on the Reading

1. Compare Smart's theory with that defended by Venner. How might Kirk criticize Smart?
2. Does Ryle's account of his view differ in important ways from Oxmore's summary of it? What further criticisms of Ryle can you think of?
3. Is Strawson's view basically a form of materialism? Why or why not?
4. How does Shafter's criticism of Smart differ from Kirk's criticism of Venner? Which criticism is the more effective?
5. Does Taylor's "solution" to the mind-body problem beg the question? Why or why not?

8

How Do We Know?

OXMORE: I'm chairman for the next two sessions, and I suppose that each of us has a somewhat different notion of what the duties of a chairman should be. My own idea is that I might make myself useful by putting on the table, so to speak, some ideas that none of us here hold or would defend, ideas which might not get mentioned if someone didn't bring them up. Our question today is, "How do we know?" The view I'd like to put on the table, as it were, is the view that we just *don't* know, the view that knowledge is really impossible. This is the view that philosophers call *skepticism*, giving that word a much stronger sense than it has in ordinary usage. Ordinarily a skeptic is understood to be a man who is hard to convince, but a skeptic in the philosophical sense is a man who is impossible to convince, a man who challenges the whole business of arriving at conclusions on the basis of evidence.

HOME: I think we might distinguish here between several sorts of skeptic. There's what I'd call the inductive skeptic, who challenges the possibility of any knowledge arrived at by induction. But an inductive skeptic may think that we can arrive at some knowledge deductively. Then there's what I'd call the epistemological skeptic who challenges the possibility of any knowledge whatever, but may think that we can have more or less justified beliefs. Finally, there's what I'd call the fundamental skeptic who won't even grant that we have justified beliefs. You seem to be talking about what I'd call the fundamental skeptic, Professor Oxmore.

OXMORE: I suppose so, although many people combine these kinds of skepticism.

HOME: True. I've just ranged them in order of strength. A fundamental skeptic is necessarily an epistemological skeptic in the sense that he denies everything that the epistemological skeptic denies. And both the fundamental skeptic and the epistemological skeptic are inductive skeptics in the sense that they deny everything that the inductive skeptic denies. It's like peeling away successive layers of our usual certitudes—first our trust in induction, then our claim to any knowledge, then our claim even to rational belief.

OXMORE: Do you intend your classification to be exhaustive?

HOME: No, these are just the most important types of skepticism. There are also intermediate types; for example, someone who rejects both induction and deduction as sources of knowledge but trusts immediate experience as a source of knowledge. In theory that's the type of skepticism Hume supported, although he often talked as if he were only an inductive skeptic, and, of course, he's best remembered for his criticism of induction. The Greek skeptics were by and large fundamental skeptics distrusting all forms of reasoning and immediate experience. Rationalists like Descartes and Plato tend toward inductive skepticism while empiricists are often tempted to be epistemological skeptics, thinking that we can get along only with rational belief, making no claim to knowledge.

OXMORE: Well, suppose that we have a fundamental skeptic, one who denies that we can have even rational belief. He's canny enough not to claim that he *knows* that his view is true, of course, or even that he's rationally justified in holding it, but he challenges us to make good *our* claims to knowledge. What sort of reply would you give to him, Professor Venner?

VENNER: I would start with the most immediate data of experience, what in the Vienna days we used to call protocol statements, and try to build up from there. As you may know, the Vienna Circle disagreed among themselves as to whether the most immediate data of experience were statements about what is given to us in experience—what we called sense data—or statements about physical objects. Carnap argued that we could use either the sense-datum language or the physicalistic language, and that neither could claim superiority.

OXMORE: Could you give us examples of protocol statements?

VENNER: We often used examples like "A red rectangle is to me here, now," where "here" and "now" were to be filled in by some appropriate spatial and temporal indexes. Or in the physicalistic language, "A red book is on the table."

OXMORE: I think that my skeptic would want to argue that you could be mistaken in all sorts of ways about those statements.

VENNER: About "There is a red book on the table," this would seem to be true, but physicalists interpreted such statements in rather a complex way that took care of many of the usual objections. For them, statements about physical objects were hypotheses about what would occur if you made certain tests. Such hypotheses are often well-supported, although they are always open to refutation. Perhaps it would be simpler to stick to the sense-datum language, which I myself prefer—it raises fewer problems and is easier to discuss without raising side issues.

OXMORE: A sense-datum protocol statement would be one such as, "A red rectangle is to me here, now"?

VENNER: Yes.

OXMORE: But I think my skeptic would say that far from being a statement just about immediate experience, this involves all sorts of generalizations, comparisons, and expectations. The words "red" and "rectangle," for instance, involve comparisons with other reds and rectangles, imply generalizations about that color and that shape, arouse expectations about what we would observe in other circumstances, and so on. And when you start filling in "here" and "now," you'll run into similar problems.

VENNER: Perhaps we might explain this statement as meaning that I have a certain experience about which the sounds "red" and "rectangle" arise in my mind.

OXMORE: But as soon as you start trying to say anything useful about this "certain experience," you run into the kind of problems I've indicated. Either you have a "pure" inarticulate experience, or you start to describe it and thus get beyond immediate experience. But even if you could get around this, there's still the problem of how you build up knowledge of anything more than immediate experience.

VENNER: This we regarded as a matter of logical constructions from sense-data.

OXMORE: Then you had to have logic as well as immediate sensation?

VENNER: Logic, of course, we regarded as conventional, a matter of meanings given to words. So that to say "This is a red rubber ball" would be to put forward a hypothesis based on past sense-data and referring to future sense-data. The meaning of "red" is fairly simple and could be taught ostensively by showing someone red objects. The meaning of "rubber" involves reference to simpler concepts, such as elastic, bouncing, and so on, which reduce to things that could be taught ostensively.

OXMORE: In other words, to say this ball is rubber is in part to say that it would bounce?

VENNER: In the appropriate circumstances, yes. Not after the rubber ball had been plunged into liquid oxygen, for example, but if it were at the appropriate temperature and so on, it would bounce.

OXMORE: But you could be wrong. The ball might not bounce in those circumstances; might not be rubber.

VENNER: This is always possible, yes.

OXMORE: Then how can you say that you know the ball is rubber if you may be completely wrong about it?

VENNER: But any empirical statement is open to disconfirmation; that is in the nature of empirical statements. Whether to speak of "knowledge" of empirical statements is a matter of convention.

HOME: I wonder if I might add to that?

VENNER: Certainly.

HOME: It *is* a matter of the meaning of the English word "know" and its equivalents in other languages; *epistēmē* in Greek, for instance. We use the word "know" in such a way that if a statement is false we don't speak of knowing it. If *p* is false, you don't know *p*. By transposition we get the equivalent statement: "If you know *p*, then *p* is true." This is a logical truth (in the narrow sense), so that we can say, "*Necessarily* if you know *p*, then *p* is true," or somewhat misleadingly, "If you know *p*, then necessarily *p* is true." But the necessity applies to the whole conditional statement, not to the consequent of the conditional. Now it follows from this that if *p* *may* be false, then we *may* not know *p*. But it doesn't follow in any way at all that if *p may* be false, we *don't know p*. Just this fallacy lies behind many skeptical arguments. The skeptic goes from the truism, "If you know, you can't be wrong," which just means "Necessarily if you know *p*, then *p* is true," to the false statement, "If you may be wrong, you don't know," which doesn't follow at all from any sound principle. Now Oxmore, I'm sure, was using this bad argument deliberately, so that we could talk about it.

OXMORE: Yes, that's one bit of formal logic that I've had quite thoroughly pounded into my head.

HOME: But many skeptics use this argument quite unconscious of the fact that it is a fallacy.

OXMORE: There's really no excuse for that in this day and age.

HOME: I couldn't agree more. But now that we have that out of the way, I'm still quite unhappy with Venner's idea that we have to start from some sort of rock-bottom protocol statements and build up knowledge from there. It seems to me that this theory itself is a leftover from the idea that we can only have knowledge of things we can't possibly be wrong about.

OXMORE: Well, what would you say in reply to the skeptic?

HOME: First, I'd start off by saying something more about the way we use the concept of knowledge. Knowledge is a concept of the kind that H. L. A. Hart called "defeasible." [1] It makes a claim that is normally taken to be established by certain kinds of evidence, but is always open to defeat by certain kinds of evidence. The logic of "knowledge" is like the logic of "champion." A champion has to win his, or her, title, then retains it until defeated. A champion isn't an unbeatable man; he's a man who hasn't in *fact* been defeated in defending his championship. When we say a man knows something, we don't mean that we can't be proved mistaken. We mean that he's established a claim to knowledge, and that claim hasn't been defeated. For example, suppose I claim to know that there are over twenty people in this room. I establish my claim to know by the fact that I counted the people in the room a minute ago, and I counted thirty before I stopped. That would ordinarily be taken as good evidence that I know what I say I know. But that claim could be defeated in lots of ways. You could show that it wasn't really true or that I didn't really believe it or that I didn't really have any good evidence for it. For example, I might be so stoned that I was counting each person three or four times. But to prove that I

---

[1] H. L. A. Hart, "The Ascription of Responsibilities and Rights," in A. G. N. Flew, ed., *Logic and Language*, First Series (Oxford: Basil Blackwell, 1952).

don't know it isn't sufficient to show that I *may* be mistaken or *may* not believe what I say or *may* not have good evidence. You have to show more than a possibility to defeat my knowledge claim.

OXMORE: What if I show that there's a hundred-to-one chance that you're mistaken?

HOME: That's OK—you can defeat a knowledge claim that way. But showing a high probability that I'm mistaken is quite different from showing a mere possibility.

OXMORE: Right. I just wanted to clear that up.

HOME: Well then, a good many skeptical arguments just ignore this fact about the way we use the concept of knowledge, or try to get us to change the way we use the concept.

OXMORE: You don't think that there could be good reasons to change the way we use the concept?

HOME: We'd just have to make the distinctions we now make using the word "knowledge" by using some other word. There is a real difference between the cases where we're right by lucky guess or have some evidence but not enough or say something true without believing it, and the case where we're right and believe what we say and have good evidence. Call this last case "knowledge" or call it "oleo margarine," but it *is* different from the other cases.

OXMORE: Oleo margarine?

HOME: It was the first thing that came into my head. Anyway, I think you got an essential point right about the skeptic in your first remarks. You said that the skeptic was one who is impossible to convince. That's right, and it's right for an important reason. The skeptic is impossible to convince for the same reason that it's impossible to defeat me in a game of cards. You can't defeat me in a game of cards because I won't play cards—card games bore me. You can't convince the skeptic because he won't "play" either. He won't enter into the process of weighing evidence, considering pros and cons, and so on. He refuses to accept any answer to his objections as satisfactory. But if a man is not convincible on principle, there's no use in trying to argue with him; just as if a man will never admit that he's lost a bet, there's no use gambling with him.

OXMORE: Then you don't think that one can argue with a skeptic?

HOME: In the same way that one can't carry on normal communication with a pathological liar—a person who lies about everything. Communication just breaks down with such a liar, because you know that whatever is true, what he says isn't. Argument breaks down with a skeptic because no matter what evidence or what argument you produce, he won't accept it. But just as it might be quite important to keep answering the liar in order to keep others from being misled by his lies, it's often quite important to answer the skeptic in order to keep people from being misled by his arguments.

OXMORE: Do you think that most people are actually convinced or affected by skeptical arguments?

HOME: Convinced, no. Affected, yes. What happens is that skeptical arguments lurking in the background tend to create a sort of climate of intellectual irresponsibility. People think that somehow *maybe* we don't really know anything, so therefore they don't take seriously certain kinds of knowledge that need to be taken seriously. Incidentally, I think that moral skepticism has somewhat the same effect of creating a sort of floating irresponsibility in moral matters.

OXMORE: That's a very interesting point. I'd like to go on to some other points about the nature of knowledge and the sorts of things we know, but Kirk hasn't had a go at the skeptic yet.

KIRK: I'm quite content with what Home has said for the moment. I think that anything I'd want to say about skepticism will come up in connection with other points.

OXMORE: Then, Home, do you want to say anything more about skepticism?

HOME: Two quick points. I think that inductive skepticism often arises from simply assuming that deduction is the only source of rational belief and then demanding a deductive justification of induction, which can't be had. But induction is none the worse for that. This may come up again later, so I'll say no more about it now. The second point is that a consistent fundamental skeptic couldn't really argue if he hopes to show anything by argument at all. Even Cratylus, who was so skeptical he gave up talking and just wagged his finger, wasn't entirely consistent, if his finger-wagging meant anything. But the skeptic can consistently argue *ad hominem* against the nonskeptic to try to "prove" that reason is self-refuting, that reason self-destructs. This, if successful, would lead to a pragmatic result—the loss of confidence in reason by nonskeptics. In other words, the skeptic could try to use reason as a tool to make skeptics out of nonskeptics. And if he just happens to want to make other people skeptics and just happens to think that this means might work, he isn't inconsistent. But if he tries to claim that he has proved that reason is self-refuting or that he knows that argument can convert nonskeptics to skeptics, then of course he's blatantly inconsistent.

OXMORE: Since we hope to get to the problem of induction in our next session, let's not get started on it now. Your other remark seems to me to be quite true. If we can go on, let me ask you this question. How would you define knowledge?

HOME: In a way, I've already defined it. I've been using in an informal way what's sometimes called the "classical definition" of knowledge, which goes back to Plato.[2] You know p just in case p is true and you believe p and you have good reasons for believing p. I think all of that is quite correct, but to give an accurate picture of knowledge you have to go on to say some of the things I've said about the defeasible character of knowledge claims, and also something about the interrelation between the three conditions.

OXMORE: What about the kind of cases where those three conditions seem to be fulfilled but we still wouldn't say that the person had knowledge? For example, there's one that goes something like this: There are three men in an office—Smith, Jones, and Brown. Smith believes that one of the other men in the office owns a Ford automobile. His reasons are that he has often been in Jones' Ford; he has talked to Jones about his preference for Fords over any other car; he knows that Jones can't get by without a car since he lives out of town, and so on. As it turns out, one of the men in the office does own a Ford, but the person who owns the Ford is Brown, who just bought one yesterday. Jones sold his Ford early this morning, planning to move into town and use the bus. Neither man mentioned these new facts to Smith, since work at the office was too hectic to give them time to chat. So, Smith believes that a man in the office owns a Ford; he has good reasons for his belief; and a man in the office does own a Ford. But would you really want to say that Smith knows that a man in his office owns a Ford?

HOME: No, I'd just agree that he doesn't know that.

OXMORE: And would you agree that all three conditions are satisfied?

HOME: I'm not so sure about that. There are several questionable things involved. What Smith has good reason to believe—if he does have a good reason—is that Jones owns a Ford.

OXMORE: You doubt that the reasons are adequate?

HOME: It's certainly enough to justify a knowledge claim. But if Smith

---

[2] Plato, see Biography (Appendix A) and Further Readings at the end of Chapter 10.

were very careful or if there were some reason to be especially cautious, he might say that what he really has good reason to believe is that Jones owned a Ford yesterday and almost certainly still owns it. Suppose, for example, someone came up and wanted to bet him ten dollars that Jones did not own a Ford. The very fact of someone wanting to bet should arouse Smith's suspicions, and the smart thing to do would be to ask Jones if he had sold his car.

OXMORE: Suppose Jones says no, either lying, although he's usually truthful, or else honestly forgetting the sale.

HOME: Oh yes, I agree that you could probably strengthen your case so that Smith's reasons would be adequate. I don't want to insist that only absolutely watertight evidence gives us good reason to believe or that every knowledge claim must contain a "probably" or an "unless" clause. But now we come to the next difficulty, which is that what Smith really has good reason to believe is that Jones has a Ford. Since Jones is a man in the office, Smith might say, "A man in the office owns a Ford." However, that would be a case of *quidam*, not of *nescio quid*. In other words, he would mean "a man in the office—I know who but I'm not saying," rather than "some man in the office—I don't know which." And the claim he actually makes, "a man in the office, I know who . . ." is, in fact, false—he doesn't know which man owns the Ford.

OXMORE: Yes, but doesn't the claim that he does have good reason to believe "Jones, who is a man in the office, owns a Ford," imply the vaguer claim "Some man in the office owns a Ford"?

HOME: Yes, but then you have to use the principle that if you have good reason to believe p, and p implies q, then you have good reasons to believe q.

OXMORE: Well, what's wrong with that?

HOME: There are several kinds of difficulties. The implication has to be a logical one.

OXMORE: That's all right in this case.

HOME: And the person has to know that the implication holds.

OXMORE: We can build that into the case. Anyway, surely any intelligent person would know that "Jones owns a Ford" implies logically "Some man owns a Ford."

HOME: But even if those conditions are met, I still have some misgivings about the principle, especially in cases where you go from a particular person to "some man" or from p to "either p or q," and then the "some man" statement or the "either p or q" statement is true even though the statement you have good reasons to believe is false.

OXMORE: Well, how would your doubts about the principle affect what you want to say about this case?

HOME: I think what you need to do is clarify the conditions of knowledge. Either you build in an extra condition saying that your evidence for p must not be "by way of" any false statement, which is rather tricky to work out, or else you have to make clear that in saying that you have good reasons to believe p you mean that p is true *for the reasons you think it is*, and not for some extraneous reasons. This is what I meant a while back by talking about the relations between the conditions. A full set of conditions might go "You know p just in case p is true and you believe p and you have good reasons to believe p and p is true for the reasons you think it is, and you believe p because of the reasons you have."

OXMORE: Going back to the skeptical position for a moment, don't these extra conditions provide more targets for the skeptic? I mean, here are more things that you have to be certain of before you can claim to know something.

HOME: That doesn't really trouble me, because again it's a matter of defeasibility. A claim to knowledge can be defeated by showing that you don't believe p *because* of the reasons you have or by showing that p isn't true for the reasons you think that it is. It seems to me that the kind of example you've brought up shows that very clearly and that any adequate definition of knowledge has to take this into account.

OXMORE: You don't think that more and more such exceptions to the classical definition might pop up, making it useless for all practical purposes?

HOME: No, it seems to me that all the vital elements of knowledge are included in the classical definition and that all we have to do is get the relation of the conditions right. No counter-example really moves us outside this *kind* of conditions to bring in something other than truth, belief, or good reasons.

OXMORE: What about a requirement that you understand what you claim to know?

HOME: That I think is implied by believing and having good reasons to believe. In fact, I'd analyze belief in such a way that this is part of the analysis. You believe p just in case you have the idea that p is true, you act as if p were true, and you have some reason to believe p is true.

And you have the idea that p is true just in case you understand that p is true and would sincerely affirm that p is true.

OXMORE: Isn't that a rather strong sense of belief?

HOME: Yes, it's what might be called "rational belief." There's a very weak sense of belief, which is about the same as just having the idea that p, and there are probably other senses of belief too. For example, I think that when psychiatrists talk about "unconscious belief," they mean just acting as if p were true without either having the idea that p is true or having reason to think p is true. And when we say someone *should* believe p, we often mean that he has reason to believe p, whether or not he has the idea that p is true or acts as if p were true.

OXMORE: But can't a man have a belief he shouldn't have?

HOME: Yes, that would be "irrational belief," having the idea that p is true and acting as if it were without having any reason to believe p is true. And we might talk about other variations of that sort, for instance having the idea that p is true and having reason to believe it true, but not acting as if it were. I don't know quite what you'd call that case.

KIRK: What would you say about religious belief?

HOME: Well, you and I would agree that religious belief is a rational belief. We have the idea that God is good, for example, and we have reason to hold that He is, and we try to act on that assumption.

KIRK: I see, and this would tie in with the idea that martyrdom is the fullest proof of faith?

HOME: Yes, dying for the truth of a belief is the most extreme case of acting as if that belief were true.

VENNER: How does your rational belief differ from the rational belief that some epistemologists would consider the next step below knowledge?

HOME: I don't think that the difference between knowledge and rational belief is a matter of steps, a matter of degree. But when people talk of rational belief in that way they usually mean a case where we have the idea that p is true, act as if p were true, and have very strong reasons to believe that p is true.

OXMORE: It bothers me that in giving the conditions for belief you have to use the word "belief." Isn't acting as if p were true just acting as if you believe p, for instance?

HOME: I don't think that this is necessarily an objection to my account. I think that we can get around using the *word* "belief," for instance. To act as if *p* were true is just to act in a way which it would be reasonable to act if *p* were true in the light of the other circumstances that obtain. It might be reasonable to drink something that contained poison, for instance, if you wanted to die.

OXMORE: Ah, but "acting as if it were true that something contains poison" is really incomplete. What you'd be doing is acting as if it contained poison *and* you knew or believed this. It could be as true as you like that it contained poison and this wouldn't affect your actions if you were unaware of it.

HOME: Yes, you're quite right about that. But I think I can explain the "awareness" that you're talking about in terms of having the idea that *p* is true. So I'd explain "acting as if *p* were true" in terms of "acting in a way that would be consistent with having the idea that *p*."

OXMORE: Yes, but you've said that one could have the idea that *p* and *not* act as if *p* were true.

HOME: But then you're being inconsistent. When you have the idea that *p* is true but don't act in the way we'd expect, people are puzzled. If an individual seems to be aware that the cup contains poison, but he's drinking it, then we think he's inconsistent. The apparent inconsistency may disappear when we become aware of other facts—for example, the individual wants to die, or he has an idea that he's immune to all poisons.

OXMORE: You're putting quite a bit of weight on this business of "having an idea that *p*." How did you define it again?

HOME: You have the idea that *p* if you understand that *p* is true and would sincerely affirm that *p* is true.

OXMORE: The "would sincerely affirm" is a disposition statement, right? Would sincerely affirm in certain appropriate circumstances, that sort of thing?

HOME: Yes, roughly.

OXMORE: But now this business of "understanding that *p*," what does that involve?

HOME: Well, having an awareness of *p*, which of course means understanding the concepts involved. I can't understand that my dog is hungry, for example, unless I understand "dog" and "hunger."

OXMORE: But this "understanding that *p*" or "being aware that *p*" doesn't imply that *p* is true, only that the person thinks it is.

HOME: Right.

OXMORE: Isn't this just what we'd sometimes call believing that *p*?

HOME: Yes, I think it is. But that's just metonymy—using the name of the whole for the part.

OXMORE: I think you mean synecdoche really. But that's an interesting suggestion. Do you think that happens with other things we call knowledge or belief?

HOME: Oh yes. For example, when someone has good reason to believe something but doesn't believe it, we say that he "really knows it but won't admit it." Or when we believe strongly but lack good reasons, we sometimes say that we *just know* that a thing is true. Again, when we talk of unconscious beliefs, not all of the conditions of belief are present. All of these are cases where we're tempted to apply the concept of knowledge or belief because some important condition of knowledge or belief is present. But we're really naming a part for the whole, like saying Washington concluded an agreement with Moscow, when we mean that the United States concluded an agreement with Russia.

OXMORE: I think that there may be better examples, but I see your point. What bothers me is the feeling that some basic epistemic notion of awareness or belief in the most minimal sense, just "thinking that," is escaping your definitions.

HOME: Well, I have some sympathy with that feeling. The most minimal sense of belief, for example, is just what's left when everything else is stripped away. It's not acting in a certain way, not affirming sincerely, not anything that can be defined in terms of something else. It's too basic to be defined, but of course we've all had the experience.

OXMORE: I'd like to come back to that point, but first I'd like to probe a little more into this business of "having good reason to believe," which you used in your definition of knowledge.

HOME: Yes, certainly.

OXMORE: Your "having good reason to believe" is something like Ayer's "having a right to believe," or Chisholm's "being evident to."

HOME: Yes, all of these are attempts to sum up in a verbal formula something that's been pretty well agreed on since Plato—that knowledge is more than just true belief, and this "something more" involves some sort of evidence or ground or rationale for the belief. Just what *kind* of evidence or ground or rationale is one of the things that people disagree about. If you state the requirement carelessly, you find yourself using the idea of knowledge in order to define knowledge, which at least *looks* circular. And a good many attempts to state the requirement carefully run into one kind of difficulty or another.

OXMORE: What would be your own attempt to state the requirement?

HOME: Well, I use the verbal formula "having good reason to believe" because I think words like "evidence," which are sometimes used, are unduly restrictive. I can know that this book is red because I see it. The book is red, I believe it is, and I have good reason to believe it is. My good reason consists of my seeing the book in good light, while my perceptual organs are in a normal condition, and so on. I *could* call this my evidence, but "evidence" isn't quite the right word. If I have evidence I can give it to you, for example, but I can't in the same way give you *my* reason for believing that the book is red. What I can do is put you in a position to have your own good reason to believe that the book is red, by letting you see it.

OXMORE: So, "having good reason to believe" is intended to be wider than "having evidence for your belief"?

HOME: Yes, and it's also intended to avoid the misleading suggestion that we must have some sort of absolutely conclusive or logically impregnable reason to believe in order to say that we know. Actually, "having good reason to believe" is probably too weak in its suggestion, but I'd rather have the suggestion too weak than too strong. I can always explain more precisely what I mean.

OXMORE: Perhaps you could do that now.

HOME: Well, one way of explaining what I mean is in terms of what a reasonable man would believe in the circumstances. If my reason to believe is such that a reasonable and prudent man would believe p in those circumstances, I have good reason to believe p.

OXMORE: That sounds rather like Aristotle defining moral goodness in terms of what a good man would do.

HOME: My "reasonable man" is a legal fiction, like the "reasonable man" in law. I don't mean that you have to look around for a flesh and blood reasonable man—what you do is apply our ordinary standards of evidence or reasonable care. It's helpful to many of us to talk about a sort of ideal "reasonable man" in this connection, but we could use other language.

OXMORE: For example?

HOME: I could say that you have good reason to believe p just in case your reasons are the kind of reasons which by our ordinary standards would justify you in believing p.

OXMORE: That sounds fairly vague. Can you describe this "ordinary standard"?

HOME: Oh, but there isn't just one "ordinary standard"; there are hundreds. That's just the unrealistic expectation that skeptics have been playing on ever since the Greek skeptics discussed the "problem of the criterion." There are ordinary standards in mathematics, and quite different ordinary standards in physics. There are ordinary standards in literary criticism, and quite different ordinary standards in matters of sense perception. The attempt to make one set of standards or rather two sets, the mathematical-logical and scientific, the sole sets of standards was just what was wrong with the verificationists.

OXMORE: But do you think that in theory we could list all of our various kinds of standards—give an exhaustive list?

HOME: Yes and no. I think that there is a finite number of standards and that they could be listed. It might even be useful to do so, in a work on practical logic or methodology. For example, there might be a section on the "reference book" standard, which would state the obvious truth that some matter of fact being stated in a standard work of reference gives us good reason to believe it true. But the section might go on to give some cautions on the limitations of reference works.

OXMORE: That's your "yes"; why did you say "yes and no"?

HOME: Sorry, I got carried away by my interest in practical logic. The "no" part has to do with the mistaken idea you might get that the standards could always be stated in a completely precise way, in such a way that they could be applied mechanically. As a matter of fact, a good many of our standards refer essentially to some specialized kind of "reasonable man," a man with expertise or experience in the relevant field, and also with sound judgment. For example, we might claim to know already that the 1975 clarets from the Bordeaux region will be great wines, because experts who have tasted the young wine would stake their professional reputations on the mature wine being great.

OXMORE: That seems to leave a good deal up to the experts.

HOME: Well, experts can be checked. We can ask how well they agree among themselves, and in some cases we can check their track records.

VENNER: If I may interject—it was precisely the consideration that there must be intersubjective agreement and predictive success that caused us to reject claims to aesthetic and moral knowledge and to give mathematical and scientific methods a special status.

OXMORE: That seems to raise the question of whether any of our ordinary standards are more basic than others.

HOME: Yes, of course, some general categories are quite basic—sense perception, for example. But saying that the way of deciding whether a new wine will mature into a great wine is "sense perception," while perfectly correct, isn't very useful. But even on that level of generality I'd want to add some general categories that Venner wouldn't admit—moral intuition, for example. At one level of generality you can talk about experience and reason as the two sources of knowledge; at another you split experience into common experience, scientific experimentation, and so on, and reason into logical intuition, moral intuition, and so on.

OXMORE: You're saying that reason is a source of knowledge?

HOME: Yes. I'm a rationalist in that sense—I don't agree with the extreme empiricist that experience is the only source of knowledge.

OXMORE: Well, that's a side issue at the moment. Would you say that our standards are open to criticism, or do you just have to take them as given?

HOME: No, I'd say that our standards can be criticized, and sometimes criticism leads to modifying or dropping a specific standard. But there are some kinds of criticism of standards that are unreasonable—criticizing one type of standard for not being another type, for instance. Criticizing induction for not being deduction, for example, is like criticizing women for not being men. If you judge inductive arguments by deductive standards, they're all invalid. If you judge women's strength by the same standards as men's strength, women are comparatively weak. But if you look at things on their own terms, you find that inductive arguments have their own kind of validity, and women have their own kinds of strength.

KIRK: Then you think that the new feminists are wrong in ignoring differences between men and women?

HOME: It's always a mistake to ignore real differences. What differences are real, of course, is a matter of dispute. But that "different" doesn't mean "inferior" is a good principle to keep in mind both in sexual politics and in philosophy.

OXMORE: But to get back to knowledge, your position is that what counts as a good reason can vary from one area to another?

HOME: Yes, and from one context to another. Good reasons for believing that a car is mine may be much less stringent in ordinary life than they would be in a court of law.

OXMORE: So in a way you give no general account of knowledge at all?

HOME: Right. But that kind of general account that I refuse to give—some sort of standard that applies to knowledge in every field—is in my view a snare and a delusion, which leaves us wide open to skepticism.

OXMORE: Well, that brings us back to skepticism, where we started. Perhaps this is a good place to call a halt to the discussion between ourselves, and open the discussion to questions from the floor. I'm sorry that Home and I have rather dominated the discussion. Professor Venner will get his chance tomorrow when we talk about the philosophy of science, and Professor Kirk will, I'm sure, have plenty to say on our final topic, the meaning of life. The title of the next session is "Has Science Failed?" and I will again be chairman. Now for questions.

QUESTIONS

Answer the following questions as you think they would be answered by the panelist to whom they are addressed.

1. Professor Venner: Whenever I see a certain shade of blue I think of my Aunt Minnie. This seems to mean, on your phenomenalistic view, that seeing that shade of blue gives me grounds for a protocol statement, "Aunt Minnie is here now." Is that correct?
2. Professor Home: If nothing is certain as a starting point, how can we begin this business of claims and challenges that you speak of?
3. Professor Oxmore: How would it help us philosophically if we were able to give a satisfactory definition of knowledge?

Do you find the following answers to questions satisfactory?

4. Venner's answer to a supposed skeptical criticism of the sense-data theory.
5. Home's reply to Oxmore's criticism that his account of belief presupposes belief or knowledge.
6. Home's use of the "reasonable man" to explain belief.

Write a short essay on the following topics:

7. How might a skeptic reply to Home?
8. Defend a theory of knowledge different from Home's.
9. How is knowledge related to belief?
10. What are the sources of knowledge? Justify your answer.

FURTHER READINGS

CHISHOLM, RODERICK, *Theory of Knowledge,* Englewood Cliffs, N.J.: Prentice-Hall, Inc., 1963.

HOSPERS, JOHN, *Readings in Introductory Philosophical Analysis,* Englewood Cliffs, N.J.: Prentice-Hall, Inc., 1968.

Bouwsma, O. K., "Descartes' Evil Genius," pp. 13–21.

Descartes, René, "Philosophical Doubt," pp. 3–13.

Malcolm, Norman, "Certainty and Empirical Statements," pp. 21–44.

WILSON, MARGARET D., DAN W. BROCK, and RICHARD F. KUHNS, *Philosophy, An Introduction,* New York: Appleton-Century-Crofts, 1972.

Austin, J. L., "Knowledge and the Search for Certainty," pp. 298–304.

Descartes, René, "Knowledge and Certainty," pp. 280–84.

Plato, "Knowledge and Belief," pp. 259–70.

Questions on the Reading

1. What elements of Plato's views on knowledge and belief would be rejected by Home? By Oxmore? Why?
2. What principle does Descartes use in his discussion of knowledge? How might this principle be criticized?
3. How would you summarize Bouwsma's argument? How could a skeptic reply to Bouwsma?
4. Briefly describe the view of knowledge taken by Austin or Malcolm. What is distinctive about this view? How might it be criticized?
5. Compare Chisholm's discussion of knowledge with that in this chapter. Criticize one in terms of the other.

9

Has Science Failed?

OXMORE: I'm chairman again today, but I may find less to say than at the last session, since philosophy of science isn't really my thing. But I would like to say something about what I think is the intent of the question posed for this session. Like many other people who grew up in this century and thought of themselves as rather humane and progressive, and like many people who are rather to the left in politics, I placed a great deal of hope for the betterment of mankind on "Science" with a capital S, that is on the discoveries of scientific research and on a scientific approach to human problems. Now I still do, to some extent, but somehow these hopes have gone sour. Science hasn't proved to be the savior we hoped that it would be, and in many ways it even seems to have made human life worse instead of better—pollution, fear of atomic war, and so on. Venner, does any of this make sense to you?

VENNER: I think that perhaps to some extent your disappointment with science is based on expectations about science which were mistaken. The purpose of science is to explain and predict. If the explanations and predictions that science gives are not to your taste, then you must not blame science—that would be like blaming the newspaper because the news is bad.

OXMORE: Yes, I do see that, and I think your analogy is a good one. I don't, I think, blame science for giving us an uncomforting picture of the universe and man's place in it. If the picture that science gives us is true, it has to be accepted. I suppose really that my disillusionment with science is partly because of the uses that have been made of scientific discoveries.

VENNER: But you must not blame the scientists for this, rather the politicians.

OXMORE: I know that's often said, but it seems to me a bit of an evasion. After all, scientists could refuse to work in certain areas or refuse to release the results of certain researches.

VENNER: I cannot entirely disagree with you on this. But for a long time scientists were very naive politically, and it was only after the atomic bomb that they truly began to realize their responsibilities. On the other hand, I would ask how what you propose could be done. In the nature of science it is impossible to keep secrets over the long run—someone else can always discover what you will not divulge. You might say that nature is a blabbermouth; it is no use your trying to keep her secrets, for she will give them away to anyone who asks. Also, although this is more difficult to speak of, there is in the scientific ideal the principle that truth should not be concealed, that the results of scientific research should be freely available to all.

OXMORE: If I may ask, what sort of "should" is that?

VENNER: It is at least partly an instrumental "should"; that is, truth should not be concealed if science is to progress.

OXMORE: Yes, but that's just what I'm complaining about, the idea that science should progress no matter what. I should think that it's far more important for human life to flourish than for science to progress.

VENNER: I think the answer that a scientist might give to that is twofold. He would point out that science has done much and will do more to make human life flourish. And he might also express his personal commitment to the value of knowledge. As you know, I do not think that such personal commitments can be rationally justified, but there is no doubt that they are deeply felt by many scientists.

KIRK: If I may come to Venner's defense here, Oxmore, I'd say that you seem to be a bit inconsistent. Earlier you appeared to agree with Venner that truth was better than comfort—that if the truth about the universe would make us unhappy, it's still better to know it. But now you seem to be arguing that scientists should suppress truth in the interests of human comfort.

OXMORE: Not comfort exactly—more survival. I can't help thinking that the truth about man's place in the universe is worth knowing, and the truth about particularly simple and ingenious ways to cause death and suffering ought to be suppressed. I don't think that I'm being inconsistent here, because as a utilitarian I think that the value of knowledge is instrumental—knowledge is good insofar as it serves happiness. I suppose you, Kirk, might agree with Ross that virtue is infinitely more valuable than knowledge and knowledge is infinitely more valuable than pleasure?[1]

KIRK: No, I agree with Ross about many things, but not about that. But I would agree with him that knowledge does have an absolute value, not just an instrumental one. In that respect I'd sympathize with the scientists that Venner mentioned. But, in fact, Venner, wouldn't you agree that many scientists hold that truth has an absolute, objective value?

VENNER: Yes, but in this I think that they are philosophically naive. Do you also, Kirk, feel disillusioned with science?

KIRK: Well, I was never really illusioned with it. When Oxmore says that science has failed as a savior, my impulse as a Christian is to say that you're bound to be disappointed if you look for salvation in the wrong place. But I will tell you one thing that I feel about science and technology and the modern world of industrial production. They've made the world a great deal uglier and a great deal less satisfying emotionally. There are all sorts of reasons for this. When things like furniture and household objects were produced on a smaller scale and closer to the consumer, there was a much better chance that they would be humanly satisfying. When collections of human beings were technologically limited by the size of buildings that could be made, and so on, we didn't have the appallingly large and unmanageable cities that create so many of our problems now. I suppose I'm wandering on about trivialities, but what I feel is really the sum of so many little things. Let me give you one vivid example. Many of us, I imagine, have seen the film 2001. Well, that film expressed a certain spirit or outlook of science, it seemed to me, and in the whole thing there wasn't one place that looked comfortable, one person you felt you liked. At least I felt that way. Now I know from talking to students that this is how science affects some of them emotionally. They

---

[1] W. D. Ross, see Biography (Appendix A) and Further Readings at the end of Chapter 4.

feel that it's something cold, remote, and inhuman, and that it tends to dehumanize those who deal with it.

VENNER: I think you romanticize the past and undervalue technology. In the modern home the furniture may not be so pretty, but more comfortable furniture is available to more people. And in the kitchen is the gas or electric stove and the dishwasher to make the homemakers' lives easier, and in the living room the television to provide free entertainment.

KIRK: I'm not sure I'm entirely happy even about that. My wife and I used to have some great talks while she washed the dishes and I dried. I won't play the curmudgeon about the stuff that comes over the TV tube, although heaven knows some of it is awful. But television has certainly made people more passive and less able to entertain themselves. Still I value some of the comforts that science and technology have brought us. What I object to is a certain draining of life and color that seems to come with scientific and technological progress. More mass production, more mass thinking, more conformity in what we eat and wear and think and feel.

VENNER: But scientific research is the most creative and exciting thing imaginable!

KIRK: Yes, I know that the real discoverers in science feel that way, and quite rightly. I never knew Einstein, as you did, Venner, but I knew Enrico Fermi slightly, and there was tremendous excitement and creativity in those people who were trying to understand quantum physics. But so many people in the lower echelons of science, doing what Kuhn calls "normal science," [2] are quite dull and plodding, and do quite dull and plodding work.

OXMORE: Your mention of Kuhn reminds me as chairman to call us back to our muttons. We are supposed to be talking about the philosophy of science and not about my somewhat confused emotional reactions to science. If I might pick up on an earlier remark of yours, Venner, you said that the purpose of science is to explain and predict. But as Kirk remarked a moment ago, a good deal of science seems to be dull plodding —not involved much at all with explaining or predicting. I remember a girl I knew at Cambridge, for example, who was doing a long series of tests on some series of compounds—fluoride compounds, I think they were —just noting their properties. She wasn't explaining anything or predict-

_____

[2] T. S. Kuhn. *The Structure of Scientific Revolution* (Chicago: University of Chicago Press, 1962).

ing anything, just finding lots of rather dull facts. But she had quite a respectable research grant to do this.

VENNER: Well, to be sensible, there is a certain amount of dull routine work in any occupation. And, of course, science must accumulate a great number of facts in order to explain and predict. These facts that the young lady was accumulating about the fluorine compounds might some day enable us to verify or disverify a theory in chemistry or physics. The dull plodding you speak of is necessary if we are to compare theory with fact at a great number of points. But I assure you that many scientists find very detailed investigations quite fascinating.

OXMORE: I agree that dullness is in the eye of the beholder, and that's not really the point, of course. The point is the vast amounts of scientific work that just don't seem to have a great deal to do with either explanation or prediction. Classifying beetles, for example, or mapping stars.

HOME: I wonder if I might suggest a view about the purpose of science which I think complements Venner's and answers that sort of question.

OXMORE: Certainly. I tend to forget that you do philosophy of science, too, as well as many other things.

HOME: Well, to start a bit back from my point, it might be helpful to clarify the sort of explanation and prediction Venner has in mind. What he's thinking of, I believe, is the sort of picture of scientific explanation given to us by Hempel. To explain something scientifically is to find certain scientific laws and certain initial conditions such that a description of the thing to be explained—the *explanandum*—can be deduced from a statement of those laws and conditions. And prediction of the kind scientists are interested in is essentially the same process—finding laws and initial conditions from which you can deduce a description of a phenomenon. Roughly speaking, the whole business counts as an explanation of the phenomenon if the phenomenon is known to occur, while it counts as a prediction if the phenomenon hasn't occurred yet or hasn't been observed to occur. For example, we have a scientific law which says that freely falling bodies near the surface of the earth fall at thirty-two feet per second per second. This means that if I drop a marble from a high tower I can explain the fact that it has a velocity of sixty-four feet per second after it has dropped two seconds by means of the law and the time it was dropped. Or I can use the law to predict that two seconds after it's dropped it will be going sixty-four feet per second. This is oversimplified, of course, but I want to give some idea of the sort of explanation and prediction we're talking about.

VENNER: This is correct, but to be complete you should mention statistical laws.

HOME: This is much more complicated, of course. When you have a statistical law, what you explain or predict is usually a certain distribution. For example, genetic laws enable us to predict a certain proportion of pure red, hybrid red, and pure white pea flowers in the second generation when we breed a pure red and a pure white pea plant and then breed two of the hybrids. Or we can explain this proportion after it happens.

VENNER: This is Mendel's classical experiment.

HOME: Yes, it's an easy one to remember, and I use it as an example in classes. Philosophers of science would disagree about whether we could be said to explain the color of a particular flower in the second generation. Is it a sufficient explanation of the white color of this particular flower to say that one out of four flowers from a red hybrid cross will be white, and this is the one that happens to be the white one?

VENNER: I would say not, and this is what makes me unhappy about statistical laws in explanation.

HOME: Well, as Venner knows, because I argued it in a thesis I wrote for him, I would take the view that we have explained the white color of the flower by showing that one flower out of four must be white and that no more determinate explanation of the color is possible. Of course, in the flower case there may be a more detailed explanation, but there are cases in quantum physics in which we know that a more determinate explanation is impossible in principle.

OXMORE: Let me be clear about this. You're surely not saying that the explanation is that the flower just happens to be white?

HOME: No, imagine this kind of case. You notice that the result of breeding two red pea flowers is a white pea flower, and you're puzzled. I then explain that the two red flowers weren't pure red but hybrids from a red-white cross, and that the result of crossing such hybrids is always a pure red—two red hybrids and a pure white. The one you noticed and were puzzled by was the white one. You ask if there's any further explanation, any reason why this one of the four is white rather than that one of the four. I answer, "No, there is no further explanation." You now have all the explanation that can be given about why this flower is white." Now, that might not be true, but suppose that it was. It seems to me that it's perfectly legitimate to regard the whiteness of the flower as explained if you have all the explanation of it that it's possible to give.

OXMORE: But you haven't explained it completely.

HOME: You haven't explained it *deterministically*, certainly. But I'd want to say that you have explained it "statistically" or "stochastically," which was the term I used in my thesis. To object to stochastic explanations as inadequate is to lay down a requirement that only deterministic explanations will be regarded as adequate. And if deterministic explanations aren't always available, that requirement is unreasonable.

OXMORE: I'll let you and Venner fight that one out.

HOME: We have, we have indeed. But if I may go on with my point; you were perfectly right, Oxmore, in saying that a good deal of scientific work doesn't have much to do, at least directly, with explaining or predicting in this sense, the sense of deriving descriptions of phenomena from laws and initial conditions. And you might have gone on to say that science isn't especially interested in explaining or predicting isolated individual facts. What it does is treat classes of cases; not why this particular sunset had red and orange and purple colors, but why you get colors at sunsets at all. Not why the Northern Lights were especially spectacular tonight, but why the Northern Lights phenomena occur at all. Of course, the general explanation of a *type* of phenomenon may enable you partly or completely to explain particular cases. Once you know that colors in sunsets have to do with particles in the air breaking up light, you may connect last night's spectacular sunset with the fact that there's smoke in the air from a forest fire. Once you know that Northern Lights are connected with magnetic fields, you may be able to explain a particularly spectacular display by discovering magnetic disturbances due to sunspot activity. But by and large it is classes of cases, not particular cases except insofar as they represent classes of cases, that science is interested in.

VENNER: This seems to me to be correct.

OXMORE: This rather reminds me of what we're inclined to say about the "generalization principle" in ethics, that a judgment we make about a particular moral situation must be such that we would apply the same judgment to any similar case. Is this a connection between science and ethics?

HOME: That's an interesting point, but I think it arises from the fact that in both cases general rules or general laws are involved.

OXMORE: Yes, I see that.

KIRK: Aristotle, of course, would have said that both physics and ethics are "sciences" in his broad sense of science, and that science always deals with the general, not with the particular.

HOME: Put in more modern terminology, that might be a perfectly sound point—when we study anything theoretically, we're always looking for general principles and are not interested in individual cases. In fact, it ties in with the point I want to make, because what I want to say about science is that its purpose is to give us an organized account of whatever knowledge we can obtain about the universe. That seems to me to explain a great many things that are otherwise puzzling about science. It explains why a good deal of science is just fact gathering, because until you have the facts you can't give an organized account of them. But it also explains why science is interested in classes of cases and not individual cases, because when you're trying to organize anything you have to classify and put similar things together, setting aside the ways in which they differ.

OXMORE: I think that you owe us a bit more of an explanation of what you mean by an "organized account."

HOME: Well, at least an account that is as simple as possible—that is, as simple as the facts will let us be—and an account that is as unified as possible. Take something like the "sea of air" hypothesis for explaining facts about how vacuum pumps work, why it's hard to pull apart two hemispheres after you've put them together and pumped the air out from inside them, and other facts of that kind. The older hypothesis was "Nature hates a vacuum," and that therefore other materials would attempt to rush in and fill any vacuum. In this view, a vacuum pump works because when you create a vacuum, the water or whatever you're pumping rushes in to fill the "hated" vacuum. The hemispheres are hard to pull apart because they're trying to rush together and fill the vacuum, but they're too rigid to do it. This seems to explain, by the way, the fact that if you try to create a vacuum inside a can or bottle or something that isn't very strong, the can will crumple up or the bottle will break and the pieces fly inward, and so on. That's nature, using whatever material is at hand to fill up that awful vacuum!

OXMORE: Of course, that way of looking at the matter is awfully anthropomorphic—talking as if nature had likes and dislikes.

HOME: Yes, but even aside from that, it doesn't explain a good many observable facts—why a vacuum pump can raise a column of water only thirty-two feet, and a column of mercury only a much shorter distance. Why a certain degree of force exerted on the hemispheres will pull them apart while a lesser degree won't. Even if we were content to speak of nature anthropomorphically, her likes and dislikes begin to seem more and more arbitrary.

OXMORE: There's something very appealing imaginatively about the picture of material rushing in to fill a vacuum—after all, that's what seems to happen.

HOME: Yes, but it happens because there is a "sea" of air surrounding the earth and it exerts a pressure of about fourteen pounds per square inch at sea level. At higher altitudes your vacuum pump won't raise water as high and your hemispheres will be easier to pull apart. Out in space a vacuum pump wouldn't work and the hemispheres would not be held together. Once we realize that most of the universe consists of vacuum, the idea that "Nature hates a vacuum" is out, but we can also create as many vacuums as we like inside other materials out in space and nothing will rush in to fill them.

OXMORE: The stuff rushes in because it's pushed by air pressure, not because of any innate tendency to fill a vacuum.

HOME: Right. Now once we see this, our knowledge about other kinds of pressure—water pressure for instance—can be linked with what we've learned about air pressure. We can calculate the increased air pressure that is necessary to offset the water pressure in something like a diving suit or a bathysphere, which goes deep under water. We can apply our knowledge of hydraulics and the mechanics of fluids to problems about the motion of air masses. We can calculate about air currents and air pressures and begin to have a science of weather. In fact, air and water, two of the "elements" of the ancients, can be seen to obey the same laws and to behave in essentially similar ways. And this is a tremendous simplification and unification of our picture of the world.

OXMORE: I see, yes. But how is this different from the kind of simplification and unification of our concepts that resulted when Russell and Whitehead showed that logic and mathematics were connected, that we could build mathematics on a logical foundation?

HOME: The answer to that would depend somewhat on your philosophy of mathematics. A formalist like Venner would say that mathematics is purely a game with marks on paper, and that in giving an organized account of logic and mathematics you wouldn't be organizing "facts about the universe."

VENNER: With some qualifications, I would agree that this is my view.

HOME: I, on the other hand, would regard mathematics and logic as dealing with a different kind of facts than the empirical sciences deal with. The kind of laws we get are the easiest place to see the distinction: logical and mathematical laws are true in all possible worlds; scientific or natural laws are true for this world, but not for all possible worlds. I might add the comment that the view I've outlined has the advantage of showing the place of classification in science. A lot of routine science *is* just classifying, and if you try to explain science as *just* explanation and prediction this is a problem for you.

VENNER: I might say that Home and I do not completely disagree on the purpose of science. I emphasize explanation and prediction with a subordinate place being given to an organized account, whereas he places more importance on an organized account with a subordinate position given to explanation and prediction.

OXMORE: I'd like to hear both your views on the nature of scientific laws and the kind of necessity they have, if any.

HOME: In my view you have at least four philosophically interesting senses of necessity. A proposition is logically necessary in the narrow sense when its denial can be shown to be self-contradictory by the meanings of the terms involved and the ordinary rules of logic. A proposition is logically necessary in the wide sense, or ontologically necessary, if it's true in all possible worlds.

OXMORE: Like Kirk's metaphysical truths.

HOME: Right. A proposition is nomologically necessary—*nomos* is the Greek word for "law"—when it has the sort of necessity scientific laws have, and a proposition is chronologically necessary if it's true at all times.

OXMORE: I'll come back to chronological necessity in a minute. Haven't you ducked saying what kind of necessity scientific laws have?

HOME: Yes, because I don't really know. Venner has quite a clear view about it, which I think is wrong, and it might be useful to start with that.

OXMORE: All right. Venner, would you oblige?

VENNER: Yes, certainly. My view, which is shared by Nagel [3] and others, is that a scientific law is a universally quantified statement that contains no reference to specific times or places or individuals. To speak more loosely, it is a statement that is true at all places and all times; for instance, a statement such as "All metals expand when heated." This was true in the

[3] Ernest Nagel, *The Structure of Science* (New York: Harcourt, Brace and World, 1961).

past; it will be true in the future. It is true here; it is true on Mars or in another galaxy. It is true of specific pieces of metal, such as my wedding ring, but mentions no specific piece of metal by name.

HOME: As Professor Venner knows, I would agree that this is part of the story, but it can't be the whole story. Take a statement like, "No hat has a brim over a hundred yards wide." That's been true in the past; it will almost certainly be true in the future. It does not mention specific hats any more than Venner's example mentions specific pieces of metal. It isn't a scientific law, but rather what's called an "accidental generalization." It just *happens* that no one ever has made or ever will make a hat that big. If I offered a large prize for a hat that big, someone would make one. My objection to the type of view Venner and Nagel hold is that it fails to distinguish scientific laws from accidental generalizations.

VENNER: I acknowledge a difficulty, but I do not see it as fatal. Many cases of scientific laws can be distinguished from accidental generalizations on the ground that the accidental generalization mentions a specific thing or place or time in some indirect fashion. Professor Home's ingenious example, which he developed in a class he took from me, avoids the more obvious pitfalls. But I think that it is convincing precisely because we have in the back of our minds real laws, perhaps psychological ones, which give us confidence that no hat so big will ever be wanted.

HOME: I'm not wedded to that case, although I admit I do like it. My point is that we recognize a difference between generalizations that just happen to be true and genuine laws, and that the Venner-Nagel theory doesn't do justice to this fact.

OXMORE: Then, what's your account of the matter?

HOME: One clue is that scientific laws will support what are called "counterfactual conditionals" or "subjunctive conditionals." I can say truly that if I had a metal hat it would expand when heated, even though in fact I don't have a metal hat. I can say truly that if the first emperor of the galaxy will have a metal crown that crown will expand when heated, even if I don't know that there will ever be such an emperor. But I can't say truly that if I offer a million dollars for a hat over a hundred yards wide, the winner of the prize would be under a hundred yards wide. Barring a miracle—that is, a suspension of natural law—any piece of metal anywhere in the universe, anytime in history, can be counted on to expand when heated. But hats can't be counted on in that way to be under a hundred yards wide, although they almost certainly will always be smaller than that.

VENNER: To this I would reply that the natural laws or scientific laws are just those completely universal statements which we do have confidence will be true always and everywhere.

OXMORE: I don't want to raise this point prematurely, but how can you be sure of that?

VENNER: There are two possible answers. You can say with Popper that we don't really know that scientific laws are true, we only have confidence in them based on the fact that they have not been refuted so far despite attempts to refute them.[4] Or you can say, with Carnap and others, that you can assign a probability or confirmation to such laws based on the evidence.

OXMORE: I want to come back to that in a moment, but first I want to ask Home why he can't define a scientific law just as a completely general statement that will support a counterfactual.

HOME: Because when you try to define a counterfactual, you find that in order to divide counterfactuals from other conditionals you have to bring in the idea of a law. If I'm justified in saying that if my hat were metal it would expand when heated, it's because I think there's a true scientific law that all metals expand when heated. So trying to use counterfactuals to define scientific law turns out to be circular.

OXMORE: What would you do then about defining scientific law?

HOME: The least unsatisfactory way I know of going about it is to say that a scientific law must be part of a system of generalizations that enable us to explain and predict a wide variety of phenomena. This connects with my idea of science as an organized account of the facts. But there are a lot of messy details that need working out.

OXMORE: If I may clear up one detail that puzzled me, what do you mean by saying that chronologically necessary statements are true at all times? Aren't all true statements true at all times?

HOME: There's a dispute in the philosophy of logic about that. The establishment view is that true statements are "timelessly true." So that statements about what will happen tomorrow are somehow always true. Some people think that this implies determinism, but all the attempts to prove this have involved fallacious arguments.

OXMORE: Like those that Ryle exposed in *Dilemmas?* [5]

---

[4] Sir Karl Popper, *The Logic of Scientific Discovery* (London: Hutchinson & Co., 1959), Chap. 4.

[5] Gilbert Ryle, *Dilemmas* (Cambridge: Cambridge University Press, 1956).

HOME: Those and others. I'd incline toward the view that we can talk of statements being true at a time, and that only necessary statements are always true. Statements about events become true or false when those events occur and are true or false ever after. But there's no statement that is now true about contingent events in the future. If you don't like this view, you can define chronological necessity in terms of sentences. Thus the sentence, "No hat has a brim more than a hundred yards wide at time t" makes a true statement for all values of t, and is thus chronologically necessary. But it's not part of a system of lawlike sentences that give an organized account of facts about the universe, so it's not nomologically necessary.

OXMORE: I think that removes my discomfort, and to explore whether your view or the establishment one is correct would lead us too far afield. Therefore, I'd like to return to the matter of how we know the truth of scientific laws. I'm thinking here of "Hume's problem of induction." Hume argued, of course, that any inference from observed facts to unobserved facts required some sort of principle of the uniformity of nature, and that such a principle could not be justified. To take a law like "All metals expand when heated" seems to refer to a good many cases that haven't been observed yet. But our evidence for it is necessarily the evidence of observed cases. So to assert the truth of "All metals expand when heated," or even its probability, is to go from observed cases to unobserved ones. This doesn't seem to be deductively justifiable, since after all, it's logically possible that all the unobserved cases could be completely unlike the observed cases. But you can't argue from past experience, or anything of that sort, because that would beg the question. Arguing from past experience is, after all, an instance of arguing from observed cases to unobserved ones. Now I know that there are lots of attempts to get around this somehow, but none of them seem to me to be successful. Have I stated the problem fairly?

HOME: Yes, very well. It might help to state it formally as a sort of dilemma, using induction as shorthand for "arguing from observed cases to unobserved ones." The dilemma is this: Induction itself must be justified either inductively or deductively. It can't be justified deductively, and to attempt to justify it inductively would beg the question. Therefore, induction itself can't be justified at all. To get out of the dilemma you either have to justify induction deductively, or else show that justifying induction inductively is not to beg the question, or else show that induction and deduction don't exhaust the possibilities—in other words, show that you can justify induction in a way which is neither deductive nor inductive. I think that exhausts the possibilities.

VENNER: Not quite, I believe. I myself would try to show that induction does not stand in need of justification—that the so-called problem of the justification of induction is a pseudo-problem.

HOME: I was thinking of the dismissal of the problem as coming under my last category. Because after all there seems to be a problem here, and if you successfully dismiss it you've justified induction in the only sense that matters. And presumably your justification is neither deductive or inductive but philosophical.

VENNER: It was then merely a difference in terminology. Reichenbach, you will remember, called what is improperly asked for by those who ask that induction be justified inductively or deductively "justification," and called his own defense of induction a "vindication" of induction rather than a justification.[6]

HOME: Yes, actually I think that there's a great deal to be said for sorting out the senses in which induction can and can't be justified, and distinguishing them in some way. For instance, when you say that the justification of induction is a pseudo-problem. Just that you can't justify induction deductively or inductively? Or do you mean that justification of any sort is somehow illegitimate? And if you do, what does that come to?

VENNER: Well, let us go step by step. The first step is easy to agree on, and this is that the skeptic who criticizes inductive arguments for not being deductive is unreasonable.

OXMORE: We can agree on that, of course. But there is a certain difficulty which has to be dealt with about the fact that inductive arguments are not deductively valid. You remember the old joke that in the first part of the usual introductory logic book, the section on deductive logic, all of the fallacies are described, and in the second part, on inductive logic, all of these same fallacies are committed.

HOME: Yes, but this arises from too narrow an idea of deduction. An argument from the fact that observed pieces of metal expand when heated to the generalization that all metal expands when heated is in one sense deductively invalid—it is an argument from "some" to "all." But we can also treat it as a probability inference. The probability of a given hypothesis on certain evidence can be calculated by using Bayes' Theorem, provided that we know the original probability of the hypothesis and

---

[6] Hans Reichenbach, "On the Justification of Induction," *Journal of Philosophy,* 37 (1940).

the evidence. If we do not know this, then we can approximate the support that a hypothesis is given by certain evidence by using the principle of maximum likelihood. We favor the hypothesis which gives the observed evidence the highest probability. Thus the hypothesis that all metals expand when heated is favored because it gives the highest probability to the observed evidence. This is all a matter of probability theory, which is part of mathematics, and mathematics is purely deductive. Thus, if we consider probability theory, we see that inductive inferences are not deductively invalid at all. Rather, the skeptic has chosen the wrong deductive model for them.

OXMORE: Wait a moment. You seem to be saying that induction can be deductively justified after all. And surely that's wrong.

HOME: No, there is still an important difference between the deductive inferences of ordinary logic and those probabilistic inferences that make up what we call inductive logic. In both cases the conclusion follows validly from the premises. But in the case of inductive inference, the conclusion is a probabilistic one. Instead of saying "If A then B, A, therefore B," we say, "We have evidence A, the probability of B given A is N, therefore the probability of B is N." The conclusion gives us only a probability, not a certainty.

OXMORE: Then the conclusion can be false.

HOME: No. Remember the conclusion is just a probability statement that follows validly from your premises. Not "B," but "the probability of B is N."

OXMORE: All right, but even though B has a high probability, it may not occur.

HOME: That's all right, it's just saying that B has a high probability but not a probability of one.

OXMORE: Yes, but isn't what worries people the idea that the whole thing could come unstuck somehow—that reasonable expectations based on probabilities might completely mislead us?

HOME: I could try to have you make that more precise, but I think I know what's bothering you. What you have in mind is the possibility that the universe is or might become what I call a "counterinductive universe"; that is, a universe in which it does no good to calculate probabilities, because probabilities are not a guide to the future. There are two ways that could happen. One is that the universe might be a "pure chance" universe with no real regularities. A fair game of chance is like that in a way. If the roulette wheel isn't fixed, there's no way of knowing which of the possible numbers will come up. In a complex universe with an indefinitely large or infinite number of possibilities which might "come up," all equally likely, you could figure probabilities, but they'd be of no use to you.

OXMORE: What is the other kind of counterinductive universe?

HOME: One with a Cartesian "evil demon" who always found out how you were going to act and then maneuvered things so as to frustrate you.

OXMORE: I see. And in either case the past history of the universe could be as we know it. There may have been "runs of luck" which deceived us into thinking that there were real regularities in the chance universe, and the demon may have been leading us on in the other case.

HOME: You've got the idea.

OXMORE: But now for the big question. How do we know that the universe isn't counterinductive? Venner, can you answer that, or don't you go along with what Home has been saying?

VENNER: It is not precisely the way in which I would attack the problem, but I am content to work within Home's approach. I would say that we cannot *know* that the universe is not counterinductive, but that it is not is a presupposition of scientific inquiry. The picture of the universe that I tried to describe when we discussed determinism, a universe governed by unalterable laws, must be an assumption of any attempt to think about the universe rationally.

OXMORE: This sounds to me rather like what Austin said about the problem of other minds—that the existence of other persons like ourselves is a presupposition of any attempt to talk at all, and there's an end to it.[7]

VENNER: Perhaps that is so. I have always had great respect for Professor Austin, and I am not uncomfortable to find myself giving an answer similar to his, although to a different problem.

HOME: I'm afraid that in both cases just saying that it's a presupposition, and that's all there is to it, isn't completely satisfactory. In the case of other minds, I'm willing to regard their existence as a hypothesis that can be justified inductively. In the case of whether or not our universe is counterinductive, I'd argue first that the mere possibility that it is cuts no ice. That's the old skeptical tactic—trying to go from a mere possibility

[7] John L. Austin, "Other Minds," in *Proceedings of the Aristotelian Society,* Supplementary Vol. XX, 1946.

to some substantive conclusion. Second, I'd treat the possibility that the universe is counterinductive as a hypothesis like any other, and argue that the observed evidence gives us good reason to favor the hypothesis that the universe is not counterinductive over the hypothesis that it is.

OxMORE: But look here. First you seem to make induction a sort of special type of deduction, and then when a difficulty arises about that, you use your inductive method itself to get around the difficulty. You combine a deductive justification of induction with an inductive justification of induction!

HOME: Yes, if you like. That may be precisely what's needed to get around the traditional problem of induction.

KIRK: If I might get a word in, I find Home's counterinductive universe very interesting. It's very much like the chance universe I described in our second meeting. But it seems to me that you can't just reject that sort of picture of the universe without putting some other picture in its place. As a theist I find that the only picture of the universe which really leaves room for human reason, either deductive or inductive, is the theistic one.

OxMORE: Well, just to join the procession I might say that I'd defend induction by analyzing our language, and trying to show that our standards for good inductive arguments arise from the meaning of the terms we use. What this proves, I suspect, is that each of us provides a justification of induction in terms of his own philosophical position. I do so in terms of ordinary language, Kirk in theological and metaphysical terms, Home in terms of logic and probability, and Venner, I gather, in terms of a scientific world view. And I suppose the moral of that is that there isn't any sort of philosophically neutral solution to the problem of induction. Or perhaps to any other philosophical problem. They all hang together, and you can't really answer one without answering them all. I know this is heresy for an Oxford philosopher, because we're popularly supposed to tackle problems piecemeal and not to try to develop a unified view. But I think that with our best people, like Austin, the objection was always to tackling the bigger problems too hastily or without getting all the pieces on the board, not an objection to handling the big problems at all.

I hope that I haven't talked too much as chairman, or let my own interests dominate the discussion too much. I've enjoyed my brief spell of power, but I'll be glad to hand the reins back to Home for our final session. The topic we've been handed is "What can philosophy tell us about the meaning of life?" which is a rather large order, but we'll see what we can do with it. Now, what about questions for this session?

QUESTIONS

Answer the following questions as you think they would be answered by the panelist to whom they are addressed.

1. Professor Oxmore: As a utilitarian, shouldn't you conclude that science is justified because it has done more good than harm?
2. Professor Venner: Since you are not a scientist yourself, how can you speak for science?
3. Professor Home: How can you call something an explanation when you can't say why A has happened rather than B?

Do you find the following answers to questions satisfactory?

4. Kirk's answer to the objection that he romanticizes the past.
5. Venner's answer to the objection that not all science is explanatory or predictive.
6. Home's answer to the objection that not all simplification and unification of our experience is scientific.

Write short essays on the following topics:

7. What kind of necessity, if any, do scientific laws have?
8. What is the purpose of science?
9. What objections can you find to Home's theory about science?
10. How would you solve "Hume's problem of induction?"

FURTHER READINGS

HEMPEL, CARL, *Philosophy of Natural Science*, Englewood Cliffs, N.J.: Prentice-Hall, Inc., 1966.

HOSPERS, JOHN, *Readings in Introductory Philosophical Analysis*, Englewood Cliffs, N.J.: Prentice-Hall, Inc., 1968.

    Feigl, Herbert, "De Principiis non est Disputandom?" pp. 111–35.

    Gasking, Douglas, "Causation and Recipes," pp. 145–52.

    Hume, David, "The Problem of Induction," pp. 107–11.

WILSON, MARGARET D., DAN W. BROCK, and RICHARD F. KUHNS, *Philosophy, An Introduction*, New York: Appleton-Century-Crofts, 1972.

Hempel, Carl, "The Covering Law Model of Explanation," pp. 425–34.

Nagel, Ernest, "The Nature of Scientific Laws," pp. 413–25.

Russell, Bertrand, "On Induction," pp. 399–404.

Questions on the Reading

1. Hempel, Nagel, and Feigl were all associated with the Vienna Circle group. How do their views reflect this? In what ways do they differ?
2. Summarize Russell's or Hume's statement of the "problem of induction." Will Home's solution to the problem work against their formulation of it?
3. Discuss Gasking's view of causation and criticize his view, drawing on the discussion in this chapter.
4. How does Feigl's discussion of justification apply to the problem of induction?
5. What criticisms can be made of Hempel's view of science?

10

Philosophy and the Meaning of Life

HOME: We've arrived at our final session. Before we close I'll have some thank-yous to say to our panelists and to the others who have made all this possible, but for the moment let's get down to business. As chairman for our final session I'm a little unhappy with the question for this time, which is. "What can Philosophy tell us about the meaning of life?" It seems to me that this breaks down into two questions at least, because the answer you give to a question like this depends a great deal on your conception of philosophy. So perhaps we could start off by asking ourselves "What is Philosophy?" and in light of that try to answer the question "What is the meaning of life?" or at least try to give such answers to it as we think are possible. Professor Venner, perhaps you could get us started off on the question, "What is Philosophy?"

VENNER: Of course. I am very happy to have taken part in this colloquium, which I understand was somewhat in the nature of an experiment. It seems to me that there should be far more discussion of philosophy than is allowed for at most meetings of philosophers. The very considerable success of the Vienna group in changing philosophical tendencies was in part due to the constant free discussion on all topics which went on in our group.

Perhaps to give you some idea of my approach to philosophy it would be useful to be somewhat autobiographical. When I was a young student at the University of Vienna soon after World War I, the prevailing atmosphere was very much influenced by Kant.[1] Our professors seemed to be very profound, but also to be very, very obscure. Some of us who were younger students began to feel that we would like more clarity, and also more justification for many of the things we were taught. Many of us, you understand, had begun in the sciences or mathematics and found ourselves interested in philosophy because of problems growing out of these disciplines. It was very difficult to discuss our dissatisfactions with most of our professors—faculty-student relationships were much more formal in those days. However, there was one young faculty member, Morris Schlick, who represented to some extent the tradition at Vienna that went back to earlier times, a tradition of critical thinking influenced by science.[2] Schlick was also very much interested in his students and very encouraging to them. So there evolved a small group of students who would meet at Schlick's home or at various cafes or beer gardens to discuss philosophy. Not all of us were philosophy students; some were in mathematics or one of the sciences. Gradually we came to an agreement on many issues and then to something like a program or almost a party platform, which we began to present at various philosophical meetings. Schlick, by a piece of tragic irony, was fatally shot in 1936 by an unbalanced student who felt that Schlick had been unfair to him. After that the dominant spirit in our group was Rudolf Carnap.[3]

HOME: May I break in to clarify something for the audience, Professor Venner? Some philosophers would say that the Vienna Circle was very much influenced by Ludwig Wittgenstein.[4] Would you say that was incorrect?

VENNER: It is at least very much exaggerated. As you know, Wittgenstein was an Austrian, but came to England before World War I to study what was then known as aeronautical engineering. This led him to study mathematics, and he became interested in the foundations of mathematics, which eventually brought him to Cambridge to study with Bertrand Russell. However, he returned to Vienna before the war, and served in the Austrian Army. He was captured and spent some time as a prisoner of war. Both in the army and in prison camp he was able to do some philosophy, and by the end of the war he had completed his first book,

[1] Immanuel Kant, see Biography (Appendix A).
[2] Morris Schlick, see Biography (Appendix A).
[3] Rudolf Carnap, see Biography (Appendix A).
[4] Ludwig Wittgenstein, see Biography (Appendix A).

the *Tractatus Logico-Philosophicus*.[5] This was a very impressive work, and when Wittgenstein came back to Vienna after the war many of us were prepared to welcome him with much respect. But he was never a great success with the Vienna Circle. We were already accustomed to free discussion on all topics, and Wittgenstein we found very didactic and overbearing. He also quarrelled very easily with those he disagreed with. Once or twice he came to our meetings; then for a time he lived somewhere up in the hills and a few members of the group went like ambassadors back and forth from the circle to Wittgenstein. But at last he quarrelled even with them.

HOME: I think it only fair to say that other people have given different accounts of Wittgenstein's influence on the Vienna Circle, Professor Venner. I accept your account, but there are those who would disagree strongly.

VENNER: This I will concede. I am certainly not neutral in the matter. I am a partisan of one side in these disagreements. Also I was a student at the time, so that some of these things I only know of secondhand. But what I have said is based on information given to me by men in positions to know, and I trust their accounts.

OXMORE: The fact is that the recent history of anything controversial is always subject to conflicting accounts. And this goes for supposedly official histories as well as anecdotal accounts such as the one Venner has just given us. If you asked me for a good history of recent philosophy I'd probably recommend one like Passmore's or Warnock's while Venner might recommend Reichenbach's book or something similar.[6] Each of these would be written from a point of view and would interpret facts in accordance with that point of view. It's not till the passions have died down that you get reasonably objective history. So instead of bending over backwards trying to be completely fair, let's just warn the audience that we all have our prejudices, and get on with it. You'd say then, Venner, that Wittgenstein wasn't the major influence on the Vienna Circle?

VENNER: Certainly we were influenced by his ideas to some extent, but I think also some ideas were in the air at that time. Many of us in the Vienna Circle wanted a scientific approach to philosophy and our ideas of science were largely influenced by mathematics and physics. The verification principles was an attempt to formalize our feeling that all important general truths were either like mathematical truths, in that

---

[5] Published in English by Routledge & Kegan Paul, 1922.
[6] John Passmore, G. Warnock, Hans Reichenbach; for these histories of recent philosophy, see Bibliography (Appendix B, Part X).

their denial was self-contradictory, or like the truths of physics in that they could be verified by experiment and observation. The attempt to formalize that insight was never entirely successful.

HOME: Some philosophers would simply identify the Vienna Circle movement—logical positivism or whatever you prefer to call it—with adherence to the verification principle and say that if any philosophical position is clearly wrong, logical positivism is. They would say that the verification principle is self-refuting. If you try to divide meaningful statements only into those whose denial is self-contradictory and those that can be verified by the methods of science, which is what I understand by the verification principle, then you find that the principle itself doesn't fall into either category. Its denial isn't self-contradictory, and it can't be verified by any experiment or observation.

VENNER: This supposes that you can apply the principle to itself.

HOME: But if you can't, then isn't there at least one important true statement that does not fall under the verification principle? And if there is one, there might be others.

VENNER: As you know, there were many attempts to rehabilitate the verification principle—as an analysis of language, as an idealization of language, as a recommendation, as a methodological principle, and so on.

HOME: But were any of them successful?

VENNER: Perhaps not entirely successful, no. For me, I think the verification principle retains the status of a useful rule of method. If you present to me a general statement, I will ask you whether it is analytic—that is, whether its denial is self-contradictory. If the statement is not analytic, I ask you how it can be confirmed or disconfirmed by experience. If you cannot answer me, then you will have very great difficulty in persuading me that the statement is meaningful.

HOME: Then, you no longer defend the principle, but you still use it?

VENNER: I no longer defend it as an absolute test for meaningfulness or truth. But as a good rule of method, I defend it on the basis of my experience. However, let me object simply to identifying our ideas at that time with the verification principle. Even the name that came to be applied to our movement indicates a wider background. We accepted the name "positivism" for our movement because we felt that its roots went back to an earlier movement of that name, which rejected metaphysics and emphasized a scientific approach. We added the adjective "logical" because we felt that the new discoveries in mathematical logic made by

Bertrand Russell [7] and others enable us to put philosophy on a really scientific basis. We also identified ourselves with the empirical tradition in England, especially with Hume, and with empirical philosophy elsewhere. Some of us were even so broadminded as to find some parts of Aristotle congenial.

In England, the movement was more often called "logical empiricism," which was the term Russell preferred at that time. We felt that Russell, and other English philosophers, were allies of our movement, if not actually members of it. And of course A. J. Ayer visited Vienna and then wrote *Language, Truth and Logic* which popularized our ideas in the English-speaking world.[8] There were also allies of our movement elsewhere—in Berlin where philosophers excited by Einstein's work were doing mainly philosophy of science, in Poland where there was a school of very able logicians generally sympathetic to our aims.

Logic was important because we felt that the solution to many difficulties in philosophy was to create a really clear and scientific language for the discussion of philosophical and scientific problems. Bernard Shaw made a joke that the way to make socialism work in England was to get rid of the English working class and replace them with sensible people. We felt, you might say, that the way to make philosophy work was to get rid of English and German and so on, and replace them with a sensible language.

HOME: Do you still feel that this will work?

VENNER: I have never entirely abandoned this ideal. The work of some Scandinavian and American philosophers offers good hope, I think, that we can find a precise language in which to state and solve certain ethical and epistemological problems. The great work of Carnap in induction logic—the logic of scientific method—was, I believe, another partial success of the idea of an "ideal language."

But along with this ideal was a very practical and piecemeal approach to many problems. The final quarrel, for instance, between Wittgenstein and Carnap was over physical research. Carnap took the position that this was a matter for empirical investigation, and that perhaps some discovery would be made which would have to be fitted into our world picture. Wittgenstein was very annoyed, and said that Carnap had no—it is hard to put it in English exactly—no intuition, no sense of what is philosophically profitable. This is not untypical of the two approaches. It was Carnap's approach to investigate patiently, to wait and see. It was

---

[7] Bertrand Russell, see Biography (Appendix A).
[8] A. J. Ayer, see Biography (Appendix A) and Further Readings at the end of this chapter.

Wittgenstein's tendency to lay down a principle and judge the facts by that principle. But possibly I am not fair to Wittgenstein. Professor Oxmore, perhaps you can fill in the picture.

OXMORE: No, not really. I believe that Bertrand Russell and G. E. Moore [9] at Cambridge felt very much the same revolt against the older generation of Cambridge philosophers that you felt in Vienna. Both Moore and Russell were very much impressed by Wittgenstein. They helped to get him a Cambridge degree, for which the *Tractatus* was accepted as a thesis, and a lecturing job at Cambridge. Russell was extremely generous in giving Wittgenstein credit for his influence on the ideas in some of Russell's writing at that period, and Moore actually attended Wittgenstein's lectures for a period of time. As Wittgenstein changed his earlier ideas and decided that philosophical progress lay in looking at ordinary language instead of trying to replace it with an ideal language, Russell lost sympathy with him, but he grew closer to Moore in many ways. Moore's philosophy of common sense and Wittgenstein's philosophy of ordinary language had many points of contact.

But you must understand that philosophy at Cambridge is a much smaller and more specialized affair than it is at Oxford. We have a couple of dozen independent colleges at Oxford, and even the smallest of them have two or three philosophers on their staffs. Philosophy is very much more mixed up with what you might call general education than it is at Cambridge. For example, a great many politicians or civil servants have read a fair amount of philosophy if they were up at Oxford. So we have a rather large philosophical community at Oxford, rather more variety and rather more continuity. There was certainly a group of so-called young Turks at Oxford after the Great War (as we quaintly called the First World War), and we were influenced by ideas from Vienna and Cambridge. But there were always some factors that made for unity, and what goes on at Oxford always seems much more important to Oxford people than what goes on elsewhere. One intellectual influence, for example, on Oxford between the two world wars was the big translation of Aristotle's works under the editorship of Ross, in which many Oxford philosophers were involved directly or indirectly. This helped to interest us in certain sorts of problems and perhaps also to some extent in questions of philology and linguistics.

One characteristic idea of the early period at Oxford was that a great many philosophical problems could be solved by paying careful attention to ordinary language, to the ways in which words were used in everyday contexts as opposed to the odd way in which the same words

---

[9] G. E. Moore, see Biography (Appendix A) and Further Readings at the end of this chapter.

were used by philosophers. I don't deny that there was some influence from Wittgenstein here, but it was indirect. We were influenced by Gilbert Ryle, who later wrote the influential book *The Concept of Mind*.[10] He in turn was perhaps influenced by Wittgenstein, but the ideas reached us in a Rylian form, not in a Wittgensteinian form. After World War II things took a rather different turn. There were people at Oxford who would definitely call themselves Wittgensteinian, and there was a group centering around John Austin who looked at language in a very systematic way.[11] But I'm trying to recapture the Oxford atmosphere at the time Wittgenstein himself was flourishing, and although we might have agreed with the later Wittgeinstein that philosophical mistakes concealed linguistic mistakes of a certain sort, we were more likely to talk in Ryle's terms than in Wittgenstein's.

HOME: And do you still feel that philosophical problems are essentially linguistic?

OXMORE: Well, like Professor Venner, I feel a certain loyalty to the enthusiasms of my youth. But although I might still say something of the sort now, I think that I'd mean something rather different by it than I did then. Nowadays I'd say that the important task of philosophy is to explore and understand the conceptual structure of our language, and I don't rule out the possibility that after having thoroughly understood that structure we might have good reason to change it. I'd agree with Austin's formula—ordinary language isn't necessarily the last word in philosophy, but it must be the first word. I think in the early days we thought it was both the first *and* the last word.

HOME: In a little while I want to try to do some drawing together, and see if we can find some areas of agreement. I think the importance of language for philosophy is one point of agreement between the logical positivists and the ordinary language philosophers, while one of the major points of disagreement is whether we should replace ordinary language with an ideal language based on mathematical logic, or spend a great deal of time trying to understand the structure of ordinary language and even its finer details and nuances.

VENNER: That is neat but perhaps too simple. As the Vienna school matured, we admitted the necessity of careful analysis of ordinary language before it was replaced with a clearer and more useful language. We also grew more modest, hoping to replace key concepts with more accurate ones piecemeal, rather than replacing the whole language. I re-

---

10 Published in the United States by Barnes and Noble, 1949.
11 J. L. Austin, see Biography (Appendix A) and Further Readings at the end of this chapter.

member Carnap talking to two young students who were very much enthused about the ordinary language school of philosophy. Carnap agreed with them that we must spend a good deal of time analyzing a concept before explicating it—replacing it with a clearer and more useable concept. Carnap mentioned a year or two as a reasonable time to spend in analysis, and it seemed to me that the young students were very much taken aback. They had thought perhaps that a day or two, or a week or two, would be sufficient to understand a concept, and here was this logical positivist recommending a year or two of careful study of a concept!

HOME: It does seem that this kind of attitude on the part of the former Vienna Circle people, and the attitude expressed by Austin that ordinary language might not be the last word, represents a coming together of the two schools, so now the difference is one of emphasis.

OXMORE: There's something to that.

VENNER: Yes, I agree.

HOME: Perhaps we should let Professor Kirk give his reaction to what has been said so far.

KIRK: My main difficulty with both the early logical positivists and the early Oxford philosophers, and both the early and late Wittgensteinians, was that they so often seemed to be trying to settle philosophical arguments by *fiat*. They would tell me that something I wanted to say was nonsense or that it was a misuse of ordinary language or that I didn't have a criterion and therefore didn't know what I was talking about. But it always seemed to me that what I wanted to say turned out to be much clearer and better supported than their theories about verification or about ordinary language or about criteria.

Perhaps a good example of what I'm talking about is the problem of free will and determinism. In the early stages all of these movements were quite convinced that there was no problem at all about free will or that the solutions was quite simple. Morris Schlick wrote a paper arguing that free will was a pseudo-problem. The ordinary language people argued that something like a happy young bridegroom getting married was a "paradigm case" of a free action, and that therefore free will must exist and be compatible with whatever science tells us about the world. The Wittgensteinians told me that the whole thing was a muddle that arose from trying to use words in inappropriate contexts. The remarkable thing was that all of these supposedly neutral answers to or dissolutions of the problem seemed to amount to assuming one particular answer to the problem—usually the "soft determinist" solution—without argument.

Or to get into my own area, philosophy of religion, almost all of the adherents of these schools were telling me that it was quite nonsensical to talk about God or believe in His existence. But none of them seemed to produce any new criticisms of the traditional arguments for God's existence, or to produce any new arguments against His existence. Those that considered the matter at all seemed to think Hume had done everything necessary, and seemed to have no idea that anyone had objections to Hume's criticisms.

The main thrust of their criticism, however, was that talk about God was nonsensical for one reason or another. But when you looked at their arguments they seemed, to me at any rate, to be far more open to question than any of the traditional arguments pro and con. If you granted their ideas about meaning, of course, the appropriate answers came out, but their theories about meaning seemed the very thing that could not be supported. For a while some of the Wittgensteinians seemed to be saying that there was no possible conflict between science and religion because science talk and religious language were two different languages. But it turned out that words like "know" and "true" belonged to science talk and not to God talk, so I was always a bit suspicious of the Wittgensteinians as friends of religion. Lately the Wittgensteinians have been helpfully clarifying religious language for us by explaining we did not really mean anything by it that we thought we meant, so my suspicions have been confirmed.

Lately there are a good many signs that the positivists and the Oxford philosophers have begun to argue again instead of trying to settle questions without argument. I understand that determinism isn't a pseudo-problem any more, and there are even some signs that we may be able to argue about God again, and even about life after death. Kant said that God, freedom and immortality are the basic metaphysical problems.[12] So if God, freedom, and immortality are being argued again I feel that we're on our way back to traditional philosophical concerns. I welcome such a return, but I feel that some of us have never been away, so to speak.

HOME: Do you really want to say that the positivists and ordinary language philosophers had abandoned argument?

KIRK: That's an exaggeration in some ways, of course. There were always areas in which arguments went on. But very often when you traced

[12] Immanuel Kant, see Biography (Appendix A) and Further Readings at the end of Chapter 4.

the argument back to its premises, you found that basic to the argument was a certain highly disputable view of language or meaning. There were a good many arguments within that framework, but not too many about the framework.

VENNER: It seems to me that the history of arguments about the verification principle belies what you say.

KIRK: Yes, but very often there the argument was started by people like me, who criticized the principle from outside. In fact sometimes it *was* me.

OXMORE: I'd also like to enter a cautionary explanation. It sometimes seems to me on looking back that we talked almost nothing *but* philosophy, about philosophy in the early days of the ordinary language movement.

KIRK: In the case of Oxford philosophy it was often very much a family fight—Austinians against Wittgensteinians, for example. You weren't always very open to outside criticism. There was that incident some years ago when Ryle refused to allow a review in *Mind* of a book very critical of Oxford philosophy.[13]

OXMORE: It was really a rather gratuitously offensive book.

KIRK: Can you imagine Socrates refusing to argue with Thrasymachus because he was "gratuitously offensive"?

OXMORE: Touché. I do think Ryle was wrong in that case.

KIRK: The case itself was a tempest in a teapot—it's the attitude it revealed that I object to.

HOME: Perhaps we could divert the discussion from old wrongs, and try to explore some areas of agreement. I take it that we can all agree on the great importance of clarity for philosophical discussion.

VENNER: Very much so. Part of our desire for an ideal language was a desire to get away from what we felt was the obscurity of ordinary language.

OXMORE: Yes, certainly. If I may quote Austin once more, "Perhaps clarity is not enough, but it will be time to argue that when we are within measurable distance of clarity on any subject."

KIRK: I think we might argue about whether clarity is enough a little sooner than Austin thought, but certainly clarity is a *sine qua non* of

---

[13] Ernest Gellner, *Words and Things* (London: Victor Gollancz, 1958).

philosophy. If you're not clear about what you're saying, how can you decide whether you're right or wrong?

VENNER: If an old opponent of Professor Kirk's may be allowed to make a comment—I have often found Professor Kirk to be wrong, but I have never known him to take refuge in obscurity. He is always admirably clear.

HOME: Another thing we might agree on is a critical attitude in philosophy—a readiness to consider both sides of every question, to leave no assumption unexamined, to test every statement by raising possible objections.

OXMORE: I'd certainly agree to that, and for that very reason Professor Kirk's accusations sting somewhat. It seems to me that discussion at Oxford has always been very frank and free and that we've always been able to accommodate a wide variety of viewpoints.

HOME: Certainly as a student I found both Professor Venner and Professor Oxmore very ready to listen to criticism and to consider' them fairly.

KIRK: I don't deny that many contemporary philosophers have the virtue of a critical attitude, or that many traditional philosophers have lacked it. In fact, the period just before this one was rather a bad one. Philosophers tended to think of themselves as members of a school or party, and felt themselves bound to defend the views of that school, almost like a partisan politician. But if you go back to the great periods of philosophy it seems to me you find a genuinely critical attitude. Plato's earlier dialogues, where the parties to the dialogue say more than "Yes " and "Certainly," are a good example of this genuine critical openness. In the *Parmenides*, the young Socrates got rather the worst of the argument, and in the *Phaedo* the arguments against immortality are strongly urged. Another example is the *Summa Theologica* of Saint Thomas Aquinas, where each question is posed, the objections to Aquinas' solution are posed first, then the argument for his view is given and the objections answered. A critical attitude seems to me to be another *sine qua non* of philosophy—if you haven't considered all objections fairly, how can you have any confidence in your own view?

VENNER: One minor point which perhaps might be raised is that if we put our arguments into formal logic then we will find whether we are making any hidden assumptions, for we will not be able to show that a conclusion follows validly from its premises unless all of the premises are stated explicitly.

HOME: Perhaps assumptions may still lurk in the premises themselves or even in our rules of inference. But I agree that putting arguments in deductive form can be very illuminating. Another possible area of agreement is the importance of argument in philosophy. Can we add a willingness to base our beliefs and opinions on argument as another of what Kirk calls the *sine qua nons* of philosophy?

OXMORE: Yes, that's so obvious that I'm going to add one qualification to it. Sometimes what is needed in philosophy is not so much an argument as an accurate description of a situation or a reminder of things that we already in some sense know. But that argument is very important, I'm sure we can all agree.

KIRK: I'll copy Oxmore by adding a caution. What counts as an argument can itself vary with one's philosophical position. But I'm quite content with clarity, criticism, and argument as the three *sine qua nons* of philosophy.

VENNER: To this I would certainly agree. But perhaps we should interrogate our former student, Professor Home, as to how much he agrees or disagrees with those who have been his teachers. He has not given his own view of philosophy.

HOME: I'd be happy to, and I think to some extent my attitude is shared by many younger philosophers. We could call ourselves analytic philosophers, and would think of logical positivism and ordinary language philosophy as earlier forms of analytic philosophy, from which we've learned a great deal. From logical positivism we've learned what I'd call the technique of logical analysis; from ordinary language philosophy what I'd call the technique of linguistic analysis. What we would reject is the idea that either logical analysis or linguistic analysis is the only legitimate philosophical technique. We feel free to learn from Aristotle or Aquinas or Kirk whatever traditional philosophy has to teach us. I like to think that we've learned a good deal from the past history of philosophy, without being a captive of any school or party or movement.

We are certainly out of sympathy with a good deal of what is called philosophy in the East, and even with a good deal of what is called philosophy on the continent of Europe and in South America. But our objections are on the basis of the lack of clarity, the lack of critical attitude, and the absence of argument in much of this so-called philosophy. Where a philosopher outside of the analytic tradition makes some effort at clarity or argument, we do our best to understand what he's driving at. For example, a few of the existentialists have attracted some attention from analytic philosophers because they're reasonably clear. Perhaps we're sometimes a bit narrow and not as ready to try to understand other philosophical traditions as we might be, but I like to think that Socrates, who in many ways started it all, would understand our standards, what we accept and reject as philosophy, and approve of them.

About philosophical positions it seems to me that there are very few that we're not prepared to consider on their merits. All kinds of religious positions, from traditional Christianity to atheism, are represented among philosophers and are debated philosophically. All kinds of political positions are held and defended by philosophers, from extreme conservatism to extreme radicalism. Some positions most of us are agreed on rejecting, but there are none that I can think of to which we are not prepared to give a fair hearing. Sometimes I wonder if we aren't a little too prepared to debate endlessly without coming to a conclusion, a little too tolerant of silly positions, a little too polite to bad philosophy. But if we have to err, I'd rather it be on that side of these questions.

Now let's turn to the second part of our question and try to give some answer to "Does life have a meaning?" By way of making the question more explicit, I'll ask you not only to answer the question, but also to say what part philosophy has played in helping you to arrive at your answer, and how your answer affects your own day-to-day life. I know that these are questions that some of us find a little personal, but they are also questions to which students are very interested in knowing the answers, and I think with some justification. Professor Venner, perhaps you would begin?

VENNER: I would be pleased to. I can answer the main question quite simply—life does not have a meaning. Words have meanings and sentences have meanings and perhaps parables or stories or works of art have meanings. But "life" is not a thing of the appropriate sort to have a meaning. Or if the question means "Does life have a purpose?" then life is also not the appropriate kind of thing for such questions to be asked about it. Artifacts such as machines, tools, and so on have purposes, but life is not an artifact. I think that philosophy has played a part in convincing me that this is the correct answer to this question, but science has played a part also, insofar as science has given me grounds for rejecting religious beliefs. As for the effect of this on my personal life, it is in some ways depressing, in some ways liberating. Certainly the knowledge that the universe is uncaring and indifferent, that man's fate means nothing in the long run, is not flattering to human vanity, nor does it satisfy the craving that we all have for reassurance and comfort. Thus if we concentrate on this aspect of the matter, it can be depressing. On the other hand, this knowledge can also be liberating. If life has no meaning or purpose, we do not have to live up to any plans or expectations imposed on us from outside. It is rather like living in a large city. Large cities are impersonal; no one seems to care if you live or die. But also no one interferes with your business or expects anything from you. I think that Bertrand Russell has expressed my feeling very well in his essay "A Free Man's Worship." I do not know, but perhaps Professor Oxmore would agree with me?

OXMORE: I suspect that I was the one that Home had in mind when he said that this question might be embarrassing to some of us. I'm sufficiently English not to like talking about my own deepest feelings. But I'll make a stab at it. Like Venner, I'd answer the question "Does life have a meaning or purpose?" with a "No." But I'd do so because I think the question itself is illegitimate. Big abstractions like "the Meaning of Life," with a capital M and capital L, are extremely suspect. If you ask a more reasonable question, such as "Do individual human lives have meanings or purposes?" the answer is obviously "Yes." They have whatever meanings or purposes we choose to give them. I think that that answer to the question is itself a piece of philosophical analysis, perhaps even an example of what one logician calls the "false contender" argument. You can take an impressive kind of question or claim and show that taken one way it's meaningless and that taken another way, it has a perfectly straightforward factual answer or meaning.

If you ask me what the effect on my own life is of this fairly routine piece of analysis, I'm tempted to say there is none. But I won't duck the issue, although I do feel that we're getting into matters that are nobody's business but mine. I suppose I am making a sort of general claim that the only meaning "life" has is whatever meaning we each choose to give to our own lives. And I suppose that, like Venner, I have rather mixed feelings about that. I don't think I'd like having to live up to anyone else's plans or purposes for me, and yet I'm not always especially satisfied with what I've done with my life or with what I see other people doing with theirs. I don't share Venner's admiration for Russell's rhetoric in "A Free Man's Worship" for several reasons. There seems to me to be a good deal of ranting in that piece, and Russell makes rhetorical use of ideas he isn't really prepared to defend. You can't reject all ideas of absolute value, and then talk about freedom or dignity as if *they* were absolutes. I don't really see why the most despicable torturer or traitor couldn't affirm his own values in rhetoric just as ringing as Russell's, if it all comes down to whatever values you choose to affirm. Some existentialists do the same thing by the way—deny all absolutes, then try to sneak in "authenticity" as an absolute—if anything goes why not be inauthentic? But I rather suspect that Venner and I represent two stages in the modern rejection of the traditional religious view of life's meaning. He's the confident morning and I'm the sad and disillusioned evening. But I suppose all of this is grist to your mill, Kirk?

KIRK: Yes, I think it is. But perhaps I'd better start by giving my own answer to the questions Home has raised. I'd go along with Oxmore in rather distrusting "Life" with a capital "L" as too vague a term. I'd say that the meaning or purpose of each human life is to know, love, and serve God in this life, and to enjoy Him in the next life, and that the purpose of human lives as a whole is to form a knowing, loving, serving community united with God forever. Insofar as any of us succeed in knowing, loving, and serving God, we have joy and peace, and insofar as we fail to do so we experience failure and frustration. I'd hasten to say that a number of us may be knowing or loving or serving God under some other name, perhaps scientific truth or social justice. But these are only aspects of God, and I think that only Christianity can give us the whole picture, can show us that God is really a person and really exists, and is not just an abstraction or an ideal. As to what part philosophy plays in my view, I think I've already partly answered that in earlier sessions. I think that philosophy can pave the way for religious belief, can show us that a theistic view of the universe is the only rational one, for example. I think that philosophy can defend the reasonableness of revealed religious beliefs. But I don't think that philosophy can take us all the way, and I don't think that it can be a substitute for religion. Like Dante's Virgil, it's a superb guide as far as it goes, but it can't go all the way. I presume that Home would agree with me.

HOME: Yes, just as I think that Venner and Oxmore are in basic agreement, but want to put their position in somewhat different ways, I think you and I agree on all the important things but that I might have a somewhat different emphasis. What I'd like to emphasize is the satisfactoriness of reason so far as it does go. Knowing is a good thing, even if it's the universe that we're knowing and not its creator. Loving and serving our fellow men is a good and admirable thing even where those doing the loving and serving don't know that in doing it for "the least of these" they're doing it for God. And for Socrates and Epictetus, philosophy *was* a sort of religion, and perhaps the noblest one that man by himself has ever arrived at. You and I, Kirk, would agree that man has a supernatural destiny, something above and beyond what is natural to him. But man's natural powers and purposes have their own dignity and importance.

KIRK: I'd agree, with one important reservation—you're ignoring original sin. You're talking as if man could attain his natural dignity without supernatural help. But since the "fall," that's impossible. And I wouldn't agree that Socrates or Epictetus arrived at their philosophical "religion" just on their own. All truth comes from the Holy Spirit.

HOME: Yes, I'd have to agree. But I feel that speaking as a philosopher, with fellow philosophers, it's the natural aspects rather than the supernatural that have to be emphasized. There's so much disagreement about the natural, so much work to do in that area, that I feel that my work is cut out for me there.

KIRK: I'm not sure that you can compartmentalize that neatly. For example, how can you really deal with the problem of evil as an objection to God's existence without bringing in theological ideas like the Redemption?

HOME: That's not a bad example for my purposes. It seems to me that an awful lot of the force behind objections to God's existence based on moral and physical evil lies in purely philosophical assumptions about free will or about what sorts of things are good. And until you answer these questions, the theological answers don't even make sense to your opponents.

KIRK: Well, I suppose that it's partly a matter of vocation—you feel called on to deal with the more narrowly philosophical problems; I feel called on to work in the area between philosophy and theology.

HOME: Perhaps you're right.

OXMORE: If I might break in, I wonder if there isn't to some extent a temperamental difference between Venner and me and between Kirk and Home. And these differences cut across agreements in belief. I know from talking to Venner about social problems that he's much more inclined than I am to think that human problems can be solved by "social engineering." I think that there are human problems that no amount of social tinkering will solve. He's optimistic, if you like, and I'm pessimistic. Similarly, Home has a much greater faith in the ability of pure reasoning to solve human problems than Kirk does. He's the optimist; Kirk's the pessimist. So we have the religious and the irreligious optimist and the religious and irreligious pessimist. Except that optimist and pessimist are the wrong terms, really. Put it this way. I know that I have much more sympathy with the anti-religious existentialists like Sartre than Venner does, and I'll wager that Kirk has much more sympathy with the religious existentialists like Kierkegaard and Marcel than Home does.[14]

[14] See Bibliography (Appendix B, Part X) under Kaufman for these existentialist philosophers.

HOME: That's very perceptive. Remember the arguments we had about Kierkegaard, Kirk?

KIRK: I do indeed. And I suspect that Oxmore sometimes feels about Venner as I sometimes feel about you, Home, that you're a little too inclined to oversimplify, to see things in black and white. A little inhuman, aren't they sometimes, Oxmore? Or perhaps a bit childlike?

OXMORE: Yes, I agree. But perhaps that's why we like them better than we like each other, if I may put it that way.

HOME: I agree that there are times when Venner and I seem to be talking the same language, although we say quite different things in it. Perhaps the fact that we're both logicians means that we both have a taste for the clear and the neat. But be that as it may, perhaps we could explore a little further this area of how our philosophical positions affect our everyday lives. Would any of us, for example, take the position that philosophy is just a job, which we leave when we go home from the campus and which doesn't really affect our everyday lives?

OXMORE: I suppose I come as close to that as any of us. The things that matter to me most in my personal life are personal relationships, which I don't propose to talk about. But aside from those, the things that matter to me most are things like music and poetry, and certain kinds of experiences of nature—country walks, not scrambling up cliffs like Venner. And I'd feel that taking an analytical attitude to these experiences would have a tendency to spoil them for me. Nothing could be worse than trying to do aesthetics at a concert, or for that matter arguing philosophy with your spouse. I don't know how relationships where both husband and wife are philosophers can stand it. But on the other hand, there are lots of departments of everyday life—politics, for example, or our general attitudes toward the other sex or other races, and so on, in which it would seem to me to be shameful for a philosopher to think as sloppily and carelessly as the average person. Wittgenstein once got very angry with one of his followers when the man uttered some vague gas about "national character" during the war. I sympathize with Wittgenstein there. A philosopher just shouldn't be a silly ass about things of that sort. I'm amazed by that philosopher we all know who is a political ultraconservative, though he seems competent enough otherwise. I'll say fair and admit that I'm not amazed in the same way about Kirk and Home being Christians and good philosophers, though I think Venner is.

VENNER: It would certainly seem to me to be an outright contradiction if someone were a logical positivist and a Roman Catholic, for instance. But other kinds of philosophical positions are more open to religious belief. Then it becomes a matter of which philosophical position is to be preferred, and like Home, I prefer to argue the question on the purely philosophical level. As to how philosophy affects my personal life, I would go further than Oxmore. I think that a critical, scientific spirit should enter into all departments of human life, even our personal relationships and our reactions to art and music. I find it hard to enjoy poetry, for example, because the ambiguities of poetic language trouble me. This is undoubtedly a loss. But I find it easy to appreciate the pure form in music and in much modern sculpture and painting. In human relationships I think that it is reasonable to try to be kind and fair, but also reasonable to realize that some people have been badly conditioned and will not respond to such treatment. I find also that I tend to distrust strong emotion, and this is perhaps a loss.

OXMORE: Yes, you and Home are Appollonians, all right, and Kirk and I are Dionysians.

KIRK: Now I think *you're* oversimplifying, Oxmore. There are a great many things that Home and I have in common that you and Venner don't share—for example, a taste for fantasy and science fiction. But to get back to the question of how our philosophical preoccupation affects our lives, there's been a rather interesting effect in my own life. A good deal of the theological excitement in the last few decades, both in Catholic and Protestant theology, has been about theologians or movements which are to some extent anti-intellectual. The effect of my being a philosopher and trying to maintain some standards of clarity and rationality in theology has been to isolate me to a great extent from contemporary movements in theology. At the same time I couldn't completely agree with those theologians who were trying to reach some kind of accommodation with Wittgenstein or with Oxford philosophy. So the effect was to put me outside the mainstream in both philosophy and theology. I'm not complaining about that—I rather enjoy being out of step. But I found myself too rationalistic for most theologians and too metaphysical for the philosophers. The same thing, by the way, has happened to others who might be called "rationalistic Christians." C. S. Lewis,[15] for example, for whom I have a tremendous admiration, was extremely popular with intelligent laymen. He brought many people into the church from outside and kept many in who might otherwise have left. But he was largely ignored by both the theologians and the philosophers.

HOME: That raises a rather interesting question. There are people who are what you might call amateur philosophers, people who reach the

---

[15] See Biography (Appendix A) and Bibliography (Appendix B, Part X).

public and manage to make a certain impact on them, in areas that are matters of concern to professional philosophers—ethics, philosophy of religion, and so on. As a fairly representative group of professional philosophers, I'd be rather interested to hear your reactions to these sorts of people. Are there any of them you admire at all, any who you think have something to say that professional philosophers ought to be listening to?

KIRK: Many of those who create a big stir in the media are charletans, of coursc, and I think that philosophers owe it to their students, and even to the public, to expose those people for what they are.

HOME: I couldn't agree more. But how about people you admire? You've already mentioned C. S. Lewis.

KIRK: A man for whom I have the greatest admiration, who had a good deal to do with my becoming a Christian, is G. K. Chesterton.[16] He's largely forgotten now, but as a sort of applied philosopher, using common sense on a good many literary, political, and human problems, he's had few equals.

OXMORE: One person who it seems to me has talked a good deal of sense about society and where we're going, over a long period of ycars, is J. B. Priestley,[17] the novelist. It's more fashionable to admire people like Virginia Woolf, but for my money Priestley, both in his essays and in his novels, has a sort of tough-minded common sense that's hard to beat. One of the younger men I find very interesting is John Wain[18] —W-A-I-N, not the movie star, the poet and novelist.

HOME: That's interesting, because one of my choices would be a poet too, W. H. Auden. I like his poetry very much, but I value his essays even more. I feel I've learned a great deal from books like *The Dyers Hand*. Professor Venner, do you have any candidates?

VENNER: In the older generation I greatly admired H. G. Wells,[19] who did a great dcal to popularize a scientific outlook. In the younger generation it is harder for me to say. Perhaps someone like Martin Gardiner,[20] who popularizes science in a truly interesting way, would be a good example of a nonphilosopher whom I admire. In the political arena it is harder to find really admirable persons, but some of our younger philosophers have been very active politically.

---

[16] See Bibliography (Appendix B, Part X).
[17] See Bibliography (Appendix B, Part X).
[18] See Bibliography (Appendix B, Part X).
[19] See Bibliography (Appendix B, Part X).
[20] See Bibliography (Appendix B, Part X).

HOME: I wouldn't say that they gave much of an example of the philosophical virtues. In fact, one effect on my own life of philosophy has been to make me very suspicious of fanaticisms not only on the right but also on the left. It's conventional enough for an academic to distrust the right wing, but many of my colleagues seem to be absolute pushovers for radical or liberal clichés. In fact, I find myself politically in a position rather like the one Kirk described with regard to theology and philosophy. I can't join the big radical "Society is rotten, burn it down" protest, and I can't join the conservative "Keep the masses in their place" counterprotest. So I find myself allied first with one side, then with the other, depending on which is being more outrageous at the moment! There's an awful lot of what Oxmore's friend Priestley calls "block thinking" going on, neat little outfits of ideas that people accept without really examining them. The only time I found myself in a reasonably congenial atmosphere was in Eugene McCarthy's campaign in 1968, and you know what happened to us then.

KIRK: I'd like to pick up on something you mentioned a moment ago—the philosophical virtues. Do you think that there are distinctively philosophical virtues, and if so do you think that they carry over to everyday life?

HOME: I do. Love of truth, for instance, is a virtue that scientists, scholars, and researchers of all kinds should have, but there seems to me to be a characteristically philosophical form of it, very much tied up with a dislike of confusion, stupidity, and deception. I don't think it's an accident that philosophers have always been involved with that area of logic which consists of exposing bad reasoning and sorting out confusions. Of course, this hatred of confusion and deception can take a variety of forms. In some, philosophers who are convinced that religion is both confused and deceptive, it can take the form of a crusade against religious belief. In others the major source of muddleheadedness and misdirection may seem to be in politics or advertising or just in everyday thinking about the world. Or, of course, in other philosophers' ideas, I think the logical positivists were really morally outraged by what they saw as the muddleheadedness of philosophers like Heidegger.

VENNER: That is true, yes.

HOME: There was something of the same feeling in the Wittgensteinians' opposition to philosophical misuse of language or Moore's rejection of the tangled metaphysics of the Hegelians.

OXMORE: I agree, but disliking knavery and foolishness seems a fairly negative and limited sort of "virtue."

HOME: I think that it's only the negative side of something positive—a desire for understanding or, if you like, a genuine "love of wisdom."

KIRK: So your characteristic philosophical virtue turns out, rather tautologously, to be the love of wisdom.

HOME: Yes, but I don't think that it's a mere tautology. Not liking to see people confused and other people preying on their confusion isn't all that common a feeling. Also, really loving truth more than personal advantage or party loyalties is fairly rare. Aristotle's "I love Plato but I love truth even more" is, I think, a good statement of one element of this philosophical virtue, and Plato's willingness to use deception as part of the machinery of his ideal state in the *Republic* seems to me to be a sin against that virtue.

KIRK: And you think that this carries over into nonphilosophical areas?

HOME: Well, here we're on rather delicate ground, because there are men who are called philosophers who don't really deserve the title. But the really good philosophers I've known—and by that I mean the most technically competent, not just those I liked or admired—have been men who were really willing to listen. Really listen to students and not just impose their own opinions on them, for example. And really listen to their opponents and try to make some effort to be fair to their positions. In fact, intellectual justice or fairness is perhaps a distinct philosophical virtue. The lawyer quite properly acts as an advocate—it's not his business to bring out the strength of his opponent's position or provide arguments for it. But a philosopher generally tries to state his opponent's position as strongly as possible, and to appreciate it as well as he can.

KIRK: I can think of lots of exceptions to that generalization.

HOME: Well, perhaps I'm really describing my ideal of a philosopher. But we don't entirely fall below that ideal, either in public or in private.

OXMORE: I agree that you're being rather idealistic, but I can accept the ideal that you're describing.

KIRK: But, of course, that's a rather limited ideal. A man who cared only for truth and understanding could be a sort of monster if he cared nothing for human desires or human suffering.

HOME: I can agree to that. The philosophical virtues aren't the only ones and to be only a philosopher is not to be a whole man. But the philosophical virtues are easy to neglect and increasingly neglected, even by some philosophers, which is what I was objecting to when I made the remark that started the whole thing.

KIRK: You don't look to philosophy to save the world, then?

HOME: Philosophy by itself can't save the world, but it can certainly help. Being able to save the world isn't the only virtue that a discipline or a theory can have. For that matter, a little philosophical reflection on what "saving the world" would *mean* is probably very much in order. Does it mean just physical survival? Or just some sort of contented populace? If so, why not get everybody high on some sort of euphoric drug and let civilization revert to lotus eating? If by saving the world you mean, on the other hand, giving everyone a good life, you have to first answer the philosophical question, "What is the good life?"

OXMORE: We'll now suppose that philosophers come to the conclusion that the good life is pleasure or activity in accordance with virtue, or whatever. What part do you see philosophy playing in bringing about this good life?

HOME: There's a gulf between knowledge and action that can only be bridged by love or desire. Philosophy is a theoretical or intellectual discipline. It can find the truth in certain matters, and thus help to guide action. But whether people choose to act in accordance with truth, whether they love the truth when they find it, is beyond the power of philosophy. If it were true that "We needs must love the highest when we see it," philosophy might solve our problems by showing us "the highest," whatever it may be. But as a matter of fact there's no "needs must" about it. We can perfectly well choose to turn away from truth or goodness, and we often do. In other words, philosophy doesn't have, and doesn't pretend to have, any solution for the problem of sin—or Original Sin, if you prefer.

VENNER: I must disagree. I still retain the hope that most people, if given a clear view of the means to solve human problems and bring happiness to the human race, would choose those means.

HOME: In other words, you're taking the Socratic position that virtue is knowledge and sin is ignorance. But I'm afraid that it does more credit to your heart than your head.

OXMORE: I'm afraid he's right, Venner. There are an awful lot of bastards about.

VENNER: On what, then, do you base your hopes for a better world?

OXMORE: I'm sorry to say I haven't any. I think the human race is probably bound for the scrap heap. Of course, that's no excuse for not acting as decently as we can on the way there.

VENNER: If, indeed, that is what you believe, and if you can find no consolation by thinking of yourself as part of the great universal process unfolding through time, then I do not see how it matters whether you act "as decently as you can."

KIRK: The answer to that, I suspect, is that Oxmore is rather a decent person, partly because her parents were. She's living to some extent on the capital of her Christian forebearers. As a matter of fact, your father was a clergyman, wasn't he?

OXMORE: Yes, I'm a child of the manse. And I'm more than happy to acknowledge my debts in that direction. But most people nowadays have no religion, and as time goes on they have less and less.

KIRK: And we see the effect in society around us.

OXMORE: Perhaps we do. I don't deny that we're going to hell in a handbasket. I just can't accept your remedy for it.

HOME: Well, I think that as philosophers we have some common ground. We can agree on the value of truth and the importance of searching for it through philosophy. We can't agree in accepting Christ, or for that matter in accepting any specific religious or political solutions to our problems. But we can all agree that we're carrying on the tradition that Socrates started. Whether or not we regard ourselves as children of God, we can think of ourselves as sons or daughters of Socrates.

KIRK: I think that you have a little too much tendency to make a religion of philosophy, Home, and if you do it's just another false religion. But if you put it on the grounds of following a great tradition, I can go along with you on that.

VENNER: This strikes an answering chord in my emotions too, but I would be false to my conception of that tradition if I said that it was more than an emotional agreement.

OXMORE: I suppose I have the greatest resistance to making too much of philosophy. There are times when it seems to me to be an essentially frivolous activity. But I can't deny that in my less cynical moments I can be moved by the sort of appeal you're making. After all it's what I've given most of my life to.

HOME: Perhaps that's as close as we can come to agreement about the purpose of life and what philosophy can tell us about it. Our time has run out at last, and I can only thank Professor Venner, Professor Oxmore, and Professor Kirk, those who have attended the sessions, and all of those who have made this series of discussions possible. Perhaps the best I can wish for all of us is that we keep on loving and pursuing understanding and wisdom. May the Great Debate continue, now and forever.

QUESTIONS

Answer the following questions as you think they would be answered by the panelist to whom they are addressed.

1. Professor Venner: In view of what you said about man as part of the universal process, shouldn't you modify your answer as to whether life has a meaning?
2. Professor Oxmore: It's all very well to talk about giving life whatever meaning we choose, but how about those who are maimed or tortured by life?
3. Professor Kirk: You claim to be a philosopher, but your answer to the question of life's meaning is religious, not philosophical. How can you reconcile these facts?

Do you find the following answers to questions satisfactory?

4. The answers of Venner, Oxmore, Kirk, and Home to the main question.
5. The answers of each to how philosophy affects their lives.
6. The answers of each to how philosophy can help deal with the world's problems.

Write a short essay on the following questions:

7. What is the purpose of your life? How do you know?
8. Does philosophy play any part in your life? Why or why not?
9. What have you learned from these discussions?
10. What is philosophy?

FURTHER READINGS

HICK, JOHN, *Philosophy of Religion* (2nd ed.), Englewood Cliffs, N.J.: Prentice-Hall, Inc., 1973, Chaps. 7, 8 and 9, pp. 97–129.

HOSPERS, JOHN, *Readings in Introductory Philosophical Analysis,* Englewood Cliffs, N.J.: Prentice-Hall, Inc., 1968.

  Ayer, A. J., "The A Priori," pp. 47–58.

  Blanshard, Brand, "A Priori Knowledge," pp. 58–95.

  Waismann, Friedrich, "Synthetic A Priori Judgments," pp. 96–104.*

TAYLOR, RICHARD, *Metaphysics,* (2nd ed.), Englewood Cliffs, N.J.: Prentice-Hall, Inc., 1974, Chap. 11, pp. 121–26.

WILSON, MARGARET D., DAN W. BROCK, and RICHARD F. KUHNS, *Philosophy, An Introduction,* New York: Appleton-Century-Crofts, 1972.

  Hume, David, "An Appeal to Passion and Understanding," pp. 771–78.

  Plato, "A Way of Living—and Dying," pp. 729–38.

  Ramsey, Frank, "A System of Definitions," pp. 744–47.

* These readings are not directly about the nature of philosophy, but about a key problem which has a major influence on our conception of philosophy.

Questions on the Reading

1. How does the question of *a priori* knowledge relate to the question of the nature of philosophy?

2. How does Plato's view of philosophy relate to the views expressed in this chapter? Which position might Plato most nearly agree with?

3. Criticize Hume's view of philosophy, or Ramsey's.

4. How does the question of an afterlife relate to the question of whether life has meaning? Contrast Taylor's views on this point with Hick's.

5. What nonphilosopher has influenced your philosophical views? Discuss the philosophical views embodied in some nonphilosophical book or article.

APPENDIXES

Biographical Notes on Philosophers Mentioned in This Book

The purpose of these notes is to briefly give you an idea of the opinions of a philosopher and of his setting in history. Further details on the life and work of many of these philosophers may be found in the *Encyclopedia of Philosophy* (The Macmillan Company, 1967).

Anselm, Saint (1033–1109) Italian theologian and philosopher, Archbishop of Canterbury, 1093–1109. An important figure in medieval philosophy, Anselm defended the view that reason should be applied to Christian beliefs and that it leads to increased understanding and conviction. His Ontological Argument for the existence of God, an attempt to prove God's existence from the very concept or definition of God, has fascinated philosophers ever since Anselm's time. For the essential parts of Anselm's work and subsequent discussions of it, see A. Plantinga, ed., *The Ontological Argument* (New York: Doubleday and Co., 1965).

Aquinas, St. Thomas (1225–1274) Italian theologian and philosopher. A member of the Dominican Order, Aquinas taught at the University of Paris and elsewhere. Perhaps the greatest of the medieval philosophers and one of the great philosophical system builders, Aquinas attempted to investigate every theological question by applying reason to the Christian revelation. The results of his investigations appear in his two great systematic expositions of theology, the *Summa Theologica* and the *Summa Contra Gentiles,* both of which contain much of philosophical interest. The *Summa Contra Gentiles* is available in an English translation under the title, *On the Truth of the Catholic Faith* (New York: Doubleday and Co., 1955).

Aristotle (384–322 B.C.) Greek philosopher and logician, and founder of one of the first schools of philosophy, pupil of Plato and tutor to Alexander the Great. The first and one of the greatest of the builders of philosophical systems, Aristotle held connected and coherent views in almost every area of philosophy. Frequently Aristotle's view is the "common sense" or "ordinary man's" view raised to a considerable degree of technical sophistication. Despite subsequent developments and changes in points of view, Aristotle's arguments and conclusions have still to be reckoned with, especially in ethics and metaphysics. Because his surviving works are essentially his lecture notes, Aristotle is not easy to read; a good beginning is R. Bambrough, *The Philosophy of Aristotle* (New York: New American Library, 1963).

Austin, John Langshaw (1911–1960) English philosopher, White's Professor of Moral Philosophy at Oxford, 1952–1960. Austin was convinced that the way to make progress in philosophy was to begin with a careful and systematic analysis of our ordinary ways of speaking about a subject. His application of these techniques to such problems as our knowledge of other minds, moral responsibility, and free will gained wide respect for his views, but many contemporary philosophers seem more inclined to argue with Austin's conclusions than to imitate the painstaking investigations which led to those conclusions. Austin's main work may be found in his *Philosophical Papers* (Oxford: Oxford University Press, 1961).

Ayer, Alfred Jules (Born 1910) English philosopher, presently Professor of Philosophy at Oxford. After graduating from Oxford in 1932 he spent some time at the University of Vienna and on his return to England published his first book, *Language, Truth and Logic* (London, 1936, 2nd edition, Dover Books, 1946), the first and most influential exposition of logical positivist ideas to the English-speaking world. He has continued to be an active and influential analytic philosopher: his views on many points have broadened, but he retains a strong positivistic bias.

Carnap, Rudolf (1891–1972). German and American philosopher and logician. As a young faculty member at the University of Vienna,

Carnap was one of the founders of the Vienna Circle. Coming to America on Hitler's rise to power, he taught at the University of Chicago and UCLA. Originally trained in science, Carnap's major interests were always in philosophy of science and the methodology of scientific investigation. Like the other positivists, he hoped to solve philosophical problems by applying the standards of science and mathematics to philosophy. Many students and colleagues owe a great deal to his help and cooperation. His major work is *Logical Foundations of Probability* (Chicago: University of Chicago Press, 1950).

Descartes, René (1596–1650)   French philosopher and mathematician. One of the major influences in the last few centuries of philosophy, Descartes turned his attention toward problems of knowledge and justification. His technique in philosophy was to attempt to doubt whatever could possibly be doubted and to rebuild our knowledge on the firm foundation of what could not be doubted; he thought our own existence and certain basic principles to be undeniable. Contemporary references to Descartes are often to his theory of mind and body as two independent substances. A good introduction to Descartes' thought is his *Meditations* (Indianapolis, Ind.: Bobbs-Merrill Co., Inc., tr. Lafleur Lawrence, 1941).

Edwards, Paul (Born 1923)   Australian and American philosopher, editor of the *Encyclopedia of Philosophy* (New York: The Macmillan Company, 1967), Professor of Philosophy at the City University of New York, and author of a number of books and papers. Edwards' orientation is generally positivist; his interests are in ethics and philosophy of religion. He is one of the leading philosophical exponents of atheism.

Hempel, Carl (Born 1905)   German and American philosopher. A member of a group of philosophers in Berlin sympathetic to the Vienna Circle, Hempel came to the United States on Hitler's rise to power. For many years he has been Professor of Philosophy at Princeton University. Hempel's primary interests have been in the area of philosophy of science, especially problems about scientific explanation and the confirmation of scientific theories. His theories have been extensively criticized by philosophers, but seem to many scientists to adequately represent scientific experience. His *Philosophy of Natural Science* (Englewood Cliffs, N.J.: Prentice-Hall, Inc., 1966) gives a good picture of his views.

Hume, David (1711–1776)   Scottish philosopher. A major figure in modern philosophy, Hume began with an empiricist position that all knowledge is confined to what we can learn from our senses and arrived at a position of complete skepticism in every department of human thought. While some philosophers accept Hume's skeptical conclusions in one or more areas (e.g. his religious skepticism) a great part of Hume's importance for modern philosophy is the formidable challenge he offers, a challenge which must be taken up by any non-skeptical philosophical theory. Two of Hume's most important works may be found in *The Empiricists* (Garden City, N.Y.: Doubleday and Co., Dolphin Books edition).

Kant, Immanuel (1724–1804) German philosopher—another great builder of a systematic philosophy. In Kant's view knowledge was confined to objects of possible experience, and the role of philosophy is to examine the limits of possible experience and judgment. The knowledge of these limits, however, provides us with a system of categories and principles with which we can either solve the problems raised by philosophers or show them to be impossible to solve. Kant's views in metaphysics are of mainly historical interest, but his ethical views are still important in current discussions. A good introduction to Kant is A. Zweig, ed., *The Essential Kant* (New York: New American Library, 1973).

Lewis, C. S. (1898–1963) British religious writer, Professor of Renaissance and Medieval Literature at Cambridge University, 1955–1963, Fellow of Magdalen College, Oxford, 1925–1954. Originally trained as a philosopher at Oxford, Lewis combined literary scholarship and the writing of fiction with clear and persuasive argumentation for traditional Christianity. Over a decade after his death, Lewis' religious works continue to be best sellers, and much of this writing is directly or indirectly of philosophical interest. His book, *Miracles* (New York: Macmillan and Co., 1963), is a good introduction to his religious and philosophical positions.

Lucas, J. R. (Born 1929) English philosopher. Fellow of Merton College, Oxford, since 1960, he is author of *The Principles of Politics* (Oxford: Oxford University Press, 1960), *The Freedom of the Will* (Oxford: Oxford University Press, 1970), *The Concept of Probability* (Oxford: Oxford University Press, 1970), *A Treatise on Space and Time* (London: Methuen, 1973), and a number of papers in philosophical journals. Lucas somewhat resembles Aristotle, both in the breadth of his interests and sometimes in the compression and difficulty of his arguments. His valuable and original work in diverse fields has not yet been fully understood or deservedly appreciated.

Mill, John Stuart (1806–1873) English philosopher. For most of his life an official of East India Company, Mill's philosophical writings have been influential outside the philosophical community as well as inside it. Mill's efforts to formulate the principles of scientific method are merely of historical interest, but his views in ethics and politics are still relevant to contemporary concerns. His classic formulation of the utilitarian ethics in his *Utilitarianism* (Indianapolis, Ind.: Bobbs-Merrill Co., Inc., Library of Liberal Arts edition) is a good introduction to Mill's ethical and political views.

Moore, George Edward (1873–1958) English philosopher, Professor of Philosophy at Cambridge University, 1925–1939. Almost entirely unknown except among professional philosophers, Moore's painstaking thoroughness, clarity, and honesty have been major influences on contemporary analytic philosophy. Moore defended his somewhat idiosyncratic version of "common sense" with arguments which appealed to ordinary ways of speaking and thinking as opposed to philosophical theories which outraged common sense. He must be considered, along with Russell and Wittgenstein, as one of the founders of contemporary analytic philosophy. His book *Ethics* (London: Hutchinson and Co., 1912), written for a popular audience, is a good introduction to Moore.

Nowell-Smith, Patrick H. (Born 1914) English philosopher, currently Professor of Philosophy at York University in Canada. He is the author of a number of articles in philosophical journals and of the influential book, *Ethics* (Baltimore, Md.: Penguin Books, 1954), which introduced to a wide audience an Oxford approach to ethical problems.

Plato (about 530–450 B.C.) Greek philosopher, founder of the first school of philosophy (the Academy), pupil of Socrates, and teacher of Aristotle. Plato had a powerful, though not very systematic philosophical intellect, which he combined with literary gifts of the very highest order. His surviving philosophical works are in the form of dialogues, usually with a fictionalized Socrates as the major figure. These dialogues have been so influential among professional philosophers and educated people in general that it is not entirely absurd to describe subsequent philosophy as a series of commentaries on Plato, though hardly any competent philosopher now accepts any view held by Plato in the form in which he held it. One important Platonic idea was that of a contrast between a nonmaterial world of pure ideals or forms and the changing world of matter and appearance. Plato's dialogues may be found in many editions; a good introduction to his work is *Plato: The Last Days of Socrates* (Baltimore, Maryland: Penguin Books, 1954), which contains four of his easier dialogues.

Ramsey, Frank (1903–1930)   English philosopher. A leading figure in early analytic philosophy until his premature death. Ramsey's papers are collected in *The Foundations of Mathematics* (London: Routledge and Kegan Paul, 1931).

Ross, W. D. (1877–1973)   English philosopher, Fellow of Oriel College, Oxford, 1902–1947, and Provost of Oriel, 1929–1947. He was General Editor of the Oxford translations of Aristotle's work and author of such important works in ethics as *The Right and the Good* (Oxford: Oxford University Press, 1930) and *Foundations of Ethics* (Oxford: Oxford University Press, 1939). Ross is in the tradition of the "rational" or "intuitionist" ethics which holds that there are objective moral principles grasped by reason, but Ross' distinctive contribution is an attempt to solve the problem of the conflict of duties by a distinction between *prima facie* and strict obligations.

Russell, Bertrand (1872–1968)   English philosopher and logician. He was perhaps the most widely known contemporary philosopher, although he was better known for his controversial opinions on matters of public policy rather than for his important philosophical work, which was highly technical. Much of Russell's early work was in logic and philosophy of mathematics; perhaps his most influential philosophical work was in epistemology and metaphysics. Russell was influenced by many philosophers, including Moore and Wittgenstein, and was always ready to change his position in response to new insights or arguments. A good introduction to Russell is his collection of essays, *Why I Am Not a Christian* (New York: Scribners and Sons, 1967).

Ryle, Gilbert (Born 1900)   For many years Waynefleet Professor of Philosophy at Oxford University and editor of the philosophical journal *Mind*. He is one of the most representative and effective members of the "ordinary language" or "Oxford" philosophers. Ryle's most important work is in the area of philosophy of mind, especially his book, *The Concept of Mind* (Barnes and Noble, 1949). Ryle's lively and informal style and his powerful though unsystematic philosophical intellect recall Plato in some ways; his latest major work is a controversial book on Plato. A good introduction to Ryle is his book *Dilemmas* (Cambridge: Cambridge University Press, 1954).

Schlick, Morris (1882–1936)   Austrian philosopher. One of the founders of the Vienna Circle, Schlick was more interested in ethical problems than many of the other positivists. A good introduction to Schlick is the book, *Problems of Ethics* (New York: Dover Publishing Co., 1939).

Socrates (about 470–399 B.C.) Greek philosopher. Probably the first person to carry on the activity of clarifying, criticizing, and arguing with regard to fundamental problems which we, in the West, call philosophy. Socrates was the teacher of Plato, but probably had no philosophical system of his own and very likely not even any philosophical theories. Our picture of him is largely based on Plato and Xenophon, who both fictionalized him to serve as a mouthpiece of their own theories. What emerges from them is the picture of a strong and recognizable personality, fascinated by philosophical problems and ready to question and challenge any assumption or theory. It is this spirit, rather than any discovery or theory, which makes Socrates the spiritual father of all Western philosophy.

Spinoza, Baruch (1632–1677) Jewish and Dutch philosopher. He refused academic appointments and earned his living by grinding optical lenses. One of the diverse European philosophers lumped together as "rationalists" whose work in some sense stems from that of Descartes, and who emphasize reason rather than experience, Spinoza used a process of reasoning based on the model of geometry to build his metaphysical system. He is the leading philosophical exponent of pantheism, the identification of God with the Universe. Few of his views would now be defended, but some of them are of more than historical interest. His most accessible work is *On the Improvement of the Understanding* (Indianapolis, Ind.: Bobbs-Merrill Co., Inc., Library of Liberal Arts).

Wittgenstein, Ludwig (1889–1951) Austrian and English philosopher. One of the most influential of contemporary philosophers, Wittgenstein spent a comparatively short time in the academic world, including a few years as Research Fellow and five years as Professor at Cambridge (1939–1947, interrupted by two years of war service in hospitals). During his life Wittgenstein repudiated every interpretation of his work and every attempt by others to develop it and would undoubtedly, if he were alive today, reject most, if not all, that is due to his influence or said in his name. Despite the temptation to find a system of philosophy or answers to philosophical questions in his work, Wittgenstein is probably best seen as a powerful and disturbing questioner of all our philosophical assumptions and theories. A good introduction to Wittgenstein's thought is *The Blue and Brown Books* (New York: Harper and Row, 1959).

Appendix **B**

Selected Bibliography

To help the reader to continue the philosophical dialectic on the problems presented in this book I have tried to find for each problem area a book representing the point of view taken by each of the parties to the dialogue. A (V) before a title represents a view at least roughly like Venner's, an (O) a view like Oxmore's, and so on. I have also included some books of readings, which are marked (R).

PART I: OTHER INTRODUCTIONS TO PHILOSOPHY

(K) EWING, ALFRED C., *Fundamental Questions of Philosophy*, New York: The Macmillan Company, 1966.

(V) HOSPERS, JOHN, *An Introduction to Philosophical Analysis*, Englewood Cliffs, N.J.: Prentice-Hall, Inc., 1953.

(O) WHEATLEY, JON, *Prolegomena to Philosophy*, Belmont, Calif.: Wadsworth Publishing Company, 1970.

(R) EDWARDS, PAUL, and ARTHUR PAP, *A Modern Introduction to Philosophy* (3d ed.), New York: The Macmillan Company, 1973.

(R) WESTPHAL, FRED, *The Art of Philosophy*, Englewood Cliffs, N.J.: Prentice-Hall, Inc., 1973.

PART II: CHAPTERS 1 AND 2

(V)   FLEW, ANTONY, *God and Philosophy*, New York: Delta Books, 1966.

(O)   PENELHUM, TERENCE, *Religion and Rationality*, New York: Random House, 1971.

(K)   PURTILL, R. L., *Reason to Believe*, Grand Rapids, Mich.: Wm. B. Eerdmans Publishing Co., 1974.

(R)   BRODY, BARUCH, *Readings in the Philosophy of Religion*, Englewood Cliffs, N.J.: Prentice-Hall, Inc., 1974.

(R)   PIKE, NELSON, ed., *God and Evil*, Englewood Cliffs, N.J.: Prentice-Hall, Inc., 1964.

PART III: CHAPTER 3

(V)   HOSPERS, JOHN, *Human Conduct* (shorter ed.), New York: Harcourt Brace Jovanovich, 1972, Chap. 9.

(H)   LUCAS, J. R., *The Freedom of the Will*, Oxford: Oxford University Press, 1971.

(O)   NOWELL-SMITH, P. H., *Ethics*, Baltimore, Md.: Penguin Books, 1954, Chaps. 19 and 20.

(R)   BEROFSKY, BERNARD, ed., *Free Will and Determinism*, New York: Harper and Row, 1966.

(R)   HOOK, SIDNEY, ed., *Determinism and Freedom*, New York: Collier Books, 1958.

PART IV: CHAPTER 4

(H)   ROSS, W. D., *The Right and the Good*, Oxford: Oxford University Press, 1930.

(V)   STEVENSON, CHARLES, *Ethics and Language*, New Haven, Conn.: Yale University Press, 1944.

(O)   TOULMIN, STEPHEN, *The Place of Reason in Ethics*, Cambridge: Cambridge University Press, 1960.

(R)   RACHELS, J., ed., *Moral Problems*, New York: Harper and Row, 1971.

(R)   FRANKENA, WILLIAM, and JOHN GRANROSE, *Introductory Readings in Ethics*, Englewood Cliffs, N.J.: Prentice-Hall, Inc., 1974.

PART V: CHAPTER 5

(H)   RAMSEY, PAUL, *The Just War*, New York: Charles Scribner's Sons, 1968.

(O)   WELLS, DONALD, *The War Myth*, New York: Pegasus Books, 1967.

(K)   ZAHN, GORDON C., *War, Conscience and Dissent*, New York: Hawthorne Books, Inc., 1967.

(R) GINSBERG, ROBERT, ed., *The Critique of War*, New York: Henry Regnery Company, 1969.

(R) WASSERSTROM, RICHARD, ed., *War and Morality*, Belmont, Calif.: Wadsworth Publishing Company, 1970.

PART VI: CHAPTER 6

(H) EWING, ALFRED, *The Morality of Punishment*, London: Patterson Smith, 1929.

(O) HONDERICH, TED, *Punishment: The Supposed Justifications*, London: Hutchinson, 1969.

(K) MOBERLY, SIR WALTER, *The Ethics of Punishment*, Hamden, Conn.: Archon Books, 1968.

(R) EZORKSKI, GERTRUDE, ed., *Philosophical Perspectives on Punishment*, Albany, N.Y.: State University of New York Press, 1973.

(R) MURPHY, JEFFRIE G., ed., *Punishment and Rehabilitation*, Belmont, Calif.: Wadsworth Publishing Company, 1973.

PART VII: CHAPTER 7

(K) MILLER, ED. L., *God and Reason*, New York: The Macmillan Company, 1972, Chap. 10.

(V) NIELSEN, KAI, *Reason and Practice*, New York: Harper and Row, 1971, Part V.

(O) RYLE, GILBERT, *The Concept of Mind*, New York: Barnes and Noble, 1949.

(R) ANDERSON, ALAN ROSS, *Minds and Machines*, Englewood Cliffs, N.J.: Prentice-Hall, Inc., 1964.

(R) CROSSEN, F., *Human and Artificial Intelligence*, New York: Appleton-Century-Crofts, 1970.

PART VIII: CHAPTER 8

(H) HAMLYN, D. W., *The Theory of Knowledge*, Garden City, N. Y.: Doubleday and Company, Inc., 1970.

(V) REICHENBACH, HANS, *Experience and Prediction*, Chicago: University of Chicago Press, 1938.

(O) WOOZLEY, A. D., *Theory of Knowledge*, London: Hutchinson and Company, 1949.

(R) ACKERMAN, ROBERT, *Theories of Knowledge*, New York: McGraw-Hill Book Company, 1965.

(R) STROLL, AVRUM, *Epistemology*, New York: Harper and Row, 1967.

PART IX: CHAPTER 9

(V) NAGEL, ERNEST, *The Structure of Science*, New York: Harcourt Brace and World, 1961.

(H) SALMON, WESLEY, *Foundations of Scientific Inference*, Pittsburgh: University of Pittsburgh Press, 1966.

(O) TOULMIN, STEPHEN, *Philosophy of Science*, New York: Harper and Row, 1963.

(R) MORGENBESSER, SIDNEY, ed., *Philosophy of Science Today*, New York: Basic Books, Inc., 1967.

(R) DANTO, ARTHUR, and SIDNEY MORGENBESSER, *Philosophy of Science*, New York: Meridian Books, 1960.

PART X: CHAPTER 10

(O) PASSMORE, JOHN, *A Hundred Years of Philosophy*, Baltimore, Md.: Penguin Books, 1968.

(V) REICHENBACH, HANS, *The Rise of Scientific Philosophy*, Chicago: University of Chicago Press, 1938.

(O) WARNOCK, G., *English Philosophy Since 1900*, Oxford: Oxford University Press, 1969.

(R) AMMERMAN, ROBERT, *Classics of Analytic Philosophy*, New York: McGraw-Hill Book Co., 1965.

(R) KAUFMAN, W., *Existentialism from Dostoievski to Sartre*, New York: Meridian Books, 1956.

SUPPLEMENTARY LIST OF BOOKS BY THE "NONPROFESSIONAL PHILOSOPHERS" MENTIONED IN CHAPTER 10

AUDEN, W. H., *The Dyers Hand*, New York: Random House, 1960.

CHESTERTON, G. K., *Orthodoxy* (reprint), Garden City, N. Y.: Doubleday and Co., 1974.

GARDNER, MARTIN, *Fads and Fallacies in the Name of Science*, New York: Dover Books, 1957.

LEWIS, C. S., *Miracles*, New York: The Macmillan Company, 1963.

PRIESTLEY, J. B., *Literature and Western Man*, New York: Harper and Row, 1960.

WAIN, JOHN, *Sprightly Running*, New York: St. Martin's Press, 1963.

WELLS, H. G., *An Experiment in Autobiography*, New York: The Macmillan Company, 1934.

INDEX

Index

M

N

O

P

ᐧ